Justice

A Question of Race

Bilingual Press/Editorial Bilingüe

General Editor
Gary D. Keller

Managing Editor
Karen S. Van Hooft

Associate Editors
Karen M. Akins
Barbara H. Firoozye

Assistant Editor
Linda St. George Thurston

Editorial Consultant
Jean Bann

Editorial Board
Juan Goytisolo
Francisco Jiménez
Eduardo Rivera
Mario Vargas Llosa

Address:
Bilingual Review/Press
Hispanic Research Center
Arizona State University
P.O. Box 872702
Tempe, Arizona 85287-2702
(602) 965-3867

Justice

A Question of Race

Roberto Rodríguez

Bilingual Press/Editorial Bilingüe
TEMPE, ARIZONA

ISBN 0-927534-69-X (cloth)
Published simultaneously in a softcover edition. ISBN 0-927534-68-1

Library of Congress Cataloging-in-Publication Data

Rodríguez, R. (Roberto)
   Justice : a question of race / Roberto Rodríguez.
      p.   cm.
   ISBN 0-927534-69-X (cloth : alk. paper).—ISBN 0-927534-68-1
(pbk. : alk. paper)
      1. Victims of crimes—California—East Los Angeles. 2. Mexican
Americans—California—East Los Angeles. 3. Racism—California—
East Los Angeles. 4. False imprisonment—California—East Los
Angeles. 5. Police—Complaints against—California—East Los
Angeles. I. Title
HV8148.A-Z.E (East Los Angeles).x
345.794'9402555—DC21   97-9913
                                                                CIP

PRINTED IN THE UNITED STATES OF AMERICA

Cover design by John Wincek, Aerocraft Charter Art Service
Back cover photo by Alicia Maldonado

Acknowledgments

Major new marketing initiatives have been made possible by the Lila Wallace-Reader's Digest Literary Publishers Marketing Development Program, funded through a grant to the Council of Literary Magazines and Presses.

Dedication

In my many years as a journalist/columnist, I have seen firsthand the courage and determination of parents in defending their children who were unjustly beaten, imprisoned, or killed at the hands of law enforcement. Because of this, I dedicate this to all parents who have had to support and fight for their children.

Specifically, this is dedicated to my family who stood by me through all these years, particularly my parents, Ricardo and Juanita.

Contents

On the Wrong Side of the Law

Foreword

Police brutality is to the United States what death squad democracy is to Third World nations. It is society at its lowest.

Police brutality is extralegal violence against the populace, carried out by official thugs, with semiapproval emanating from the highest quarters. Police brutality is the breaking down of society where law enforcement functions as the judge, jury, and the prosecution.

Sadly, this violence is directed primarily at the Black youth and Brown youth of this nation and, up until very recently, was either denied or tolerated.

In 1979, riot sticks to my head introduced me to that underworld of police brutality—to an Orwellian world of legal, judicial, and political dyslexia, a world in which nothing is as it appears to be and in which everything is the opposite of what it is supposed to be.

In this surreal world, I, the victim, became the villain. I, the good guy, became the bad guy. I, a 24-year-old journalist who had never committed a single crime, was branded a criminal. The crime was witnessing and photographing a brutal attack on a defenseless man by the very officers who almost killed me.

By the time I left the hospital, by the time I was bailed out of jail, barely able to walk on my own, I walked out a different man, having been charged with attempting to kill the officers who had nearly ended my life.

From the moment I walked out of the hospital, an incredible ordeal began: a perilous seven-and-a-half years that almost cost me my life a number of times; a period in time in which I lived in constant fear while attempting to prove my innocence. In the end, that wait culminated in a dramatic, emotion-charged trial from which I am still trying to recover.

During this traumatic and agonizing ordeal, I also struggled to return to normalcy, to regain my youth, dignity, and humanity.

The following, related in two parts, is an attempt to explain what happened to me during those seven-and-a-half years. An epilogue, written 10 years after the second part, brings closure to this nightmare.

Assault with a Deadly Weapon is an account I wrote five years after I almost faced my maker and two years before I went to trial. When I wrote it, I was still in fear for my life. In fact, I wrote it because I believed that my trial was right around the corner and that the police would not permit me to live to testify. It was written with the idea that if I were to be killed, people would know what the police were trying to suppress.

Assault with a Deadly Weapon was published independently, through the assistance of a church. It is reprinted here, without significant change from its original form.

When it was written, I was not only still living through this ordeal, but in a sense, I was living in a different world. If I would have rewritten the account of the first five years, it would have read much differently. I don't write that way anymore, and today, the threat of an impending trial is no longer hanging over my head.

On the Wrong Side of the Law doesn't just pick up where *Assault with a Deadly Weapon* leaves off. Now that there are no legal actions pending, I can tell my story, without the fear of it being used against me in court and without the fear of retribution.

On the Wrong Side of the Law is an account of what I experienced in my torturous pursuit of justice.

The epilogue simply brings my thoughts together, examining that legal, judicial, and political world that permits police brutality, post–Rodney King, to continue to flourish.

The following is my contribution toward getting our nation's citizens to understand one of its worst nightmares and to finally put an end to it.

Roberto Rodríguez

Acknowledgments

The African saying that it takes a village to educate a child applies to this book; it took an entire community to publish this book. All along the way, I was helped, supported, and inspired by countless individuals, not the least of which were family and friends. It was their support that enabled me to march forward, especially at times when I no longer wanted to move forward. I would like to thank the following individuals who helped not simply with the book, but in fighting my trials and in either supporting me or carrying on the struggle of accountability within law enforcement and the judicial system.

First and foremost, my witnesses who stepped forward, Josie, Dina, Rick, Kiki, Reyes, and my attorney who pulled off miracles—twice—a man who has dedicated his entire life to the cause of human rights, Antonio Rodríguez. To those who have supported and inspired me throughout these years: Raquel Salinas, Gil Jasso, María Jiménez, Roberto Martínez, Antonia Hernández, Dionicio Morales, Armando Morales, Gloria Romero, Julián Samora, Susan Alva, Sam Paz, Margarita Rosario, Richie Pérez, Virginia Chacón, Dr. Arnoldo Solís, Demetria Martínez, Reyna García Ramos, Julie Wilson, Dennis Britton, Mike Hamilburg, Rosa Guerrero, Rudy Acuña, Arminda Ayala, Noemí Pérez, and Vivian López. Thanks also to my colleagues at the California Chicano News Media Association, and to Rubén Blades, Culture Clash, and Latins Anonymous for providing support and laughter when I needed it most.

A special thanks to all the people from my neighborhood, who at times provided sanctuary and at other times assistance in actually tracking down elusive witnesses. For that matter, thanks to all the barrios that provided me sanctuary throughout the years. Thanks also to those who helped in the actual writing and editing, particularly my wife, Patrisia Gonzales— who also has provided me with support and moral strength—and the editors of Bilingual Review Press, for believing in my work.

Also, to all those who have given their lives in fighting for justice, that you may never be forgotten.

Assault with a Deadly Weapon

Dedication

(October 1984)

To all those who have ever cruised the Boulevard.
To all those who will step forward.

Preface

On March 23, 1979, a little after midnight, while taking photographs of the cruising on Whittier Boulevard in East Los Angeles, I, along with others, witnessed the senseless beating of an innocent and defenseless individual by members of the Special Enforcement Bureau of the Los Angeles County Sheriff's Department. In turn, I was severely beaten and had my head cracked, camera confiscated, and life threatened. It is a night I will never forget.

For the next three days, I lay in a hospital bed, in the prison ward of the L.A. County Hospital, charged with assault with a deadly weapon and assault and battery on a peace officer. For witnessing and photographing an incident of police brutality, I ended up not only as another victim but also as the one who ended up being charged with a crime.

As a result of the incident, 538 people were arrested, countless individuals were beaten and harassed, the Boulevard was shut down, and by the end of the weekend, Whittier Boulevard in East L.A. resembled a war zone. Nine months after the incident, after endless court appearances, the charges against me were finally dropped. However, as of this writing, I have a lawsuit pending against the sheriff's department. To this day, I don't know what happened to everyone who was arrested or beaten the weekend of March 23–25, 1979. What I do know is that a few months later, on August 31, 1979, as the tension created by the sheriffs in East L.A. increased, Whittier Boulevard was permanently shut down. Now, almost five years later, the barricades still go up every weekend on the legendary one-mile strip of Whittier Boulevard, remnants of a bloody past, a testament to the powerlessness of an exploited people.

Originally, as the incident began to unfold, there was a sense of outrage. As the sheriffs began to arrive, as they began to pursue the individual, as they began to subdue him, as they began to beat him and take turns on him, everyone watched in disbelief. As more sheriffs arrived, sensing danger, my first instincts were to split, to leave the scene. The cries from the victim, the horrified expressions and the pleas from other witnesses, kept me there. The barbaric brutality, the animalistic behavior displayed by officers of the sheriff's department sent chills of disbelief. What was the victim's crime? Wearing a sarape in the middle of the street? Being Mexican? The man who was beaten was not merely subdued but was subjected to a malicious free-for-all by peace officers who fought with each other like scavengers to see who could get in the best licks.

In my mind, the scene is frozen. Every time I snapped a picture, the camera recorded something that was already ingrained in people's minds.

That was the sad part: that what I was seeing, that what I was photographing, that what everyone was seeing, was not unusual. It was business as usual, another beating of a Mexican. The guardians of justice were acting as enforcers. They had become the prosecution, the judge, and the jury.

The camera I used to photograph this incident wasn't supposed to be there. Peace officers were not supposed to be caught in the act. Besides, the ganging up on a Mexican by sheriffs is not considered a crime, and most of all, it is not news. This was not L.A. in the forties. This was L.A. in 1979. When I was arrested, my camera was confiscated. It had become a "deadly weapon." This deadly weapon was returned to me, nine months later upon dismissal of the charges. The film was no longer inside the camera, but the incident, that night, is ingrained in my mind.

This book is not about hatred or vengeance nor is it an exposé of the sheriff's department. It is about an incident that has left me mentally and physically scarred. It is about Whittier Boulevard; it is about East L.A.; and it is about lawlessness. It is about 1979, but it is also about the wheels of justice and the lack of justice.

Acknowledgments

(October 1984)

Thanks to all those who have helped me through my trial and lawsuit. Thanks also to the following people who have helped with the publication of this book: José Montoya, Dolores Huerta, Porfirio Miranda, Alma Cervantes, Lorenzo "Toppy" Flores, Tammy Ramírez, and the band Califas.

A special thanks to Frances Carrasco and Consuelo Preciado for their help in proofing and editing.

Also, I would like to borrow a quote from a friend: "Un gran abrazo for all those who helped, and una gran patada for all those who got in the way."

1 / Introduction:
The Victim on Trial

Not long ago, in November 1983, I was talking to a few friends. It was about 6:30 P.M., so at that time it was already dark. Since I hadn't eaten, two of us went down the street to Nick's Hamburgers on Whittier Boulevard, in East L.A. There were a lot of people out. Club 47 was jumping, the cars were cruising. The poppers were popping. The Raza were out enjoying a Sunday evening. I sat down at one of the tables, checking things out. Suddenly, the sheriffs came out of nowhere, red and blue lights flashing. They began to barricade the Boulevard. As I was eating my hamburger, I couldn't help but feel like I was some kind of criminal, as though the Raza out cruising were criminals. Here, the sun had barely gone down, and the sheriffs were barricading Whittier Boulevard, as though something heavy was coming down. Indeed, something heavy was coming down.

How should I describe what the sheriffs were doing? I looked around to see if there was a gang fight in progress. All I saw were guys talking to girls and girls talking to guys. Across the street, the poppers were doing their thing, and further down the street, there were a lot of people outside of Club 47. Cars were cruising by in both directions. At the hamburger stand, every table inside and outside was packed, and there were a lot of Raza standing around, eating their food, and checking out the scene. A couple of homegirls were on the phones telling their boyfriends that they were home babysitting or that they were at the laundromat doing the wash. In the parking lot, my friend was talking to some other friends.

In front of us, the sheriffs were slapping up the barricades on the corner of Whittier and Hendricks. After they put them there, they moved on to the next corner. They didn't bother anyone at the hamburger stand, so no one paid any attention to them.

It was as though everyone had become accustomed to that scene. It didn't escape my attention that the sheriffs putting up the barricades were white. I was probably bothered by what I saw more than most everyone else. I don't cruise or lowride every weekend. In fact, I don't cruise Whittier Boulevard or any boulevard at all. Since the sun goes down at about 8:30-9:00 P.M. in L.A. in the summer, I hardly ever find myself on the Boulevard when the cruising is going strong. However, since the time changes in November, it gets dark around 5:30, and that night I found myself on Whittier when the cruising was happening.

I didn't see any criminal activity going on around me. Of course, everyone around the Boulevard is aware that since 1979 the Boulevard has been closed on Fridays, Saturdays, and Sundays. But the ban on cruising is supposed to cover only Whittier Boulevard, from Atlantic to Eastern in East L.A. I knew I had been gone from L.A. for a few years, but I wasn't sure whether another law had been passed that said you can't cruise anywhere in East L.A. What I do know is that no matter where the Raza cruises—whether it be Olympic, Atlantic, Hubbard, or Whittier Boulevard between Atlantic and Garfield—it seems to be illegal. I'm not sure the sheriffs have the legal right to do what they do, but regardless, they do it.

When I was there eating my hamburger that night, I was aware that many of the residents didn't like the cruising, but it's funny because almost everyone out there lives around there. It bothered me to see what the sheriffs were doing. They were in effect declaring Whittier Boulevard off limits, and it was off limits. I didn't see any machine-guns blazing, yet they were declaring everyone to be a criminal.

After we finished eating, the question was, "how do we get home?" We in effect were now subject to arrest. We paid for the hamburgers. I admit I might have asked for a little extra ketchup for my fries, but I wasn't aware of any crime we might have committed. We were only going three blocks down, and yet the possibility existed that we could get arrested for . . . for what? We weren't wearing headbands. We weren't hopping and scraping up a storm. We weren't even out cruising. Even though the Boulevard was barricaded, we went down Whittier anyway. Luckily, we didn't get pulled over because the sheriffs were busy pulling over everyone else.

How do you express the feelings you get when you're in a situation like that? It was absurd. You stop to think. You get mad. You say to yourself or you say it out loud, "Who are these sheriffs anyway? Who gave them the right to do what they're doing? Aren't we supposed to be innocent until proven guilty? Sure, there are criminals, but is every Mexican a criminal? Is everyone who goes down the street a cutthroat hoodlum?"

Something's wrong in East L.A. Something's wrong on Whittier Boulevard. The last time I checked, East L.A. was still a part of the United States, but you would never know it by the way the Raza are treated on the streets.

As you begin reading this, you may wonder if this is a history of East L.A. or a history of Whittier Boulevard. Instead, it is a retelling of an event that took place in 1979, but it is also about a situation that continues to this day. It is also about a million other things. Getting hit on the head does a lot to a person. For me, it made me want to win my court case and split the country. At times, I wanted to see real justice—I wanted to see the guilty officers behind bars. Other times, I was all excited about the lawsuit. But time also does a lot to a person. Sometimes, people ask me if I hate cops or if I hate white people. I usually respond by saying,

"How would you feel if you were sent to the hospital by four or five sheriffs?" I don't hate cops, and I don't hate white people—although that issue will probably come up in court. It will probably be the classic: "put the victim on trial."

My lawsuit shouldn't be whether I like cops or white people. It should be about a specific incident. What happened on March 23, 1979, on the corner of Whittier and McDonnell in East L.A. was very simple: I witnessed the beating of a Chicano by about nine sheriffs. I photographed the incident. In turn, I was severely beaten, was sent to the hospital, my camera was confiscated, and I was charged with assault with a deadly weapon and assault and battery on two peace officers. There were probably fifty to a hundred people who witnessed this series of events. Despite this incident, my ideas haven't changed regarding cops. I have always been against police abuse. Who isn't? And as for whites, I don't like to see our Raza treated like animals. I had those ideas before I got hit on my head. The reasons I had those ideas existed prior to the incident. I mention this because I've learned a little about the justice system. But does a real justice system exist? Will I be tried based on my ideas or based on what occurred that night? What happened was very simple and should be viewed that way in court.

The ridiculous charges against me were dropped, but will I win my lawsuit? I don't think the lawsuit will be about whether they cracked my head, but, rather, it will probably go something like this: "Isn't it true that you were caught writing on the walls of East L.A. in elementary school?" Then they'll bring out some photographs and continue, "Isn't it true that you were involved in a food fight and a walkout in the eighth grade at Eastmont Junior High?" I'll probably slap myself on the head, and the lawyer will continue, "Isn't it a fact that you used to read *La Raza Magazine* in high school?" Then they'll probably top it off by, "and isn't it also true that your girlfriend in college was a troublemaker?" By this time, I'll probably get up and say, "Yes, it's all true, but what about March 23, 1979? Are these officers ever going to stand trial? Am I ever going to get true justice?" Then they'll probably say that I'm out of order and that I'm in contempt. Then the lawyer will probably continue and say, "Isn't it true that some of your friends are in prison?"

That's how I expect it to go. I've already had a taste of law enforcement and the justice system. Maybe my faith in the justice system can be restored, but what happens in court will be another matter.

I used to tell people that I didn't want to publicize my case because it might affect my lawsuit. Actually, I didn't want publicity because I was scared for my life. Many incidents convinced me of that. I thought that every time I got behind the wheel of my car, it might be my last. I don't think I went anywhere near East L.A. for at least two years. But the fear wasn't limited to East L.A. Fear was driving alone anywhere at night, expecting the red and blue lights to turn on behind me and then to be shot for making an "unexpected" move.

Why am I writing this? Probably because of something that happened in East L.A. on August 29, 1970. That is the day Rubén Salazar was killed. I was sixteen then. His death and the events of those years made a sizable impact on the youth of my generation. The era of the late sixties and early seventies, which produced walkouts in the schools, protests, demonstrations, and marches in the streets, is known as the height of the Chicano movement. At that time, the Raza rebelled against anything and everything that put down our Raza. During that era, conditions for the Raza were intolerable. Police brutality was rampant; the educational system was failing and pushing out 50 percent of our Raza. Everything that affected the Raza was owned or controlled by whites. At that time, the whites had the attitude that they knew what was good for us, and if we didn't like it, we could go back to Mexico. Our access to higher education was practically zero. Across the country, there were only a handful of Raza at the universities, but that was probably because universities weren't built for the Raza. The prisons, on the other hand, seem to have been built especially for us. Nobody could complain that the Raza was underrepresented in the prisons, nor could we complain about the lack of representation of Raza in the military.

In fact, the rally of August 29, 1970, was a protest against the Vietnam War, and even more specifically, it was to protest the disproportionate amount of Raza casualties in Vietnam. At least, that was the theme of the rally. I think the residents had other ideas. When the Raza were attacked by the sheriffs, the Raza exploded, taking out their pent-up anger on the sheriffs and anything white. Not surprisingly, Raza-owned businesses were not damaged. In an incident that is still shrouded in mystery, amidst the rioting, a prominent journalist, Rubén Salazar, News Director of KMEX and columnist for the *Los Angeles Times,* lay in a pool of blood at the Silver Dollar Cafe on Whittier Boulevard. He lay there for three hours, gunned down by a deadly projectile fired by a member of the sheriff's department. Rumors circulated through the streets for three hours until it was confirmed that the lone journalist who spoke out about the problems afflicting the Raza had been gunned down by a sheriff. Speculation persists to this day about whether Salazar was assassinated. That night, as the Raza huddled around their TV sets, people watched in amazement as it was revealed that Salazar had been silenced. Tension was so heavy that night that a virtual state of siege was declared. The curfew imposed added to the rising tension. Between August 29 and the annual 16th of September Parade, tension on the East Side was so thick that it cannot be adequately described in words. The inquest into his death was seen as a kangaroo court, which contributed to the mounting tension.

Those days are gone now. There was another riot after the parade, and there were a few more, but since the early seventies, the Raza truly have not been heard from. The Raza who protest now do it in a different way. So, in effect, the Raza have been silenced for many years. It's kind of sad because all the reasons that gave rise to the revolt of the Raza are still there. Even sadder is that conditions are actually worse. The Raza have little if any political power. The educational system is in worse shape than it was when all the walkouts took place. The dropout rate is still around 50 percent, and unfortunately, despite opposite claims, there are still only a handful of Chicanos at universities. On the streets, police abuse is as rampant as it ever was, and the media still have a field day blaming all of the country's problems on the Raza without papers. When the protests began about fifteen years ago, there was good cause to revolt. Now, with our population doubled and still skyrocketing, our prospects are even worse. For sure, there has been some progress, but only for a few. We are still as politically powerless as we've ever been. What's really sad is that the generation that revolted is now silent, and the youngsters of today take for granted that we are supposed to be powerless.

The problems that afflict our Raza are serious and many. Police abuse is one of the problems, but it is not the only problem nor is it the most important. The reason I write about police abuse is because in the process of doing a story on police brutality, I became a victim of law enforcement and the judicial system. Police abuse is not from out of our past nor is it history. Because this abuse is directed primarily at the youth, those in the position to combat this either are unaware about the extent of this problem or, if they are aware, don't do anything about it because it doesn't affect them.

My thoughts are not bitter nor full of anger. My thoughts are those of many, voices that are seldom heard. There are very few written examples that you can point to and say, "This is how a real Chicano thinks." *La Raza Magazine* used to express how we thought. Now we don't have *La Raza*. The true voices of La Raza have been replaced by government hispanics. For a buck, now we are "hispanics." But that's not really us. Despite what's seen on the surface, below our real thoughts are ready to explode, are ready to surface once again. There's a lot of blood in East L.A. I myself have seen a lot of blood, including my own, probably more blood than most people will see in a lifetime. But what I have seen, others have also seen, and the thoughts I have belong to many others. I am one voice in a sea of voices waiting to be heard. There are Raza who have seen ten times what I have seen, and there are youngsters who have yet to see anything at all. Hopefully, we ourselves can do something to let those voices be heard. If those who have been here since the '40s can teach us about those days, maybe we can do something to avoid repeating those mistakes. There are still abuelitos and abuelitas in our barrios who survived the Mexican Revolution. Those voices are the ones we need to hear. I am but twenty-nine years old, but it probably won't be those of my age who speak up but rather those who are in junior high and elementary school today.

I'll continue to fight against this probably because I am still influenced by the events that took place when I was growing up. As of now, I am still waiting for my lawsuit to come to trial. I haven't and don't intend to drop it. Nothing can alter the facts. If I lose, it will be based either on total lies or some fancy legal maneuver pulled out of the hat. If I lose, it will not be based on the truth. Because nothing I say can alter the facts, the reason I write this is so that the Raza can benefit from it, so that people can see we don't have to bargain our rights away, that we can fight and can win, that we can file lawsuits, and, most of all, that we speak up about it, that we no longer have to remain silent.

2 / Before *Lowrider:* From Mexico to the Silver Dollar

Probably the hardest thing for me to do is to write about myself. When I was awaiting my trial, I had to do it, so this won't be the first time. What I wrote in '79 was an appeal, and in a sense, this is also an appeal because the incident is not yet over, for me or for the Raza that gets harassed routinely. This section is the most difficult because I do write about myself, but it is necessary so that the readers know who they are supporting.

I do not live in East L.A. right now, although if the circumstances permitted, I would. I was not born in East L.A. I was born in Mexico. My family moved to Tijuana when I was four years old. We lived there for about a year and a half. When my family moved to East L.A. in 1960, I was five or six. I lived in East L.A. from kindergarten through the end of my first year in college. In other words, East L.A. is where I grew up.

Either due to economic reasons or fate, we were only one of a handful of families who lived on Whittier Boulevard in East L.A. It seems like since the first day we came to the United States, I can't get away from the Boulevard or from East L.A. Whittier Boulevard and East L.A. are special places. For a lot of people, these landmarks are symbols. To me, this is where I call home. My roots are Mexicano. That can never be taken away. All the ideas I grew up with about East L.A. were formed in East L.A. I did not get my ideas from outsiders. My ideas, I'm sure, are not even unique because millions of people have grown up in East L.A. All the things I have done or have observed must have been done or observed by many others. The thing is, a lot is written about East L.A. which is actually written by outsiders. There have been very few instances in which the gut feelings of the Raza have been expressed about East L.A. Gut feelings cannot be invented or perfected. Gut feelings are anger. Gut feelings are protest. Gut feelings are dissatisfaction. People have always written about the surface of East L.A., both from within and from outside the community. There is a lot more than meets the eye. One thing is for sure, nobody represents East L.A. There are groups or organizations that represent certain segments but no one group or person can make a claim to be the sole representative or the sole voice of East L.A.

Twenty-three years ago, when I first came to the United States, East L.A. was very different in that people's minds were different at that time. East L.A. was a Mexican area that had undergone much discrimination in the previous decades. The response of the people had been to reject U.S. society or to try to emulate it, or both. At that time, you found a lot of Raza who denied their Mexicanidad. They had been forced to deny it. Many refused to speak Spanish either because they actually didn't know it or because they were made to feel ashamed. At that time, a lot of successful Raza had emulated white ways, refusing to teach their sons or daughters their language and true culture. It's a long story that couldn't be dealt with in one book, but the result was that those who rejected the white ways also at the same time rejected their Mexican traditions. So you had Pachucos who stood against everything that U.S. society stood for, and, at the same time, they themselves hated Mexicanos. At the other end of the spectrum were the Mexicans who had changed their names, accepted the U.S. ways, and turned out Mexican surfers who hated "beaners" and, still more, hated "wetbacks." I think the reason that Mexicanos who had been living here thought that way was because of the heavy discrimination that existed when they were growing up. I don't think they wanted to be seen as "wetbacks," and maybe that's why they, too, joined in on the discrimination against the Mexicano.

That's the atmosphere I moved into. Maybe the fact that I lived in an area in which Montebello was only six blocks away had something to do with my perception. Even though 100 percent of our activities were directed away from Montebello, I'm sure its closeness influenced the area. At the time, Montebello was like a bastion for whites. As for the Mexicans who lived there, you wouldn't know they were Mexican except that they couldn't bleach their skin. From firsthand experience, I didn't know anything about the fifties or the forties. What I did know is that the Raza still carried an extreme hatred for sailors and surfers. I didn't realize until later that it was a carry over from the Zoot Suit Riots of the forties and the gang fights of the fifties.

In 1960, when I went to Eastmont Elementary, the only tension of any consequence seemed to be that there was a lot of hatred of Mexicanos by Mexican Americans. Although Eastmont Junior High is technically in Montebello, the majority of the students were from East L.A. In 1968, while in the eighth grade, the first signs of a different kind of tension surfaced. The anger now seemed to turn toward the whites. Although I was only in the eighth grade, I knew all about racism the day I crossed the border. At Eastmont Junior High, about 98 percent of the teachers were white, so racial flare ups never really surfaced. But everyone knew tensions were there. The thing about Eastmont Junior High is that the majority of the students were clearly from East L.A. This didn't mean much while we were going to Eastmont, but when those of us from Eastmont went to high school, we had to go to Montebello High. By then, Chicanismo—pride in being Chicano, in being Mexicano—was sweeping through all the barrios of Los Angeles. Montebello seemed to be untouched by this movement. The majority of Mexicans from

Montebello, it seemed, were surfers who thought they belonged to another race. I don't think I ever really came into contact with a totally brainwashed Mexican until I went to school at Montebello High. The thing, too, was that not many of us from Eastmont Junior High seemed to be going there. There was a revolution going on in the streets a few blocks away, but it seemed as though there was a gigantic barrier on Garfield Boulevard or something, because the revolution didn't seem to have any effect on many students at Montebello High.

As a thirteen, fourteen, and fifteen year old, I knew there were walk-outs going on, and I knew that people were protesting police brutality and things such as that, but nothing that had happened till then, except crossing the border, had really made any impact on me. On August 29, 1970, it was as though reality set in on East L.A. There was a big riot that day. It was to protest the high rate of Chicanos being killed in Vietnam. I think the organizers had one thing in mind and the plebe had another. The event set the stage for a cataclysmic volcano. East L.A. erupted, and till this day, it will never be the same again. If Rubén Salazar, noted journalist for the *Los Angeles Times* and News Director for Channel 34, hadn't been killed, who knows how we would've looked back on that day. To the youth, like myself, we had other things to think about. It might have gone down as just another riot during a turbulent era. That was the time of the Vietnam War, but youngsters didn't really care about it until they got to be of draft age. The reason this day became different is because inadvertently Rubén Salazar became an instant martyr. Everyone still remembers the Silver Dollar and Laguna Park. Now, it is the New Silver Dollar, and Laguna was renamed Rubén Salazar Park.

Consciously or subconsciously, I know that event influenced me probably more than anything that had ever happened to me, until what happened to me in 1979. In 1970, I was in the tenth grade. In 1979, I was three years removed from college and one year removed from teaching. After the incident in 1970, I continued to go to high school, determined not only to graduate but to go to college somewhere. Through fate, I ended up getting accepted to the University of California, Los Angeles during my senior year in high school. I not only couldn't believe it, but I also didn't know how I had been admitted. I had good grades and all that, but I didn't even remember applying. Either someone had put in a good word for me, or I had forgotten that I had applied. I still remember, to this day, the shock I got when I opened the letter. I think it read something like, "Congratulations, you've been accepted to UCLA." I practically flipped. I think that, at the time, it was the aspiration of every young Chicano to go to UCLA. Mentally, I had already prepared myself for going to Cal State L.A. I was ready for Cal State L.A. When the letter came, it blew me away. If it blew me away, you should have seen what it did to my friend. My friend Trini and I were the only Raza in the college prep biology class. She was a righteous Chicana if I ever met one. The two of us and another friend had taken an overnight tour of UCLA while in the tenth grade. We had gone with some students from Garfield and Roosevelt. When we came back to the East Side (we passed through another demonstration and march at Belvedere Park), we, like little kids, vowed that we would all go to UCLA. So here, a couple of years later, in my senior year, I had gotten this letter of acceptance from UCLA. I couldn't wait to show it to Trini. We were in biology class and the teacher was giving his rap. She sat behind me, and I took out the letter. I had to be real quiet because the whole class was very attentive. Like they say, you could've heard a pin drop. Without turning around, I passed back the letter. It is difficult to describe what happened afterward. She practically threw a couple of somersaults and a mean grito. We were hugging each other like you wouldn't believe. The whole class was looking at us, but since they were white, they couldn't understand what it meant for a Chicano to be accepted to UCLA.

If I wrote all about UCLA in detail, it would take at least two books. I went there from 1972 to 1976. The only thing I could say about college is that I left disillusioned. I graduated from UCLA in four years just so I could prove a point, take the degree, and split. There, in spite of the university, I learned to write. I still remember the first story I ever wrote like it was yesterday. While still at UCLA, a friend who said he worked for the newspaper *La Gente* asked me if I wanted to write a story about César Chávez. At the time, *La Gente* was a very prestigious Chicano newspaper in the community. It was probably second only to *La Raza* magazine in importance. One of my older neighbors in East L.A. who attended UCLA worked for *La Gente*. I thought about checking with him, but I figured that if my friend Mando Cagando said it was OK to do the story, it must be OK. I think that because of the article I did on Chávez, that was the worst quarter I ever spent at UCLA, and to top it off, the article wasn't accepted. Not that it wasn't good. Everyone liked it, but they said somebody else had been assigned the story. They said that Mando was on the staff but that he wasn't the assignment editor. I felt like killing the guy, except I think I would have had to wait in line.

Despite this first experience, I got to hear César Chávez, and later, I got to meet the guy. I continued to write articles from my freshman year through my senior year when I became the editor. It was more than just a writing experience; it was a commitment to La Raza. I liked school a little, but it was more the newspaper that kept my interest.

As I said, I could go on for days about UCLA, but that's another story. What I could say is that in the summer of 1974, my sophomore year, I worked in a summer mural program in El Sereno and Cypress Park. In that program, we worked with Raza from Cypress Park, the Avenues, Happy Valley, East Side Clover, and El Sereno. A day didn't go by without an incident. I remember, we tried to put up a mural in front of El Sereno Junior High. For whatever reasons, throughout the whole summer, we couldn't put up the mural. Actually, a big reason was because to put up a mural, the wall you paint on has to be white, and it has to be left clean for two days so that the paint can dry properly. Are you kidding? The mural never stood a chance, although we did have a lot of fun trying to put up murals in Cypress Park and El Sereno.

The following summer, in 1975, I ended up working at a recreation center in Culver City. At the time, I didn't know how rowdy it was in that area. I saw a fancy recreation center, so I figured it must be for whites. It was supposed to be for everyone, but there was a rule that residents of the nearby Mar Vista Housing Projects could not use the facilities. Most of the time, people ignored the rule, but sometimes the people upstairs tried to clamp down on the regulation. On the West Side that year, things were pretty hot. There were four varrios that made up the West Side (west of the San Diego Freeway): Culver City, Santa Monica, Sotel, and Venice. A lot of blood was spilled in 1975. I didn't know the West Side very well, but I did know that just as much blood was being spilled on that end of town. A lot of Raza I met in those days are no longer around. In 1975, when things were getting out of hand, a few parents got together and decided to try to do something about the violence. I remember Birdie from Venice and Romie from Sotel. If you have ever met a mother who has lost a son, that is reason enough to try to put an end to the killings that stalk every familia in every barrio. Nothing in the world can compare with the grief of a mother. During that summer, they got together to try to prevent more outbreaks. Sadly, a fourteen year old was killed that summer. A call went out to have a meeting of the four varrios. To this day, I have never witnessed anything similar to the events that transpired. So much tension filled the hall as it was packed by the four varrios. Somehow, Channel 7 was there. As the events unfolded, the hall became even tenser. The varrios were there to talk, but because of the seriousness of the situation, some weren't there to talk. Just as everything was going to go down, the little homeboy's tía broke out emotionally. I wouldn't even want to describe what happened, except that she stopped a possible bloodbath. A lot of innocent people might have gotten hurt. While this was going on, the people from Channel 7 were told not to air what they had just seen. They didn't have to be convinced because even they knew that they had seen something that shouldn't be seen on TV.

Because of that meeting, Barrios Unidos West Side was formed. At first, the meetings, which took place once a week, were jam-packed. Each week, they took place in a different neighborhood. All the meetings were pretty tense, but I don't remember any incidents taking place at the meetings. I do remember going to parties afterward in which everyone got together. A lot of plebe think that the conflict never really stopped, but at minimum, they figured Barrios Unidos slowed it down. I don't remember how long Barrios Unidos met, but I know that by the end of the summer, the varrios were no longer meeting regularly. One meeting I do remember taking place after that hot summer was held in Culver City in which a guest speaker brought a film. It was called, "What to Be." The speaker, Gus Frías, was a dynamic speaker. He was a student at the University of Southern California who had been involved in wanting to end varrio warfare on the East Side. It was too bad that he came at the end of summer rather than at the beginning, because by then the four varrios had stopped meeting the way they had begun. Barrios Unidos had become an organization, and even later, a barrio newspaper came out of the organization. The main thing I remember about those days and Barrios Unidos is that a lot of Raza from those days are no longer around. A lot of Raza I met from those varrios are dead. There were a lot of good people who were killed senselessly. Every year, one by one, someone is killed. I still remember a lot of them, and I still remember talking to some of the mothers, especially Romie of Sotel. I remember that when I was at *Lowrider* I went to see her, and she ended up writing us a couple of letters so that she could express her grief about her son who had been killed trying to break up a fight. Many people read her letter, entitled, "A Message to a Cholo." Unfortunately, a few months later, she wrote another letter of sorrow.

Hopefully, her letters did some good.

In my senior year at UCLA, my best friend, someone who I figured should have been up there with me, fighting for the Raza, died. It was hard to take. If it hadn't been for my girlfriend, I probably would have quit school.

After I graduated from UCLA, I spent a year at Hollywood High as a bilingual teacher's aide, waiting for my girlfriend to graduate from UCLA. Meanwhile, I began to write. Although I had written since my freshman year, this time I began writing fiction. It was much harder than writing for *La Gente*. Luckily, all the Raza at Hollywood High helped me with my writing. That year, I ended up winning two national writing awards and one statewide writing award. I think at the end of that year I ended up going to Mexico for the first time since my family and I had left when I was four. It was a mind blower of a trip. I got to know family who knew me, but I didn't know them. It was like a part of me I didn't know existed. When I came back to L.A., I knew I had to return to Mexico. Unfortunately, I couldn't. The following year, I taught in Whittier.

This isn't supposed to be an autobiography, but I do want people to know where I grew up, where I went to school, and what influenced me. A couple of other partners I grew up with also got blown away around '77 or '78. There's much to be said about that, but if you're wondering, I never was from a gang. The barrio I grew up in is a pretty cool place in East L.A. Those of us who hung around together hung around our neighborhood, off of Whittier Boulevard. I don't ever remember cruising the Boulevard except when I was about fifteen when my older brother took me down the Boulevard. Other than that, I didn't cruise the Boulevard. I don't know about anyone else, but I thought the Boulevard was for those who had nowhere to go. I did go down the Boulevard to hang out at Jack-in-the-Box now and then, but nothing regular. In fact, I met a girlfriend there. I also met someone there who later turned out to be a real good friend. She ended up going to UCLA. I still crack up about how I met her. She was in her mother's car going one direction, yelling at her brother, who was going the other way, to come home (or he was yelling at her to go home) all in the middle of bumper-to-bumper traffic. Seriously, even though I lived on Whittier Boulevard and was always around it, I never really went down the Boulevard until after I got into *Lowrider Magazine*. A big reason I probably didn't cruise the Boulevard is because my partners in college rarely came down to the East Side, and as for the partners I grew up with, we partied right there where we grew up.

Going to college was like being in two worlds. The hard part of it was that none of my partners I hung around with went to college, and the partners I went to college with were from somewhere else. Whatever the case, the main thing I always kept in mind is that, no matter how much education I got, I would never abandon East L.A. I would never abandon the Raza that had sent me there in the first place.

Maybe one last thing I should say is that in East L.A., when I was grow-ing up, most everyone made a decision about lowriding when they were about fifteen or sixteen years old. In a way, it wasn't much of a decision, because at that time, lowriding is what you did. A lot of Raza dropped out of high school for economic reasons, got a job, a nice ride, and par-tied through the best years of their lives. For a lot of people, quitting school had nothing to do with economics. Since school had little to offer to most Chicanos, the lure of lowriding was a better alternative. Getting a nice ride was tempting because you'd have to be blind not to see that a lot of the fine looking Chicanas always seemed to be with the nice rides. On the East Side, when you're fifteen, there are probably two things on your mind, getting a nice ride and picking up with it.

Everyone has to decide if they want to live in the streets and have a good time, or sacrifice their youth and hit the books. The pressures I had probably were about the same as anyone else on the East Side. One thing for sure, although before very few people went to college, around the time I was fifteen, a new climate was setting in. The older Raza were telling the younger Raza to go to college, to get educated. It was a differ-ent message than the one that was given in the schools. In the schools, even today, what they say is "Study hard and one day, you will make it. If you try hard enough, you can even go to college and make something of yourself." The new message that was being heard in the streets was "You owe it to your Raza to get educated. It's a responsibility! If you want things better for your familia, for your Raza, go to college, but come back. Don't abandon your barrio, don't abandon the Raza." That was the new message. It was a powerful message. I don't know if that message in itself is what made me decide. I do know that because we had come from Mexico, my jefito would always say that we didn't come for nothing. He would say, "Go to school. I don't want you to be like me, having to work in a factory all your life." I probably heard that about ten thousand times. We were as poor as anyone on the East Side, so I didn't need an economic incentive. There were nine of us living in an alley house built for two. It was pretty bad but not unique. Almost every Raza family I know was poor or is poor, and I never knew one family that didn't encourage their sons or daughters to go to college or to at least make something of themselves. I think that with all these common factors, the death of Rubén Salazar triggered the determination to strive to go to college. I was sixteen at the time. If you ask Raza who were sixteen years old in 1970 when Salazar was killed, maybe you will find that his death made a sizable impact, an imprint on all the youth of the East Side. I know that after that, I wanted to do something about it. I wanted to go to college, no matter what the cost. I knew that I would be giving up the lure of the lowriding lifestyle, but it was a sacrifice I was willing to make. I remember at the time thinking that I was going to be the only Chicano on the East Side who would grow up not knowing how to tear an engine apart.

I don't know if it is irony or what, but I did go to college, graduated, I taught. Then I got into a magazine that covered the streets, the varrios, the lowriding lifestyle that I had passed over in favor of a chance to help my Raza. Maybe that's the way it was meant to be because now I can't get away from the East Side, nor can I ever get away from the street where I grew up, at least not until the barricades come down.

3 / *Lowrider Magazine:* Cruising the Streets of Aztlán

I don't really remember how or when I met the editor/publisher of *Lowrider Magazine.* What I do remember is that in the summer of '77, when I came back from Mexico, a partner of mine told me that Sonny, the owner of the magazine, had been looking for me. I had talked to Sonny a few times during the year. What I remember is that he said that he had started or was starting a magazine about the lowriding lifestyle. At that time, I was working at Hollywood High. A few partners and I had been talking about starting a barrio newspaper in L.A. We had gotten our ideas and our experience working for different Raza newspapers. I had written for *La Gente* newspaper out of UCLA since I was a freshman in 1972. In 1977, a year after I graduated, I still had too much ink in my blood to stop. Since this guy Sonny wasn't from L.A., I didn't exactly run into him everyday. The second time I saw him, as I recall, he had the premiere issue of *Lowrider.* It was OK. It had a beautiful Chicana from Soledad in color on the cover, but there was nothing much else inside. Nonetheless, I thought that after a few issues, it would probably get better.

Of course, many years before, L.A. had given birth to Raza newspapers and magazines that had made quite an impact throughout the country, mainly *La Raza* and *Con Safos. La Raza* was a political magazine from the late sixties and early seventies that focused on what was then known as the Chicano movement. *Con Safos* was a cultural, political, and artistic magazine that was the heart and soul of East L.A.—of Chicanismo. They were both magazines that will never be duplicated. They were born at a time when Raza were rebelling against anything that oppressed La Raza.

When I first saw the premiere issue of *Lowrider,* I wasn't exactly impressed except for the front cover. It was nothing like *La Raza* or *Con Safos* nor like the newspaper I had worked on, *La Gente.* The first issue of *Lowrider* was fresh and unique. It was kind of crude, but despite its crudeness, you could tell that it was on its way. It was aimed at the streets, the heart and soul of the barrios. The message was unity. The magazine was not the best example of Chicano talent, but you could tell it was going to get somewhere. Later, during the year, I was surprised to see the publisher with about two or three more issues. A few months later, after I came back from Mexico, I got in touch with Sonny and told him that I couldn't really help him full time because I would be teaching in Whittier that upcoming year. If I wasn't that much impressed with the magazine, the young Raza were. I started teaching at Cal High as a long-term substitute, but by the end of the year, I had been at La Serna, Pioneer, Santa Fe, Sierra, and Whittier High. At all these schools, I brought *La Gente* newspaper from UCLA and *Lowrider* to give to the students. It was as though the Raza were starved for reading material. Everywhere I went, the students wanted something to read. They liked *Lowrider* for the pictures and *La Gente* because it had a lot of stories about the Raza. By the end of the 1977-1978 school year, I had seen how students ate up Chicano material. In truth, it wasn't that *La Gente* or *Lowrider* or any other Chicano medium were super good, it was that students were getting trash to read from school. Maybe trash isn't the right word, but maybe irrelevant is a better word. Imagine growing up as a Chicano and always hearing the white version of history, always seeing blondies on TV. Most of the reading material that was being used (except Chicano studies classes) was boring, irrelevant, and full of stereotypes and lies. You couldn't help but sympathize with students who were ditching their English or history classes. The material for the most part had little to do with the students. When Chicano material written by Chicanos was introduced into the classroom, it was as though night had turned to day. Students became interested, intrigued, and even mad. In other words, with Chicano material, the educational process began to impact the students.

Right before the end of the school year, the publisher of *Lowrider* hit me up to help him introduce *Lowrider* to Southern California. I knew the impact *Lowrider* was beginning to have with students, but at the same time, I didn't think the magazine really had too much to say. That summer, I was going to teach a Chicano studies class at Santa Fe High School. I was also scheduled to teach for the following year, but when Proposition 13 passed, that cut out summer school. Since I had nothing to do that summer, I decided to join the magazine. I figured that if *Lowrider* was a little more like *La Gente*, like *La Raza*, it would be cool. So around May or June, I joined the staff full time. I came in with certain ideas, with certain conflicts, and with a lot of enthusiasm. From the end of that school year until September 1981, I stepped from one world into another, into an ordeal that will probably be with me for as long as I live.

When I joined *Lowrider*, I knew how to write, and I knew the streets of L.A. pretty well, or so I thought. What I ended up finding out is that there's a big difference writing for a college audience versus writing for a street audience. I did learn how to write, not just to eggheads but to everyone. In other words, what I learned to do is communicate. It was hard in a way, but experience was the best teacher. For whatever was written in the magazine, the readers let you know what they thought. As far as the streets are concerned, I thought I knew the L.A. area, but I found out it was bigger than a lot of countries, not only in population but also in area. I found out about barrios that I hadn't even known existed. I couldn't even begin to list the number of barrios in the L.A. area. The main thing that amazed me is that, from the northern end of the San Fernando Valley to the southern part of Orange County, from the East Side to the West Side, from the Pomona-Ontario area to the South Bay, from the Long Beach-Harbor-Wilmington area to the Pasadena area, all of these areas did have some things in common. Off the top, Whittier Boulevard was like a magnet that brought together Raza from all these different areas. Whittier Boulevard was more like the hub, the center of a spoked wheel. The barrios were like the spokes; they all met on the Boulevard. It's hard to imagine the size of the area until you actually stop and meet each and every barrio.

I received an education at UCLA, but it was nothing like the one I got on the streets. Going from neighborhood to neighborhood, from varrio to varrio, it was hard to accept the fact that a lot of the varrios were at war with each other. Many of the varrios were virtually the same. They even had the same names. Of course, there were reasons for all the wars, but it was hard to accept. A lot of homeboys and homegirls who were getting hurt were not vicious criminals. A lot of them were youngsters who just happened, for whatever reasons, to get into a madness they couldn't escape from. From '77 to '81, many homeboys were killed in Southern California. Never before had so many been killed. Throughout the state, probably over 2,000 homeboys were killed during these years. Many were in the pages of *Lowrider.* Before I joined *Lowrider,* I had never taken photographs. After a couple of months, I was given a camera (I paid for it) and was told to go out and take my own pictures. The only instructions I was given was to always have it with me, "You never know when you're going to need it." The reason I mention this is that I took a lot of pictures of a lot of varrios, a lot of groups, and a lot of car clubs. Many times I was hit up for the negatives because someone, a few months later, was calling to say that their homeboy had gotten killed. They wanted to know if we could give them the negatives because ours was the last picture with all the homeboys.

There was a lot of violence on the streets; much got reported, and much went unreported. One of the main things that always concerned me was whether *Lowrider* was contributing to the violence and whether it was encouraging a negative lifestyle. I know that when I joined the magazine full time, I felt there was a lot wrong with the magazine. I felt the magazine could really succeed if it took care of some of its faults. I was in conflict with the publisher's ideas from day one. Throughout my time at *Lowrider,* I don't think either one of us changed. His ideas about how the magazine should be always conflicted with my ideas. There were three major complaints about the magazine when I first joined. The first one was about how Chicanas were portrayed in the magazine. The second one was that *Lowrider* was encouraging a negative lifestyle, contributing to projecting false stereotypes. The third complaint was that *Lowrider* was not contributing anything of substance to the youth. In other words, there was nothing worth reading in the magazine. Most people felt that the publisher thought the Raza were too dumb to read. Throughout my stay at *Lowrider,* I tried to do something about these three major complaints, and to this day, I feel I contributed something positive to a magazine that influenced a whole generation.

In this atmosphere, I worked at *Lowrider.* I had conflicts with almost every idea the publisher had. Amidst the criticisms of the magazine, I do have to say that a whole book will probably be written one day about the magazine because *Lowrider* was more than a phenomenon. It grew from a few thousand magazines per month to over one hundred thousand almost overnight. A lot of work went into it, a lot of sacrifice and, in my case, a lot of blood. When the dust settles, people will recognize *Lowrider* for something that no other magazine has ever done. That is, it penetrated into every neighborhood in the southwestern United States. It even reached into the border regions of Mexico, into the Midwest, Chicago, and eventually beyond the Midwest (not counting the military bases around the world). The magazine definitely impacted a whole generation, from California to Texas. The rise and success of the magazine says nothing for the publisher's morals or scruples, but it does say a lot in terms of business. It was a unique magazine that sprung up from a seed and blossomed into a huge financial success. The question in everyone's mind is whether the youth were influenced positively or negatively. Many people will argue night and day either way till their faces turn blue. I can't answer with a yes or no, mainly because I feel there was some good in the magazine. However, I can never defend some of the things that occurred or came out in the magazine. Nonetheless, I have to share some of the responsibility because I could have quit earlier. I put a lot into it, but in the end, as much as I hated to quit, I finally felt that the bad finally outweighed the good in the magazine.

4 / Whittier Boulevard: A Chicano Disneyland

Whittier Boulevard is a legend. It is a lot of things to a lot of people. Whittier Boulevard throughout the country is seen as the lowriding capital of the world. For people outside of the area, it was first made world famous by Lil Willie G. and Thee Midnighters in their classic song, "Let's Take a Trip down Whittier Boulevard." Whittier Boulevard is probably the equivalent of the Sunset Strip in Hollywood or Rodeo Drive in Beverly Hills. But to compare it to those streets is actually to minimize the importance of Whittier Boulevard. The Boulevard is more like Disneyland or Magic Mountain, and even then, it does no justice to compare the Boulevard with amusement parks.

I didn't really know the significance of Whittier Boulevard until after I had moved from Los Angeles. Outside of L.A., almost every Mexican neighborhood has a cruising spot, an area where the Raza goes to show off their rides, where guys pick up on girls and girls pick up on guys. In San Jose, it's Story and King; in Phoenix, it's Central; in Albuquerque, it's also Central; in San Francisco, it's Twenty-Fourth Street; and in the San Diego area, it's Highland in National City. Also, El Paso, San Antonio, Denver, Española, Tucson, and almost every city in the Southwest has either a street or a park where the Raza cruise on weekends, particularly Sunday afternoons and Sunday evenings. All of these cities, all of these cruising areas look at Whittier Boulevard as the birth of lowriding, as the lowriding capital of the world. It's like the Rose Bowl; it's the granddaddy of them all.

Many people associate Whittier Boulevard with violence. Probably nothing damaged the image of lowriding more than the movie *Boulevard Nights*. Up till that point, people looked at Whittier Boulevard as a place where people would have a good time. It really was like Disneyland except that it didn't cost that much. All it cost was a tankful of gas, and you were set for the night. Of course, there was violence on the Boulevard, there was drinking, and there were also drugs. Any different than society in general? Whittier Boulevard was a place where young Raza went to have a good time. Since we do not control the media, only the negative images were portrayed in television, movies, or the newspapers. If you believed the media, you would have believed that everyone who frequented the Boulevard was a hardened criminal, ready to kill on sight. How do you put a stereotype to rest? You probably can't. People will believe what they want to believe. If there had been so much killing and violence, nobody would ever have gone to the Boulevard. The thing that people don't seem to realize is that cruising Whittier Boulevard is a tradition.

Thousands upon thousands of people cruised the Boulevard weekly. It is probably safe to assume that almost everyone who grew up in the area has cruised Whittier Boulevard at least once, not to mention those that come from surrounding areas. I'm sure nobody has the exact statistics, but I would say that probably less than 5 percent of those who came to cruise came to look for trouble. The figure is probably closer to less than 1 percent. In other words, the vast majority of those who came down the Boulevard came to have a good time.

Whittier Boulevard was not all glamour. It was not all shining new cars; it was not all expensive show cars. Not every car that came down the Boulevard had a $2,000 paint job, nor did every ride have an expensive interior. Many of the cars were lowered. Some had nice rims. But not all were hydraulically equipped. The majority of the rides were family cars. On some weekends, there were more nice rides than on other weekends. By far the most popular cars were the bombs. Everyone who ever cruised the Boulevard had a respect for bombs, probably because bombs represented the veteranos. And everyone knows that people in bombs don't go looking for trouble. Although most people who don't know the area look at Whittier Boulevard as a haven for car clubs, the fact is that most car clubs have parking lots they hang out in near the Boulevard. But Whittier is not bumper-to-bumper car clubs. There are many reasons for this. One reason is that car club members take a lot of care of their cars, so they really can't afford to get hit in bumper-to-bumper cruising. In some cases, there are actual conflicts, so sometimes they stay away. For the most part, the majority of the cars are like party mobiles. You have two, three, or four to a car, out having a good time. The worst thing I could do is present a false image of the Boulevard. There was violence on the Boulevard, but there was also violence off the Boulevard. In other words, the Boulevard wasn't unique in its problems with violence. The difference was that Whittier was a major attraction, so if a killing took place, the Boulevard was blamed for it. I wouldn't dwell on the Boulevard so much except that it's important to clarify misconceptions. The main thing I wanted to say here is that there were a lot of dishonest people involved in the controversy. Many were saying they wanted to close down the Boulevard because of the violence, but the truth is, those who wanted the Boulevard closed were not interested in curbing the violence. All they were really interested in was moving the violence away from the Boulevard.

At the time of the incident, cruising was at its height. The Boulevard had been made world famous by Lil Willie G. and Thee Midnighters in the sixties, but cruising on Whittier had its roots in the forties. Where did cruising originate? Probably nobody really knows. One of my neighbors claims he started lowriding in El Paso and that when he moved to L.A., he brought the tradition with him. A likely story, but nobody can trace lowriding to any one particular incident or location. What is known is that a similar tradition existed in Mexico prior to the invention of the automobile, that is, cruising around the placita where the guys court the girls. As far as customizing cars, its tradition may go back to a time when people were customizing carts and animals, even to many hundreds of years ago when our ancestors used to adorn or tattoo their bodies. Whatever the case, the origins go back a long way. What is definitely known is that the modern era in lowriding is traced to the midsixties, when Whittier Boulevard transformed from a drag strip into a lowriding area. Since that time, the Raza have been lowriding from Atlantic to Eastern on Whittier Boulevard. When people were racing down Whittier, it is said that people would cruise from Soto all the way down past the town of Whittier into La Habra. After the Boulevard changed from racing to lowriding, the cruising was mainly from Eastern to Atlantic, occasionally further East to Garfield Boulevard, the border of East L.A. and Montebello.

During the time of the incident, the cruising was mainly from Eastern to Atlantic, although when it was super-packed, it would go all the way to the K-Mart area. It was not unusual for a car to be caught in the K-Mart area before Atlantic for an hour. Many times, people would complain about the tremendous traffic jam, the inconvenience. As far as residents were concerned, everyone knew the situation, so it was extremely rare for someone "to get caught in traffic." The rest of the people were there "in the middle of traffic." That's what cruising on Whittier Boulevard is . . . bumper-to-bumper traffic . . . taking an hour to get through an area that would normally take less than five minutes. The complaints about the traffic were not realistic because people who were going somewhere used the side streets, but there were other real inconveniences. To paint an inaccurate picture of the Boulevard would be a disservice. A real problem was the litter left on the side streets, beer cans, bottles, etc.

Whittier Boulevard in early 1979 was at its peak. Cruising had expanded from Sunday nights to Friday and Saturday nights, Sunday afternoon in Montebello, and Sunday nights in both East L.A. and Montebello. There was violence, litter, and other negative aspects, but the cruising was a tradition. It was a Chicano alternative to Disneyland. It brought Raza together from all parts of Southern California. It was unequaled entertainment for a minimal price. It wouldn't be an exaggeration to say that love and romance flourished on the Boulevard. Thousands upon thousands of Raza came from all parts of Southern California. It was not uncommon for Raza from the military bases in San Diego area to frequent the Boulevard. San Diego had its own cruising boulevard. So did San Fernando, Oxnard, Orange County, and the Inland Empire, but Whittier was the big time. Nothing could compare with a night on Whittier Boulevard. The majority of Raza who went down the Boulevard did not go looking for trouble. Fights did take place, but the majority were not involved. Logic tells you that if it was as violent as they say, the Boulevard would not attract thousands upon thousands, week after week, year after year. It was not a gladiator's arena; it was a tradition unrivaled probably anywhere in the world.

In 1978, some people decided to make a movie about Whittier Boulevard. They called the movie *Boulevard Nights*. A lot of controversy surrounded this movie because it came on the heels of another movie called *Warriors*. *Warriors* was a movie about gangs in New York uniting to fight against the New York City Police Department. *Boulevard Nights* was a romanticized version of Whittier Boulevard. Another movie, *Walk Proud*, was supposed to be about two West Side gangs. It was so stupid it was never released on the West Coast. In fact, its only outlet was cable TV.

The movie that really made an impact was *Boulevard Nights*. It was controversial for a number of reasons. The world premiere took place on Wednesday March 21, at the Picwood Theater in Westwood. The movie was greeted by a picket line. I, along with a number of people, had seen a preview at the studios, and because I had seen it, I found it hard to tell other people not to see it. What I told people was that it was a stupid movie. I felt that the movie should never have been made, that nobody should have cooperated in the filming of the movie. It was too bad that for fifty bucks, white directors were given the keys to East L.A.–"the most violent barrio in the U.S." Everyone who was involved was given a few bucks for their participation, from security, to extras, to cars. Those who allowed their cars to be used were paid the most.

It wasn't so much that the movie distorted East L.A. The damage that was done was probably subconscious. The movie glorified the so-called gang lifestyle. The damage did not occur in L.A., rather it occurred outside of L.A. The movie projected a lifestyle that was already known in L.A. and a few other urban areas. After the movie was released, instant gangs sprung up all over the barrios of the Southwest. Youngsters began to emulate Chuco and his Mickey Mouse cholo friends. If it was just the talk or the dress that was imitated, it would have been cool, but coincidentally, a lot of violence spread with it. Varrio warfare throughout the Southwest escalated to new heights. Was it the result of *Boulevard Nights*, or was it magazines like *Lowrider Magazine?* I don't know if ten psychologists could agree, but definitely, the media has tremendous impact. *Boulevard Nights* is probably the first time Chicanos anywhere had seen Chicanos on the screen. We had been seen in Mickey Mouse roles once in a great while, but this was the first time a Chicano could take some kind of distorted pride. The TV show *Chico and the Man* was probably the ultimate disgrace. It had provided a baboso who was supposed to be a Chicano, but he reminded nobody of anyone. He looked like a white man's version of a Chicano, a silly clown, subservient to a white patron, supposedly in East L.A. *Boulevard Nights* on the other hand starred a rebellious Chicano, a vato loco, someone who cares about nothing or nobody except his homeboys. Across the Southwest, it was easier to glorify Chuco rather than a full-fledged baboso named Chico. The result was that a thousand Chucos sprung up out of nowhere. Danny de la Paz, the baboso who played Chuco, denies that *Boulevard Nights* did any damage. In his fantasy world of movies, no one gets hurt. Unfortunately, many people were killed in 1979, 1980, 1981, and so on. Even if only one had been killed directly or indirectly as a result of being influenced by that movie, it would be one too many. Having seen more than one friend fall victim to senseless warfare, I know that anything that contributes to gang warfare shouldn't be glorified. It's nothing to be proud of.

On Wednesday March 21, 1979, the movie premiered. On Friday March 23, 1979, *Boulevard Nights* opened throughout the city. The weekend before, March 16–18, the Boulevard was jam-packed. The weekend before that, March 9–11, the Boulevard was also jam-packed, bumper to bumper, from sundown till 2:00, 3:00, and 4:00 in the morning. In other words, prior to the opening of the movie, the Boulevard had been at its peak. No doubt, the influence of *Lowrider Magazine* had made an impact. Lowrider fever was spreading. The Boulevard had created other boulevards in other cities. The Boulevard and cruising had created *Lowrider Magazine,* and it had also created *Boulevard Nights*. This is because, although *Boulevard Nights* influenced many cities and many towns, it did not influence L.A. in the same way. *Boulevard Nights* brought "La Vida Loca" to other cities. It brought with it a distortion and a glorification of a lifestyle. In L.A., that lifestyle was already here. Unlike what some people would like to think, Whittier Boulevard created *Boulevard Nights,* not the other way around.

On the night of Friday March 23, 1979, the night *Boulevard Nights* opened, Whittier Boulevard was jam-packed, bumper to bumper. The weeks preceding that Friday night's opening, the sheriffs had been warning that they were expecting a lot of outside cruisers and lowriders to converge on Whittier Boulevard, just as they had been doing since the midsixties and even before that. Whittier Boulevard was jam-packed that weekend but not because of the movie. The movie had been made because of the phenomenon of cruising on Whittier Boulevard. If no movie had ever been made, the cruising would have continued as it continues to this day.

If the Boulevard was extra crowded that night or that weekend, it was because the sheriff's department had deployed over 100 sheriffs, members of the Special Enforcement Bureau. The sheriffs were out in force that weekend for reasons that only they seemed to know. There was nothing special or extraordinary about that weekend. Chuco wasn't taking a cruise down the Boulevard. As far as the Raza were concerned, Whittier Boulevard was going to be just like the weekend before. There would be rides; there would be bombs; there would be girls; there would be guys; and probably there would be a few fights. It would be like a carnival atmosphere. People would be coming from the San Gabriel and San Fernando Valleys, from Orange, Riverside and San Bernardino Counties, from Central L.A., from the Harbor-Wilmington area, from the West Side; and there would even be visitors from San Diego and Arizona. That's the way it was March 23, 1979. That's the way it was the weekend before and the month before and the year before, and ten years before that. Whittier Boulevard was unlike any other street or Boulevard in the world. Most came to meet each other, to pick up. And yes, some, a few, a small minority, came to fight. Unfortunately, many of those who came looking for trouble were wearing badges. It's too bad that hostilities exist between the sheriff's department and the residents or the cruisers because nowhere else does a relationship like that exist.

In 1979, there were about six other cruising areas in the L.A. area. There was "The Mall," San Fernando Road in San Fernando; there was Van Nuys Boulevard in the Valley; there was Whittier Boulevard in Montebello (the park); there was cruising in Santa Ana; on Pacific Boulevard in Huntington Park; and there was cruising on Whittier Boulevard in the town of Whittier. All of these cruising areas experienced problems with the police. However, in Van Nuys and on Whittier Boulevard in the town of Whittier, which are frequented more by whites and highriders, the harassment seldom if ever escalated into police brutality or outright confrontation. All of the other areas in a sense were created by Whittier Boulevard. When all the problems started happening on Whittier, the other areas got bigger because people did not want to deal with the police abuse that was occurring on the Boulevard. A lot of police measures in the other areas were taken to prevent the spill-over of the so-called gang violence that was plaguing Whittier. One boulevard after another began to be shut down, from Whittier in Montebello to San Fernando Road in San Fernando. Although police harassment did take place in other areas, it was nowhere near the scale of Whittier Boulevard in East L.A. Harassment in other areas consisted of road blocks, tickets, and trips to jail. On Whittier Boulevard in East L.A., it was not uncommon to see police abuse in the form of brutality. On a normal three-night weekend, over a hundred people were usually arrested on the Boulevard. That's an extremely high average for a one-mile area. On the weekend of March 23–25, it was reported that 538 were arrested Friday, Saturday, and Sunday nights. There were conflicting reports in the news media ranging from close to 400 to 538. Whatever the actual figure, it was unusually high even for Whittier Boulevard.

The deployment of over a hundred sheriffs of the Special Enforcement

Bureau obviously had something to do with the high number of arrests. However, there was nothing special about that weekend. Movie or no movie, the Boulevard would have been bumper to bumper from sundown till 3:00 or 4:00 in the morning.

5 / The Assignment: Zoot Suit, Glitter, the Sleepy Lagoon, and Tripping into the Past

On the night of the incident, I was taking pictures on the corner of Whittier and McDonnell for a story I was finishing. My original assignment was beyond stupid; it was silly. The original assignment, given to me by the publisher, was to do a fashion story on how East L.A. dressed. When I heard the assignment, I almost died with laughter. I didn't think he was serious. When I realized he was serious, I told him he should get some white reporter to do his kind of story. I couldn't believe the guy. Here we were protesting every time some white reporter made a mockery of our people, and now he wanted the same. I ignored him. A few weeks later, I was asked how the story was going. I told him that I wasn't an anthropologist, that if he wanted someone to snoop around to see what East L.A. was all about, there were plenty of whites who were willing to do it. At the time, every magazine and newspaper was discovering East L.A. I guess those who didn't live in East L.A. were fascinated that the Raza didn't act, talk, walk, or dress like whites. To them, it was a phenomenon, something for *National Geographic,* something for the *New Yorker.* To whites, stepping into East L.A. was like stepping into the Twilight Zone, another dimension. Story after story talked about the tattoos, the single mothers, the vatos locos, and the meaning of the red and blue bandanas. In 1979, we were under a microscope. It was a field day for sociologists, anthropologists, psychologists, and zafados. There are too many stories to mention, but they were all the same. The thing I couldn't understand is how the Raza could get tricked into it. Anyway, if I would have done a story like that, I might as well have changed my name and dyed my hair blonde.

At that time, I had just finished doing a big story about the Sleepy Lagoon, the incident on which "Zoot Suit" was based. The story had featured original photographs from the Leyvas family, the actual family that the movie was based upon. I didn't want to follow up that story with a white-oriented story. Instead, I figured I would just go from varrio to varrio and play it by ear.

I don't remember where I went to first, but I ended up going to about twenty-five to thirty varrios, mostly in the L.A. area. I came across some heavy stuff. I got into some pretty heavy situations, but for the most part, I came out OK. Sometimes, however, I found myself in the middle of neighborhoods at 3:00 A.M., wondering what I was doing there. Night-time or daytime, it was the same thing. Everywhere I went, I was given a history of each varrio. It was like no education I had ever had. I was going to neighborhoods where I wouldn't have thought of going without cannons. Not only was I given history, I was also told of their current situation. For some unexplainable reason it seemed like every varrio was under siege.

I was going from neighborhood to neighborhood, and I was getting the same kinds of stories. The next time the publisher hit me up about what I was doing, I told him I wasn't sure yet. I wasn't sure because I hadn't figured out a story. I went to Anaheim, to Long Beach, to Venice, to Eighteenth Street. Those are neighborhoods that had been in the news. In each case, the police had conducted mass arrests for one crime. Fi-nally, it hit me. The Sleepy Lagoon was a case in which twenty-two Chicanos were arrested for the murder of one Chicano in 1943. The case had made the big time news because of the unprecedented mass trial for one crime.

It happened forty years before, but it was not forgotten. The Pachuco era was still with us in that a lot of veteranos were still around us as a reminder, as a testament to those days. Carey McWilliams, a noted histo-rian, and Rudy Acuña, probably the foremost Chicano historian, both kept it alive in their respective history books, *North from Mexico* and *Occupied America.* Now, Luis Valdez, the director of Teatro Campesino, had brought the Sleepy Lagoon on stage. He made a very successful play about the Sleepy Lagoon and the Pachuco era. The play premiered in Los Angeles, then went to New York, and later became a movie called "Zoot Suit." The play broke every box office record in the world. Luis, who is also the founder of Teatro Campesino, happened to produce the right play at the right time. He has produced many plays in the past and will continue to do so in the future, but because we don't control the enter-tainment industry, that feat may never be repeated again. Hopefully it will, but the intensity, the interest it created, is even hard to describe. Some called it Zoot Suit Fever.

Amidst this Zoot Suit Fever, people were forgetting the real message of the play. It was about racism and the justice system. It was about rac-ism and racial hysteria. People got lost in the lights of Hollywood and treated it as simply an unjust event out of the past, "but now, that stuff didn't exist." It was OK to romanticize the forties but the present was a taboo subject.

Here, as I was going from varrio to varrio, there was a lot of anger. Everyone liked the play, but a lot of Raza were mad that people were ignoring the present. In neighborhood after neighborhood, mass arrests were taking place routinely. That's what the play was all about—22 were arrested for one crime. The difference between 1942 and 1979 is that it was OK to sympathize with history, but not with today's reality. Anyway you looked at it, the plebe of 1979 were the modern Zoot Suiters. The same conditions had produced both. I'm sure some eggheaded sociologist could come up with a theory, but whatever the case, the real message in the play was not glitter, it was happening in and around L.A. Since everyone was caught up in the glitter and the glamour, I decided that the story I would do would show that from the forties till 1979, nothing had changed except the sophistication of society. I went to almost every varrio in Los Angeles. At first, I had planned only to go to about ten, but since every varrio seemed to tell the same story, one varrio led to the next. The story I got on the streets was that the Sleepy Lagoon wasn't history, that mass harassment and mass arrests were common.

I remember when I went to Long Beach, and the Raza there can tell you better what happened in their barrio in 1979. A disturbance that had originally involved the barrio versus the fire department turned into a mass dragnet. Every Chicano over three feet tall became a suspect in the disturbance. If it sounds like an exaggeration, talk to someone who was there. Not only was everyone susceptible to getting stopped and interrogated, but after the illegal interrogation, the Raza were stamped like cattle to show they had already been interrogated. Imagine the scope of the dragnet. Every Mexican was a suspect. I wouldn't doubt that a book will one day be written about what happened that Sunday afternoon. If Long Beach sounds like the exception, it wasn't. Similar dragnets occurred in Venice, on Eighteenth Street, and in Anaheim. Mass arrests were occurring in almost every neighborhood. What shouldn't be forgotten is that there indeed was a crime committed by someone. That is not in question. In the case of the Sleepy Lagoon, nobody disputed that a crime had been committed. The controversy arose over how the police rounded up their suspects. They judged people by the color of their skin and by the clothes they wore. Similarly, when the crackdowns in Venice and on Eighteenth Street occurred, crimes had been committed, but laws were violated in weeding out the suspects. Maybe it sounds like I or others defend criminals. Nobody I know defends criminals. Everyone I know is for just punishment of those who commit crimes, whether the crimes are serious or minor. The point is, in the atmosphere on the streets in 1979, it seemed every brown-skinned person was a suspected criminal. If the Raza was khakied down, or wore a bandana, that person had no rights. That's where the anger stemmed from. A lot of injustice was going on, and those who could have done something about it were drowning in glitter, tripping on history, and ignoring reality. It was even worse than that. Many who idolized the Zoot Suit scene were actually tapados who had a contempt for the streets. They could romanticize the Zoot Suit era on the one hand and, on the other, put down the Raza who wore khakis and a bandana as a uniform. The modern Zoot Suiter was put down by those who were blinded by Hollywood. That is what produced a hostile response on the streets. Where were all the defenders of the Raza?

The year 1979 was one of unprecedented gang murders. There's no denying that violence was definitely on the increase during the year, but not everyone stood and watched. Many people tried to curb the violence: groups from Santa Ana to San Fernando; from veteranos from the South Bay area to righteous Chicanos from the East Side; from Raza from the Whittier area to Raza from Long Beach. Because Los Angeles is huge and the problem massive, a real organization never formed to combat the problems of the streets. The Coalition to End Barrio Warfare is the closest thing to a successful effort, but its efforts were limited to attempting to curb the violence that plagued every barrio. But the problems in the streets were not limited to varrio warfare. As mentioned earlier, the escalating violence brought on some heavy retaliation by law enforcement. In Venice, they brought in CRASH, Community Resources against Street Hoodlums. In parts of Los Angeles, they have Operation Safe Streets. The crimes were serious, but so were the measures taken to find suspects. Law enforcement should always be free to apprehend suspected criminals, but people should not be treated as suspects just because of the color of their skin or because they wear a black, red, or blue bandana.

The problem got so serious that in many areas, as in Pacoima, the young Raza were getting arbitrarily stopped, interrogated, then photographed. I remember that the Proyecto del Barrio in Pacoima was fighting to stop that harassment. But it wasn't limited to Pacoima or to a few barrios. This practice was spreading everywhere. It probably culminated with the publication of a series of police manuals listing ways to recognize gang members and how they dressed. Everyone probably has some idea of what a gang member looks like: someone tattooed down and wearing khakis, sunglasses, and a bandana. Simple, isn't it? What about a chola? What is her dress? Khakis and heavy makeup?

It may seem hard to believe, but law enforcement agencies really did come out with these types of books, claims that they knew how to identify gang members. You see, the crime isn't in claiming to know how to identify a gang member, it's the ramifications of having such a method that is the crime. In other words, if a rookie officer sees someone fitting these descriptions walking down the street, according to his or her manual the person is a gang member. What does that mean? Does it mean the officer has the right to interrogate the already assumed guilty suspect? What is the person guilty of? Being Brown? Dressing the way someone doesn't approve of? Remember that in 1979, the United States was still a democracy. Even Mexicans were supposed to have rights.

That's the story I heard on the streets. When I first started the story, I really wasn't sure what I was getting into. There was a lot of heavy stuff going down in every neighborhood, practically every day. About that time, I decided to write about the similarities of the 1940s and 1979. One barrio led to another, and after a while, I decided that it would be a two- or three-part story. All of these mass arrests were happening in the L.A. area, but I figured that maybe it was happening only in L.A. Maybe, I thought, a zoot suit isn't considered gang dress outside of L.A. I had already gone to a lot of barrios in Southern California. I figured my next step was to show the rest of the state.

That night, when I went down the Boulevard, I planned to photograph the Raza having a good time. I wanted to show that just because Raza wore bands around their wrists or wore bandanas, it didn't mean they were out to kill. The Boulevard was heavy, but it wasn't as though 100 percent of the Raza were there for war. The majority were there for picking up. The Boulevard was more about romance. It was a place that probably couldn't be compared to anywhere in the world. There were fights all right, just like you have fights at parties for looking at someone's girlfriend, for saying the wrong thing. Whatever, the thing is, if you avoided fights at parties, you could avoid fights on the Boulevard. The way it was described by the police, you would think there was a murder every night on the Boulevard. If over one percent of those who came to cruise came to fight, that was too many. The majority who came were there for romance. A carnival couldn't compare with the atmosphere, neither could a circus. At a carnival, you didn't have a thousand chances to fall in love in one night. On the Boulevard, you did. That's where legends were born and romances flourished. People met from all parts of L.A. Varrios met varrios, and if you were at war with each other, it didn't mean automatic violence, although it could lead to it. When taking pictures, I would see Raza from three or four neighborhoods together. The reason the majority weren't fighting is because the main reason for being on the Boulevard is that the guys were trying to pick up the girls and the girls were trying to pick up the guys. That was the real Boulevard. A few cagapalos gave it a bad name, and likewise, the sheriffs came down hard on everyone as if everyone was there to wipe out the rival neighborhood. That's why they shut down Whittier Boulevard, because a few cagapalos blew it for everyone. The sheriffs couldn't distinguish the good guys from the bad guys, so they took the easy way out by punishing everyone.

When I went out on the night of the incident, I didn't know what was going to happen. All I knew was that I was going to go to the Boulevard to show the Raza cruising, to show the side of the barrio that was never shown. I was going to photograph the Boulevard the way it was, the way I saw it. I knew the hazards of the Boulevard. I went out there fully aware of the situation, making sure that my partner and I didn't drink anything. As I remember, I wouldn't even have been there that weekend except that I needed pictures from the Boulevard.

The week before, a partner and I had been cruising, taking photographs, when another incident occurred. I was driving the magazine's black van. Actually, I think my partner was driving it because I was taking pictures. That night was no different than any other night on the Boulevard except that there was a light sprinkle. That didn't stop the cruising. In fact, at that point, I had known nothing that could stop the cruising, nothing short of a nuclear attack. So that night, it was packed like always. The traffic was bumper to bumper. As we reached Arizona, or the block before, a carload of girls in a van was stuck in the left-hand lane going west. Since we were also westbound in the right-hand lane, and since traffic was slow anyway, we got out and gave them a hand. It was only a dead battery. Since I always had cables, I took them out, and at that time a sheriff started getting hysterical. He started yelling, telling us to quit tying up traffic. It was funny in that what he said was true; the traffic was stopped, but who cared? That's what cruising was. Nobody behind us was complaining; nobody was in a hurry or on their way to a fire. It was funny because he was yelling as though we were causing the traffic. Now it sounds funny, but at the time it was intimidating. He kept threatening. We told the sheriff that if he waited a few seconds, we'd take care of the traffic problem. He didn't want to hear any of it. We connected the cables anyway and started up our van, and the girls started up their van. Their motor kicked over, but by this time, the guy was steaming. I mean, here we were doing a good deed, acting like boy scouts, and we were told to pull over. Another ticket, I figured. Both of us were directed onto the side street. I'm sure it was Arizona because the street seemed to be pretty wide. The Chicanas in the van were from Ontario. They thanked us, but because of the situation, we didn't get to talk. They got their ticket first and then were told to leave. With my partner and me, the sheriffs, I think, wanted to take their time. We told them that all we were doing was helping out the girls. We told them that anyone who was halfway Chicano would do the same. We told them that, because of the rain, we couldn't do anything else. I don't even remember whether they gave me a ticket that night, but what I do remember is that a few more sheriff squad cars arrived on the scene. They held us, interrogated us, and ran a make on both of us. But we were both clean. Not satisfied, about two or three of them climbed into the van and proceeded to search for something. After an hour of harassment, they gave back both of our licenses. I had it for the night. I told my partner, "It's cool, I think I got enough pictures." We were going to split, but then I said, "let's go down the Boulevard one more time." An incident like that wasn't going to scare us away. We cruised east, past Atlantic, looking for the girls in the van, but we didn't find them. So, I dropped off my partner and then split to my house on the East Side. To my surprise, the incident wasn't over then. In the morning, when I awoke, I had to photograph a wedding. That was one of the big things about an East Side wedding, that is, having cherry rides to caravan in. The classiest ones were the bombs, which everyone seemed to prefer. That day, I don't know who was getting married, all I know is that the wedding was in East L.A. and they were going to be caravaning down Third Street, not far from where I lived. I left my house and took my camera with me. When I got to an underpass around the East L.A. interchange, I took out my camera and climbed on top of the van. It would be a perfect picture of the caravan. I guess I was always in the habit of checking my camera before I took pictures. I noticed that I had no film because the indicator said "s." That meant that either I had just put in a new roll of film or that it was empty. It kind of startled me. I stopped to think. The last I remember is that the night before, the window indicated that I was on number 30, meaning I had six left. I had another roll of film, so I hurried and loaded it because I could see the caravan approaching. It didn't hit me until I started photographing that the reason my camera had been empty was because the night before, when the sheriffs had taken a long time in the van, they had taken out the roll of film. I couldn't believe what had happened. I lost interest in photographing the wedding because I realized that the sheriffs had ripped off my film. No wonder they let me go, I thought. This way, I didn't even have proof that I had been stopped. I couldn't believe it. I remember thinking that I should file a complaint, mainly because I was mad. You see, the photographs I had taken could not be reshot. I had pictures of different neighborhoods I had been to. I also had pictures of the Boulevard and some shots of a hair outfit that wanted to put an ad in the magazine. I couldn't believe it had happened. Well, I figured I just learned another lesson: Always check your camera after you've been stopped by a cop.

Due to that incident, I postponed the trip up north until I had gotten some good pictures of the Boulevard. Since my Boulevard pictures had gotten ripped off, I had to take some over again. I didn't mind that much because Whittier was like nowhere in the world. Besides, it was kind of fun to see how the Raza would get crazy in front of the camera. So instead of leaving for Northern California, the following weekend, March 23–25, I found myself once again photographing on Whittier Boulevard. Unfortunately, I didn't make it through the weekend nor did I ever end up going north for the story I had been doing.

On March 23, the incident took place, but because of publication deadlines or other complications, the story about the incident did not appear in the pages of *Lowrider* until the May 1979 issue. In that same issue, parts of the story I had been writing were put together, by the publisher I presume, and presented as "Los Varrios del Sur." I guess I got mad because that's not what I had written about nor was it the title I had given the story. I was mad, but in a way, the story had become second priority in that now I was facing criminal charges.

6 / The Incident: "I'm Alive to Talk about It"

After I was released from the hospital, I had to tell and retell a lot of people what happened to me that night. I didn't like talking about it, but once I got started, I would get into a type of trance. I would actually visualize the incidents of that night, the series of events leading to the incident, the incident itself, and the ride to the hospital and the threats. Every time I would start talking about it, I would remember how I felt in the sheriff's car.

The incident itself had happened in a split second, but the ride to the hospital is what actually traumatized me. I actually believed that they were driving me to my final destination, that I was not going to get to a hospital. Those moments that took place between the time of the incident and my arrival at the county hospital are moments I wish had never happened. It was a feeling worse than total helplessness. I think that between the time of the incident and the time I arrived at the county hospital, two hours must have elapsed. Those two hours produced a type of emotion that I couldn't describe. To say that a million thoughts went through my mind, to say that my whole life flashed before me, would be an understatement. Probably it's a feeling that survivors of death or disasters feel.

Right now, as I've been writing this, I saved this part for the last, although it appears at the beginning, because I didn't really know how I would feel or what I would say about the actual incident. Because I do have a pending lawsuit and because I don't really want to get graphic about what happened to me, I am reprinting a letter I wrote in the form of a news story that appeared in the July 1979 issue of *Lowrider*. Most people who know I'm on trial probably heard about what actually took place that night because of that story.

Roberto Rodríguez Awaiting Trial

Q-vo Raza:

Kicking back at my pad, I sit here just thinking about my trial—assault with a deadly weapon and assault and battery on a police officer. Sometimes I wake up and forget what happened, then I look in the mirror and I am reminded by the scar on my forehead.

It was Friday night, March 23, 1979. Me and my partner got to the corner of Whittier and Atlantic a little before midnight. The huda were all over the place. The boulevard was packed like it always was. The cruising was moving too slow. I hung a right and then a left on Hubbard, going all the way until I made another left on Arizona and then back on Whittier. Hanging a right, I reached McDonnell St. I hung a left and parked my car in front of Pueblo Liquor Store. There, me and my partner got out. There were blue and red lights all over the place. I took my camera out and there I ran into another dude who had a camera and was taking pictures. We talked a little about the Magazine and about all the busts that night. I started taking pictures that I needed for this story I was finishing up on. I had gone to maybe 30 neighborhoods—the story I was getting was one of harassment. I couldn't believe the amount of police harassment there was.

From Venice to Long Beach, Tercera, Cucamonga, El Hoyo, Sotel, White Fence, San Gabriel, Casa Blanca, Frogtown, Pacoima, Anaheim, 18th St., Lennox—everywhere I went, it was the same thing—mass arrests and mass harassment. Why? That's what I was trying to find out. That night on the Boulevard, I was taking photos to finish up the first half of the story. Saturday morning I was going to Oxnard, then Santa Maria, Salinas and then San Jose, the bay area and Sacramento and the rest of the State. I ain't lying. Some of the accounts I had already gotten were horror stories—tortures, kidnappings and shootings at point blank by the police and this is 1979!

"Run, so I can shoot you in the back like a dog—that's what you Mexicans are anyway." Yeah, 1979, and it's like we were back in the Zoot Suit days. In fact, that's why I was doing this story—to show that the days of the Sleepy Lagoon were not over.

So that's where I was at that night—on the corner of Whittier and McDonnell—observing a lot of harassment. The huda were foot patrolling, dragging people out of their cars, insulting both Chicanos and Chicanas alike. This night was different. There was tension in the air because it was the opening night of *Boulevard Nights*. I took some pictures of people cruising. A little after midnight, some cops were busting some Chicanas in front of the liquor store.

Me and the other dude with the camera took pictures. We went back to the liquor store. Some time later, some dude with a bright colored sarape was standing in the middle of Whittier Blvd., a few steps west of McDonnell St. He was saying something about God.

Me and the other dude with the camera went out there and took a couple of pictures. At this time everyone in the area was aware of this guy with the sarape. The cruising had stopped. It was only a matter of seconds before the sheriffs came. First about 2 or 3 approached him, then as he ran backwards, a few more arrived on the scene. They knocked him to the ground and dragged him to the sidewalk. Right about here, I took a picture. I waited about 15 seconds for the flash to recharge. At this time, more sheriffs joined in on the beating. Some came at him with kicks to the stomach or wherever they landed. Me and the other dude took another picture. While this was going on, more sheriffs were arriving.

The people who were around me and the people who were on the boulevard were pleading with the sheriffs to leave the defenseless guy alone. They (sheriffs) kept beating the guy. I was about to leave, but they kept beating and choking him worse. I took my last picture—and, by this time, the boulevard was crawling with sheriffs. The sheriffs started yelling at me and the other witnesses, including the other guy with the camera. They were yelling for us to leave. As we were leaving, more of the sheriffs were arriving. One of them yelled at me, "LEAVE!" and I responded, "I'm leaving."

As I crossed the street towards Pueblo Liquors, I could see a lot of people in the store. Next thing you know, I got pushed from behind and then I heard him say, "Get the guys with the cameras." I got scared. I thought they were going to do me in. I figured if I gave the camera to somebody, they could split with the evidence.

This was all happening in a split second because after I got pushed against the car, I got hit from behind. I threw my camera so that they could hold it. I saw it in midair and by then, I had gotten hit with the riot stick in the back. I had gotten punched and kicked and, by this time, I had been knocked to my knees. I remember seeing at least four or five of them. As they turned me around, I could see the black stick going right at my head. I got hit and I was stunned, dazed—I hit the cement. They kept going away. Finally one sheriff began yelling at me. I didn't know he was yelling at me—I was still in a daze. The blood was spurting out pretty bad. The sheriff kept yelling. Then I knew he wanted to handcuff me. So first the right hand, and I forgot about the left. He yelled again. Then my left arm. They left me there bleeding. I was on my stomach, not really aware of what was going on. I could see the sheriffs running back and forth. Finally, after about five minutes, they picked me up and put me in the sheriff's car. I was bleeding bad. I asked them to take me to the hospital.

They laughed and joked about how it was a good hit. Meanwhile, I kept bleeding. All the blood was rolling off my jacket and onto my pants. I asked the different sheriffs that came around at least ten times to take me to the hospital. I was a bloody mess. Everyone knew what had happened. While in the sheriff's car, I looked out—some Chicanas flinched as they saw me—they acted like they had seen a monster. I tried to tell them to call *Lowrider Magazine,* but they couldn't hear me. I looked at the mirror and my face was full of blood. I couldn't tell where I was bleeding from—there was blood squirting out of my forehead. There was blood all over my eyes, nose and mouth. Finally, after about ten minutes, two of the sheriffs stepped into the squad car. The cop riding shotgun pulled his riot stick out and said, "Motherfucker, you act up and I'm going to finish the job." From then on in, everything he said was a direct or indirect threat. Everything he said was intended for me to get scared—to make me believe they weren't going to take me to a hospital.

They drove away from the liquor store and into a dark street at about 5 miles an hour. The guy driving didn't know or was pretending he didn't know where he was going. He acted confused.

After going from one dark street to another, the guy riding shotgun unscrewed the back of my camera and said, "So you had the lens cap on all the time, huh?" I didn't answer. He turned around and I assume he either exposed the film—or took it out. After a number of threats, and being in the position I was in, bleeding and in a dark street, the shotgun rider turns to his partner and says, "Do you think we can convince him how he got that cut?" The driver says, "I don't know, ask him." The shotgun rider pulls out the riot stick and asks me, "How did you get that cut?" I answered him, "I hit the cement." I told him that because I was under threat, we were going 5 mph through dark streets, they were pretending to be lost, and no one knew where I was.

He again asked me if I was sure (with the riot stick in his hand). Again, I said "yes." Because of the circumstances, I stuck to that story until I was released three days later. I've gone to arraignment, pretrial, discovery motions. That's where I'm at right now. I can't believe they've gone this far. I thought by now they would have dropped the charges. The sad part is that things like this happen every weekend like it was nothing.

Pura Raza

*   *   *

As I said, this letter came out in the July 1979 issue of *Lowrider.* At that time, I still hadn't won my case. When I wrote it, I was still kind of scared, scared that I could wind up in prison. What I wrote then was an appeal, and I think it worked in that because of that story, a lot of Raza rallied to my support.

I'm sure that today, if I wanted to, I could probably write about what happened that night in more detail, and I could even be more graphic. But in a way, I think I'm still trying to block out the incident.

7 / The Legal Defense: Flying the Bandera High

As soon as I came home, after I was finally released from the jail ward of the County Hospital, the first thing I did was make a phone call to a friend and tell him to meet me at my house in East L.A. I told him to bring his camera. Between the time I called and the time he got there, I called another friend and told him I needed a lawyer. Since we had both gone to UCLA, we both had a few friends who were lawyers, although I hadn't kept in contact with any of them. He suggested that I talk to a friend of ours, Eddie, who was just starting out as a lawyer. I called him, but he wasn't able to help me out. However, he said that maybe he could recommend someone. He mentioned Sam Paz, someone who I slightly knew. He had been one of the founders and first editors of *La Gente* newspaper at UCLA before I had attended. He had gone on and become a lawyer. He also mentioned Antonio Rodríguez, a lawyer who also had a reputation for defending the Raza.

For whatever reasons, I didn't want to see those lawyers. Eddie suggested going to see the head of the legal center near the projects on Olympic. In a way, I didn't really want to go there because that's where Antonio worked, and I didn't feel like running into him. He said to ignore that and just go see the head of the place. I hung up the phone and called my friend back and told him I had talked to our lawyer friend. When I told him about the legal clinic, he cracked up and said, "Why don't you get Antonio to defend you. That way you can write for *Lowrider* from Quentin." It was kind of funny in a way, but the reason he said that was because I didn't really care for that lawyer. I knew him, and I knew of him. After laughing, I told my friend that I would tell him on Monday what happened. I must have still been in a daze because, after hanging up, I started feeling kind of dizzy. After a while, my friend got to the house. He reacted like everyone else did. He couldn't believe that the battered person he was looking at was me. I didn't look anything like myself. He took out his camera and took some pictures in color and in black and white. It was near sunset or thereabouts. I know I told my friend what happened. I don't know who else I told that night but I don't think I really wanted to talk. I just wanted to think. I needed some time to think.

Here I was, a college graduate, a former teacher, and now I found myself charged with assault with a deadly weapon and assault and battery on a peace officer. I was thinking to myself, "This isn't supposed to happen!" Before this, I had heard about people pinching themselves to see if they were awake, if it was for real. It was happening to me. No matter what I did, I couldn't believe it had happened. It was like a nightmare. When I finished thinking about choosing a lawyer, I went to the mirror, and I couldn't believe what I saw. My face was disfigured. The main blow from the riot stick had hit me square on the forehead, above the nose and between the eyebrows. It had created a perfect "T," a cross. My face was black and blue, and my forehead was puffed out. The stitching that held the skin together was blood red. I was a mess. I looked like one of those dudes with a big forehead from the "Outer Limits." That whole night, I thought about a million things. Besides choosing a lawyer, the second thing on my mind was finding out what had really happened that weekend. I found out that Whittier Boulevard had been shut down Friday night, "as a result of a riot"!

When I was in the hospital Saturday night, I didn't realize what was actually going on. When people started coming in with cracked heads that night, I knew something big was going down. The jail ward was packed to capacity. After coming home Sunday night, I was tempted to go down to the Boulevard. On the Boulevard, a lot of people had already heard about what had gone down on Whittier Boulevard on Friday and Saturday nights. Apparently, there had been massive arrests on both nights, and more were expected that Sunday night.

Somehow, a friend had heard about it and called Channel 7. Estela López, an assignment editor for Channel 7, called me and asked if I would give an interview. I froze. I didn't know what to say. The cops had threatened me, and since I was always out on the streets, I didn't know if it was a good idea to put my face out on television. That was my prime concern. I didn't want to be recognized and harassed on the streets. I didn't want to be killed. At the time, the fear was real. I had just barely got out. I told her that I didn't have a lawyer yet, so that when I got one, I would ask the lawyer and let her know. I told her that I was too mad at the time, that I probably wouldn't know what to say or would say all the wrong things. I told her that since I didn't have a lawyer yet, I had to make sure that what I said wouldn't affect my case. The real reason was that I was kind of scared. I still didn't believe it was real. I hadn't finished thinking things out. I had to worry about getting a lawyer.

I don't remember if I slept or how I slept that night, but in the morning, the first thing I did was go to that legal office where I was supposed to see the head of the legal center. Since legal centers are for those who can't afford lawyers, and since they get their money from the government, I figured they probably couldn't even take my kind of case because it involved the sheriffs. I didn't want to go, but I went anyway. A week before that, or two weeks before, I had gone to that center where I met Gus, a partner of mine. He was there to see Antonio about him taking a case of a young Chicano from some nearby neighborhood, who was in some kind of danger or trouble. When we went in to see Antonio,

I had been uneasy because I really didn't like him. I don't remember what happened as a result of that meeting except that I don't think he took the case.

Whatever the case, here I was going to this legal clinic to see if the head of it would defend me. When I got there, I hesitated. I was going to change my mind and walk right out, but before I could, the first person I saw was Antonio. He was with a client or something, and I think he was leaving. When I walked in, he was startled to see my face. I probably was as startled as he was. I remember the look on his face as he asked, "What happened?" I began telling him of the incident, and in the middle of my explanation, he said, "I'll take the case." I don't know how I responded, but I was shocked. I froze. I didn't know what to tell him. I practically hated this guy, and in a split second, I was supposed to decide. I hadn't asked him to take my case. I was there to see the head of the place, but there was no time for a debate. I knew I didn't like the guy, I didn't really know what he thought of me, but I thought that if he was willing to offer, then it was as good a time as any to let bygones be bygones.

As for his determination in defending the Raza, there was no questioning his credentials. In a split second, I thought to myself, "I would lose gladly as long as I knew that a fellow Chicano, a fellow Mexicano defended me to the best of his ability." I knew that I could lose, that I was taking a big chance, but just the decision to have him represent me became for me more important than whether I won or lost. It was like I had to decide whether I was willing to put aside all the conflicts I had with him. I knew he stood for the Raza, so the decision wasn't hard in that sense. It was more a thing of pride. In that frozen split second, I decided that this was as good a time as any to put the past behind. It seemed I was being tested. If I righteously believed in the Raza, I had to put aside petty differences, and that's what they were. I decided "yes." He probably didn't know that I had frozen, that my mind was racing a million miles a minute. When I agreed to let him take my case, it was like I had instantly matured. It was a hard decision to make. It was the right decision, and I'm glad I made it.

I probably never thanked him enough for defending me because the victory probably meant a lot more to me than it meant to him. For me, the fact that he defended me was a victory. It had proved something that I had long suspected. I had felt that a lot of Raza couldn't get along for Mickey Mouse reasons, but in the end, when push came to shove, all those who were for the Raza would still fly the bandera high, and all those who didn't really have the interests of the Raza at heart would show their true vendido colors. It was important to me because thereafter everyone who had ever been my enemy, I no longer considered my enemy. I know that all those with whom I had had conflict in the past were ready to back me up at the drop of a hat. That was true carnalismo.

Up to that point, I thought all the former Chicano leaders had sold out, that they had betrayed the Raza. What happened to me restored my faith in myself and my own Raza in that I got to see what carnalismo was really all about. It was not a theory, it was strength. I know, because of the experience of getting defended by someone I didn't like, that in the future, when the need arises, there is an army of Raza ready to pick up the flag, ready to fight and die for our Raza, despite petty differences.

It's too bad that it took this incident for me to realize this. I know that because of it, I can see things differently. I value life more. I learned to appreciate honesty; I learned to distinguish things that are important from things that are trivial. It's too bad that it had to happen that way because I know a lot of Raza who could use a crisis so that they could see who their friends are. It's been over three years since I won the case, and in a way, there's some unfinished business regarding my lawyer, in that I didn't thank him enough, not only for winning but for learning and understanding the true meaning of camaraderie, of carnalismo.

8 / Plea Bargaining: A Bargain for the Guilty

Many times you hear the saying, "It ain't nothin' but a misdemeanor." It's a carefree attitude that allows a lot of youngsters to participate in crime, to be on the edge of the law, knowing that if convicted, it means nothing more than a slap on the wrist.

Plea bargaining is like a loaded weapon. It can work for you, or it can work against you. If you are guilty, plea bargaining is good for you. I think the reason it exists is for expediency. The way it works is like this. Let's say a person is charged with murder. If the police know that the person is guilty but do not have sufficient evidence, the prosecutor may make a deal with the defense lawyer for the guilty party to plead guilty to a lesser crime, say manslaughter. If the person is guilty, it's a pretty good deal. For the courts, it must be good because it saves the state a lot of money. In other words, rather than having a lengthy trial for a major offense, the lawyers work out a deal that reduces the charge. The prosecution gets an easy conviction; the state wins; and if the person is guilty, he also wins. If you are guilty, it is a bargain.

Probably the biggest travesty of justice is the misuse of plea bargaining. It's hard to pinpoint how many instances or what percentage of plea bargaining is a misuse. The way it's used is this: Someone is charged with a crime or a number of crimes. The party involved is innocent. The prosecution offers to drop all the charges except one or to reduce the more serious crime to a lesser crime. The deal is, "We'll reduce the charges if you plead guilty to at least one minor crime." In addition, the defendant is assured that if he pleads guilty, he can also get off with a few days in jail or that he can get off free altogether with just probation. The innocent party is under tremendous pressure, due to lack of money, time, and good legal representation, just to get it over with.

This preoccupation with "getting it over with" is where the abuse comes in. The abuse is being committed by law enforcement, the justice system, and the individuals who are actually guilty. The losers are those individuals who are wrongfully charged and society that has to deal with the violent criminals who, for reasons of expediency, are let off the hook with nothing but a misdemeanor.

Before the incident ever happened to me, I was aware of this common practice of plea bargaining. I really didn't understand it until I ended up in the hospital room where many were bruised or had their heads cracked. There I saw what "travesty of justice" meant. If I'm correct, everyone who was locked up in the jail ward was Chicano; many had also been charged with being under the influence of PCP (Angel Dust). That was the initial charge. The other charges ranged from resisting arrest to failure to disperse, assault on an officer, etc. In the many cases that I observed, people were routinely stopped, and before you knew it, verbal abuse was followed by physical abuse. The victim ended up with a series of charges, but the abuse was not limited to Chicanos; Chicanas were frequent victims of this brutality. After being harassed and many times beaten, the victim ended up in jail as the criminal. Sure, there was always a pretext, but the main pretext was the color of your skin. Those who were stopped often either had a can of beer in their car, or they talked back—crimes that hardly called for the use of riot sticks. It's easy to understand how confrontations occurred, because often times there indeed was a criminal element operating on Whittier Boulevard. Sometimes, the sheriffs did find weapons, etc., but people aren't automatically guilty. The problem that was occurring is that people were routinely stopped, harassed, and beaten and then charged with a crime. The officers rarely come to trial when they themselves become disrespectful of the rights of people. Plea bargaining almost ensures that the police will always get off scott free.

When police abuse occurs, the recourse is to file a complaint against the officers involved. If the victim of a police beating is making a complaint, that victim probably has been charged with a series of crimes. What's a police complaint? Most people view it as a paper that's thrown away, and if it does go on their record, it is less than a slap on the wrist. Most people don't even bother reporting police abuse because they have to file it at the police department in the area where the incident occurred. Most people figure that police just file it away or they get a simple reprimand. If a person off the street actually beat and assaulted a police officer, the civilian would not only be charged with the serious crime of assaulting a peace officer, he would also be considered a dangerous criminal. Most likely, the person would spend some time in prison. Now, if a police officer beats someone, all he or she gets is a pat on the back or maybe a reprimand, if that much. You would think that if it could be proven, a guilty officer would at least stand trial for assaulting a person. When incidents of police brutality occur, the police department doesn't consider the officers as criminals even though they've committed criminal acts by abusing their police powers. The only recourse for a person off the streets is to defend himself from the charges against him and, at best, file a meaningless complaint. That's where plea bargaining is abused.

Plea bargaining is detrimental to an innocent person who has to worry about defending himself against false charges. The main concern is to fight the charges. There is rage. Everyone's instinct is to see the guilty officers behind bars, but as the prospect increases of an innocent person going to prison, the concern is to just get it over with. Plea bargaining does just that. Most people would rather not go through a lengthy, expensive trial, where there is no assurance of winning. People have to worry about getting a good lawyer, lawyers fees, missing work, etc. When they offer you freedom in exchange for a guilty plea to a lesser crime, 99 percent of innocent victims will take the freedom. That is how the guilty police get away with criminal police abuse. After you plea bargain, after you plead guilty to a lesser crime, you have all but waived your legal right to seek damages via a lawsuit. Sure, they tell you that being guilty in a criminal court does not prevent you from filing a lawsuit, but if you plead guilty to, say, resisting arrest (rather than assault of a peace officer), in the eyes of the jury you are not innocent. Your testimony is tainted because you have stated that you were guilty. What are the chances of a person, a victim of police abuse, pleading guilty to a crime and then winning a lawsuit against the police? The chances are probably ZERO. Worse, I don't even think that many people, after plea bargaining, consider a lawsuit. The main reason they agree to a plea bargain is because they want to put the incident behind them. Besides, they figure that they don't have a chance in a million to win a lawsuit against law enforcement. For obvious reasons, very few lawsuits are filed against law enforcement officers, and even less win. Even if someone refuses to plea bargain and they eventually are exonerated of all the charges (by the District Attorney dropping the charges or by winning in a trial), the chances are also very slim that someone who goes through a draining ordeal will want to continue pursuing the matter further via a lawsuit. It is expensive, it is draining, and it is time consuming. It's a long time to wait.

So in essence, those officers who do violate the law by using excessive force are protected by a justice system that almost guarantees many officers will take advantage of the system, knowing that nothing will ever happen to them. It is a sad commentary on law enforcement and the justice system that permits it.

If we were talking only theories in a university classroom, the arguments could be excused as intellectual rhetoric. But the fact is, at the time of my incident, harassment and police overreaction were a common occurrence on Whittier Boulevard. The abuse may have been even more widespread than anyone really knows, but a lot of people can tell you about the real violence that was occurring on the Boulevard.

While the press and the media were harping on the gang violence that was plaguing the Boulevard, little was heard about the police harassment and the beatings that occurred nightly on Whittier Boulevard. Some people could tell you horror stories of police abuse that occurred to them on the Boulevard. When you ask them what they did about it, the standard response was that they did nothing or that they filed a complaint but nothing came of it. A lot of them ended up doing time until the charges were dropped or until they plea bargained.

Maybe my perception wasn't that good, and maybe I really couldn't get a feel for the Boulevard because I worked for the magazine, but from what I saw, the gang violence that the media talked about did exist. But it was nowhere near the comparison to police abuse. On the Boulevard, everyone was fair game for the sheriffs. I remember that people would always scream bloody murder when someone was wrongfully killed by law enforcement officers. The only problem was that police abuse was more widespread than an occasional mistake killing. When a killing occurred, people were quick to react, but how many people were being killed senselessly by law enforcement? Five or maybe six per year? The killings got a lot of attention, but the real abuse is that probably hundreds were being intentionally abused daily. On weekend nights on Whittier Boulevard in East L.A., many senseless beatings were taking place. Maybe they're still taking place, maybe not. I'm not hanging around Whittier Boulevard at night to find out.

Someone might ask, "What is a senseless beating?" Probably nobody can produce a set of rules to distinguish when a beating is senseless or not. The thing is, beatings should never be allowed. I could never or will never understand the motivations or pressures of a cop, but I have witnessed defensive action versus senseless beatings. Obviously, there is a proper time for the use of force. Who determines when is the proper time? The police? Or the residents they are sworn to serve and protect? Regardless of who makes the rules, there is a big difference between giving a gun or a riot stick to someone who has no respect for the people he or she is supposed to protect and giving this equipment to an officer who is truly serving the people. The best regulations in the world are of no use when the person behind the badge is no good. People probably have argued about the role of police in society for thousands of years and will probably continue to argue about that forever. Maybe things will get better. Maybe in the future someone will devise a law enforcement system that everyone likes. The future may be different, but in 1979, people were routinely beaten on Whittier Boulevard. Then they were arrested on charges of assault on a peace officer.

When I was assaulted and then arrested, my case was probably as routine as you can get. The only difference was that I had a camera at the time. From what I remember, 538 people were arrested on the Boulevard on the weekend of March 23–25. When I was in the county hospital, the jail ward was packed. I couldn't believe the amount of people who were there because they had been beaten on Whittier Boulevard. If Friday night was bad, Saturday and Sunday were worse. The only thing that came to my mind is that I thought that, from what l had seen, the majority of the victims were innocent, but I also knew they had been charged with serious crimes. While I was in the hospital, Friday, Saturday, and Sunday, I was quiet. I kept my thoughts to myself. With everyone talking about how they got arrested and what they had been arrested for, I also wanted to say what had happened to me, but I figured I had better be quiet until I got out. For some reason, I felt sorry for everyone who was in there. Here I was with my face disfigured, and I was feeling sorry for them. The thing was, I knew I would win my case. I knew that I would win not because I was more innocent than anyone else but because I had a camera. Because I worked for the magazine, I would get a good lawyer. I would not back down, and I would sue the hell out of them. I was mad because I knew that, because of the nature of the case, I would win. I was actually mad because I knew I would win, but most everyone else would lose. I knew that I personally couldn't afford a fancy lawyer but that, through the magazine, enough publicity would be generated to obtain the services of a good lawyer. That's all I could think about that whole weekend. I knew I would win, but what enraged me was that, due to financial and other circumstances, most everyone would end up plea bargaining. Some would eventually get their charges dropped altogether, but I figured very few would file complaints, and even less would file lawsuits against the county.

From the point of the incident until they finally dropped the charges, nine months had elapsed. A lot happened during that time. They wanted me to plea bargain. As determined as I was to win, the offer was tempting. The last thing I wanted was to do time in prison. As innocent as I knew I was, I was tempted because I was actually scared of the possibility of going to prison for a crime I didn't commit. I figured if they were crazy enough to put me on trial on trumped-up charges, the possibility existed that I might get a jury that would actually believe that I attacked the sheriffs with a camera. Despite the knowledge that if I accepted the plea bargain, I would probably get off with just probation, that wasn't the point! I was innocent. Why should I plead guilty even to jaywalking when I knew that I didn't do anything wrong. It took a lot of faith in my lawyer because I knew that if I rejected the offer, we would head into a trial, despite my innocence, with the possibility that I could lose. We rejected their offer. We had called their bluff, but they didn't respond by dropping the charges. As the months went by, I began to worry. They hadn't dropped the charges as everyone had said they would. I thought I might have made a mistake. I began to think I would lose, not because I was guilty but because I didn't believe in the fairness of the legal system.

9 / The Mass Denial of Rights and the Battle over the Boulevard

In 1979, there was so much violence in the streets of Los Angeles that certain areas resembled war zones. The news media reported all the gang-related murders and gang-related crime, but what they failed to report was the violence committed by the police. In East L.A., police brutality was as common as a smog alert. Who's to say how much of that police violence was justifiable? One thing for sure is that the influx and use of Angel Dust in the barrios made the problem worse.

If you think that police violence doesn't exist, it's like saying that gang violence doesn't exist. People may call it by another name such as justified use of force or excess force. Whatever it's called, it exists. In 1979 police violence was rampant. I no longer go out on the streets twenty-four hours a day to see if it still occurs. Sometimes, before I ever really observed a lot of it, I used to drive by police who had pulled people over and I'd see them roughing up Raza. My first reaction was an angry one. I used to see that all the time, but later when I got to see more of that, I realized that sometimes there was more to it than met the eye. Sometimes, when officers pulled over suspects, I did see that the occupants of the car were abusive and/or under the influence. When people were under the influence, it changed things a little. A few times, when I would drive by and see something happening where officers were using force, I thought that maybe the suspects had just finished shooting someone or had just robbed someone. I learned not to prejudge. The reason I mention this is because at the time, there was a lot of senseless violence by Raza against Raza. When someone got hurt, the thought that would come to my mind was, "would the perpetrator get caught?" Sometimes, when I would see officers roughing up Raza, I would think "don't jump to conclusions, maybe they just committed a serious crime." If I had learned not to jump to conclusions, the Boulevard changed all that.

The streets were dangerous in 1979. That, nobody can deny. That's why I had learned not to jump to conclusions. Prior to that year, I had seen the effects of gang violence on our Raza. It was destructive. Words cannot come close to describing the effects a single murder could produce. All the worst came out of our Raza: hatred, vengeance, revenge, followed by more hatred and retaliation. These reactions produced an endless chain of killings that seemed to never end. Most Raza can probably name at least one person they grew up with who is now dead. Unfortunately, some people know two, three, ten, and sometimes even more people who have fallen victim to gang violence. Just by living and growing up on the East Side, I know that 99.9 percent of everyone is against gang violence. Nobody I know is for it. Probably as far back as everyone can remember, Raza have always talked about uniting the Raza to stop the senseless killings. I was aware of that in 1979.

Until 1979, I was aware of gang violence as much as anyone, but up to that point, I was not fully aware of the extent of police violence. Probably I had heard of hundreds of cases of police harassment and abuse prior to 1979, but around that time, when I began to take photographs for *Lowrider*, I saw how routine and widespread police abuse was. When I first went out to take pictures on Whittier, I did see a lot of violence among the Raza, but it was nowhere near the amount of abuse by the police. That was 1979. It wasn't the 1940s. What I saw is something that probably cannot be adequately described. It is one thing to know of or to be aware of police violence. It is another thing entirely to see it. What I saw time after time was not hypothetical nor did I jump to conclusions. A routine stop of people on the Boulevard was always presupposed by the assumption of guilt. In other words, anyone who was pulled over was guilty even if proven otherwise. The sad part is that any minor infraction was grounds for rude behavior, for provocation, for abuse, for arrest, and many times for violence. The reason it is sad is because when the plebe went out to cruise, not everyone was a santito or santita. When people go out to have a good time, oftentimes there is drinking involved. Even rich people and gabachos do it. When the Raza would get pulled over, an open container would give officers the license to do whatever they pleased, because once it had been established that someone was under the influence, the officers had a justification. I could count and recount incidents of police abuse, harassment, and brutality till I turned blue. The thing is, it exists, or it existed in 1979. In relation to the number of cases of police abuse, few of the victims are killed. The problem was ten times worse than gang violence because junior gangsters are not paid to keep the peace whereas the police are paid to "serve and protect." The reason police brutality is not headline news is because the brutality is almost always accompanied by serious charges against the victim. If a cop beats somebody on the head, the cop can say that the victim was resisting arrest. The brutality is then justified. The brutality is not seen as brutality but, rather, it is seen as proper use of force. The victim ends up facing criminal charges, so cries of police brutality seem hollow when they are reported in the media.

Another reason police brutality exists is because of the widespread use of drugs, alcohol, and specifically Angel Dust (PCP). When a person is actually under the influence of PCP, it does cause erratic and many times violent behavior. There is ample proof that many who come under the influence of PCP are apt to commit crimes. When an individual is stopped, the police do have trouble arresting the individual. The problem is that in attempting to subdue someone under the influence of PCP, force almost always is used. In those kinds of cases, there is a fine line between proper use of force and excess use of force. The problem is that not everyone on the Boulevard is always under the influence of PCP. Yet, at the time of the incident it seemed like everyone was treated as though they were. There's a big difference between having a six pack in a car among friends versus being under the influence of PCP.

Maybe the problem of police violence has always been serious, but to me, it seemed like it peaked in 1979. Between March 1979 and the closure of Whittier on August 31, 1979, it seems that a battle intensified between the sheriff's department and the lowriding plebe.

When the incident took place on Whittier and McDonnell, I was not the only person arrested or sent to the hospital. If I had been singled out, if I had been the only victim, then my case would have been altogether different. It would have been an isolated incident, involving one individual. But that's not the way it happened. On the weekend of March 23–25, the media reported that 538 people were arrested on Whittier Boulevard. Later, apparently to diffuse the situation, the number was reduced to close to four hundred. The number, 538, even though an unusually high number, still does not adequately paint a vivid picture of what went on that night, what went on that weekend, and what was going on every weekend. Even if only 100 were arrested, that would have been a high number. The statistic that's missing is how many people were harassed that weekend. How many people were victims who were not arrested? Believe me, it wasn't a nice sight to see Chicanas getting dragged out of cars by sheriffs. It wasn't a pretty picture. Worst of all, it didn't start or end that weekend. From what I heard, the harassment had been going on for years; and from what I have seen personally, it was society at its worst. Authority had fallen to the days of the Wild West, and we were the Indians. We were the bad guys. That was the sad part, that it was a racial thing. It was mainly white sheriffs, exerting authority over an indigenous population. Every weekend, it was the same thing. Every weekend, over 100 Chicanos were routinely arrested on the Boulevard. Every weekend, the sheriffs made wild claims that it was outsiders who were causing the trouble, and they were right, because when the sheriffs went home, they didn't go home to East L.A. They went home to everywhere but East L.A. It was the sheriffs who knew nothing of what it was to live in East L.A. and to grow up among Raza. To them, East L.A. was a territory to be conquered every night, and Whittier Boulevard was the highlight every weekend. When the incident happened to me that night, I probably didn't realize what was happening until later when it became apparent that the sheriffs had declared an all-out war against Whittier Boulevard and the "outsiders."

At the time, by default, *Lowrider Magazine* was the closest thing that people could call the "voice of the Raza." When the war against Whittier Boulevard intensified, it was the sheriffs on the one hand and the lowriding plebe on the other. Because of what had happened to me, I was determined personally to fight against those who wanted to close down the Boulevard. They were saying that they were concerned with the gang violence and all that, but that's what got me mad because not even one word was said about police violence. The merchants who were in support of the closure were concerned for economic reasons. U.N.O. (United Neighborhood Organization) was concerned about the problems caused by loitering and by the ensuing gang violence. One thing is for sure. The U.N.O. had legitimate concerns which they have shown over the years. The problem in regard to Whittier Boulevard is that their desire to see an end to gang violence and their desire to see the Boulevard closed said nothing about the prevalent problem of police violence. For whatever reasons, they chose not to speak up about the widespread police violence that was plaguing the Boulevard. Maybe they weren't aware of the extent of police brutality because it wasn't commonly reported in the papers, but on top of the gang violence, the police violence made the streets even unsafer. This call for the closure of Whittier Boulevard by the merchants and U.N.O., plus the zeal of the sheriff's department, culminated in its closure on August 31, 1979.

The way that battle was won was through the media. From March to August 31, 1979, there was a concerted assault on lowriders and Whittier Boulevard. Actually, the battle started long before March and continued after the Boulevard was closed. The campaign against the plebe and against the cruising did not stop. Even to this day, those who claim that the Boulevard was closed because of gang violence cannot say that even one life was saved, because the closure did not stop the killings. The years 1979, 1980, and 1981 were the years with the highest rate of gang killings. Nothing was solved.

Before the incident in March, there were always rumors that the sheriffs were going to close down the Boulevard, and in fact they did close it down a number of times, but they did not have the legal authority to barricade the Boulevard. The reason they needed that legal authority is that when the sheriffs closed down the Boulevard without the barricades, people would get diverted onto the side streets, but somehow, everyone managed to get back on the Boulevard. Either that or people would start cruising Atlantic, Olympic, or the side streets. On March 23–25, when *Boulevard Nights* opened up, over 100 Special Enforcement Bureau officers of the Sheriff's Department were sent out to Whittier Boulevard in East L.A. The result was that the Boulevard was shut down. All of the arrests that weekend focused people's attention on the Boulevard, but rather than getting the true picture, they got the sheriffs' version. From that point on, Whittier Boulevard became national news. Whittier Boulevard, in the eyes of many, became *Boulevard Nights*. The problem is that, by focusing on gang violence, the sheriffs shielded themselves. They came out as the defenders of peace, justice, and the American way. Nothing was said of the mass arrests, of the widespread police brutality, of the routine abuse, or of the blatant disregard for rights that were taken for granted. From March, after that weekend, a malicious campaign was carried out that culminated with the closure of Whittier on August 31, 1979.

What was happening on the streets between March and September wasn't just a media war. There was war in the streets. One thing I should say again is that I don't know anyone who is for gang violence. A solution to all the violence did take place even before the closure. The Raza, the plebe, had enough. By the summer of 1979, cruising Whittier Boulevard in East L.A. wasn't the big thing anymore. The big thing was cruising Whittier Boulevard in Montebello.

I remember that when I was in elementary and junior high, the Volksmen car club hung out at Montebello Park. That was in the mid- and late sixties. In the seventies, a lot of Raza used to hang out at the park just to have a good time. By the summer of '79, hanging out at Montebello Park wasn't just where the cool Raza spent a Sunday afternoon. By then, the Boulevard there was bigger than the Boulevard in East L.A. The cruising was so heavy that at times it would stretch from Garfield Boulevard to the bridge in Pico Rivera that led into Montebello. The cruising in Montebello went on from about noon or 1:00 P.M. on Sundays till about 10:00 or 11:00 P.M. and sometimes even later. For those who were totally addicted, after the cruising in Montebello, many would go back to East L.A. to continue the all-night cruising. Cruising was definitely at its peak in '79. The cruising plebe hated gang killings as much as anyone else. What got everyone mad was that the police and the media would make it seem as though everyone who liked to cruise was a criminal looking for someone to shoot or stab. No matter where the Raza cruised, they were harassed, and always on the pretext that gang elements were causing trouble. Of course, there were problems, but the real problem for the majority was the police harassment.

If anything, as I prepared for my trial while all this was going on, I was confident that my lawyer would expose the truth, that the sheriffs would be put on trial and that the trial would actually not be me versus the sheriffs but rather the Raza versus the sheriff's department, or the lowriding plebe versus the sheriff's department. I actually saw it as a battle over the truth about Whittier Boulevard. They had the media on their side. We had the magazine. But at the trial, I figured that the media would finally see the truth about the Boulevard, about how the sheriffs had ceased to function as peace officers.

That's how I saw my trial. The Boulevard had been closed on August 31, 1979, but my trial had not come up yet. I thought that with the closure, the sheriffs had won a momentary victory but that when the trial came around, the Raza would be exonerated. The media would see a different face of the Boulevard. I would win, and possibly, I would lose. But no matter the verdict, unless we were prevented through some legal maneuver, people would see that there was a common pattern of police brutality that existed on Whittier Boulevard.

Throughout this time, I have actually regretted that my charges were finally dropped. They were dropped in November 1979. I was glad and still am that I did not have to face the possibility of going to prison, but I do regret not going to trial because to this day the sheriffs have not been exposed. Five years have passed, and maybe today it's different, but in 1979, things were pretty bad. Nobody was backing up the Raza. A lot of the organizations that were supposed to be there in the defense of our Raza were not there. To this day, the barricades stand as a testament that nobody was willing to come forward and fight the abuses. Maybe it's all for the better because if the Boulevard would have been reopened in '79, the sheriffs probably would have taken it as a personal insult. If the Boulevard is ever reopened, I hope it's because the people of East L.A. had a say-so rather than through a court decision because it could be easily reopened. I know lawyers who are willing to take the case. It could be done. But without a restraint on the sheriffs—on those who are supposed to serve and represent us—what would be the price?

10 / The Dismissal: The White House, Mariachis, and the Red Carpet

I know it may sound funny, but the last few days before the dismissal on November 7 were filled with the type of suspense, tension, and drama mostly found in movies. When I joined *Lowrider* the year before, I was going to places that I had never gone to or even heard of before. As a result, I rarely saw anyone who I had gone to college with. After my case, it was even rarer in that I was practically a mole. I surfaced here and there, but the only people I ran into regularly besides the cops and the staff of *Lowrider* were a few partners I had grown up with. Even though the neighborhood I grew up in is in East L.A., which is patrolled by sheriffs, I always felt safe there. So if I was in East L.A., I was in my old neighborhood. Most weekends I was somewhere people didn't know me.

Sometime in September, I went to a big political event at East L.A. College. I was doing something else earlier that day, but after I got through, I went over to the political event. I don't know why I went, maybe because César Chávez was speaking there, but nonetheless, I ended up going. When I got there, Chávez had already finished speaking, so almost everyone was leaving. As I was walking around the stadium, I began to run into all kinds of people I had known in college. I got kind of uneasy because I really didn't want to explain or recount what had happened to me. Since I hadn't seen any of my friends in a few years, I figured they had heard about what happened to me either through my lawyer, who knew almost everyone, or they had read about it somewhere. I was there only about five minutes when I decided to leave. I kept running into people as I was leaving. I don't remember who, either a friend of mine or someone from Proyecto del Barrio in Pacoima, but someone introduced me to some people who were talking pretty fast. They were into a real heavy conversation. I wanted to leave right away because I didn't really like the scene. Besides, I had somewhere else to go. Either that or it was getting dark, and at that time, by sundown, I was usually long gone from the East Side. Anyway, when I was introduced, there was this one guy who seemed to be kind of hyper about whatever he was talking about. He started telling me that he knew about my case or that he had just heard about it. Whatever the case, he said that he could help me. I told him that I already had a real good lawyer. He kept insisting, telling me that he was the head of some Civil Rights outfit from San Jose for the GI Forum. One of the guys he was talking to was from Pico Rivera. His son had allegedly been involved in the murder of two highway patrolmen in Sacramento. The hypered-up guy kept insisting that he was innocent and that he and the GI Forum were going to help him. All I remember is that he kept saying that he could help people. I thought that he was probably a well-meaning guy but that he probably really couldn't help anyone. Whatever the case, we exchanged numbers, and he said he would see that my case was investigated by the Department of Justice or something and that he would personally conduct the investigation. I just looked at him like, "right." I thanked him, ran into a few more people, and then booked. When I left, I really didn't think much of that chance meeting in that I was more disappointed I hadn't gotten a chance to talk to Chávez. I figured if anyone could help, he could.

I didn't think about that guy again until I got a phone call from him. I think it was on Friday November 3, 1979. He said that I should come to San Jose the next day because on Monday there was going to be a big hearing regarding police brutality and abuses by the Immigration Department against Mexicanos. He said that his outfit would fly me in as a secret or surprise witness or something and that those conducting the hearing would not know that I would be testifying. He said to catch a flight the next day so that we could prepare the testimony I would be presenting. At that time, in early November, I think I was giving up hope of avoiding a trial. It already had been nine months since the incident, and, although my lawyer kept insisting from the beginning that the prosecution would drop the charges, they hadn't. I had another court appearance scheduled for November 7, so I asked the guy: "Will I be back in time to go to court?" He said I could leave right after I testified. I wasn't too sure, but I ended up saying yes. I figured I would think about it overnight, and if I changed my mind, I just wouldn't go.

At the time, I had two lawyers, one who was handling my criminal case and one who was preparing the lawsuit that I would file as soon as I won my criminal case. I figured I better tell them that I was going up north, because I wasn't going to tell anyone else. My defense lawyer, Antonio Rodríguez, wasn't there so I went to see my other lawyer, Miguel García, the one that was handling the lawsuit. I talked to Miguel about what I should say and what I shouldn't say. Before I left, I told him to hold onto some negatives because the guy who called had told me to bring the photographs I had. The photographs weren't of the cops beating that innocent guy. They had taken that film. The negatives I gave him were of photographs taken of me almost immediately after I had been released. I looked like a mess in those photographs. Those were the photographs that had appeared in *Lowrider,* and I was taking them with me up north. I told him I was leaving the negatives with him in case something happened to the photographs. He wished me good luck. I left the next day to go to San Jose with about 30 copies of the July 1979 issue of *Lowrider* and the two photographs. The July issue explained everything about what had happened to me and the 537 other people. The photographs of my face that appeared in that issue were, for the lack of a better word, graphic.

When the plane landed, I was met by the guy who had called me, and I was welcomed by a Mariachi band. It kind of freaked me out. I thought, "I guess it's true what they say about the Raza from San Jose. They really roll out the red carpet for a fellow Chicano." And they really had rolled out a red carpet. There was only one catch, the red carpet and the Mariachis weren't for me. They were there to greet Esteban Torres and Gilbert Colón, the highest ranking Raza at the White House. They were there for the hearing. Anyway, after recovering from the disappointment, we went to the guy's house. I met his wife and family. They were one of the nicest families that I have ever met. The guy's name is Gil Jasso, the head of the Office of Civil Rights for the GI Forum. His wife's name is Molly.

At the time, Gil operated the Civil Rights Office out of his house. It was a pretty big responsibility which was matched only by his dedication. The San Jose GI Forum, through the Office of Civil Rights, had been monitoring deaths of Chicanos at the hands of law enforcement. The list was big. I got kind of uneasy because I didn't want to be on that list. I learned a lot in a couple of days. I learned more about the GI Forum and about the Jasso family. Before, I didn't really know too much about the GI Forum except what I had read about them. I had read that they were a Raza organization of ex-GIs which had been started in Corpus Christi, Texas. The organization was supposed to be on the conservative side. When I met Gil and his family, I didn't judge them as conservative or radical, rather I saw them as sincere, as a concerned family committed to trying to prevent police abuse. I left San Jose with a lot of respect for them.

When we sat down to discuss the upcoming hearing on Monday, I let him know everything about the case, showed him the photographs and also the magazines. He was confident that the evidence would shock everyone and that it would prompt an investigation by the Attorney General if not the White House itself. I wasn't really convinced that anything would come of it, but I was prepared.

I forget how, but that weekend I went to Story and King, the area where the Raza cruise in San Jose, to see how it was. The last time I had been there, I had cruised till the car broke down around the time the sun was rising. This time, I just passed through and went to some kind of party which was being thrown by some barrio organizers. I didn't really go there to meet people, but a couple of years later, when I moved up north, I got to meet some of the organizers I had met at that party. I stayed at that party, thinking about my court appearance the following Wednesday and the hearing on Monday. I don't remember what I did Sunday, but Monday I got ready for the hearing. It was bigger than I had expected. When I got there, representatives were there from the Department of Justice, the U.S. Office of Civil Rights, the Attorney General's Office, and the White House. I had expected a hearing with the representatives but what I hadn't expected was the big crowd that showed up. In addition to all the government representatives, many Raza groups were represented. The GI Forum, of which Gil was a part, was there. Other groups included MAPA (Mexican American Political Association), LULAC (League of United Latin American Citizens), MALDEF (Mexican American Legal Defense and Education Fund), MECHA (Movimiento Estudiantil Chicano de Aztlán), and a few other groups. Since Gil had said they were going to be secret hearings, I didn't expect such a large crowd of people. At that time, I used to try and avoid crowds. In the crowd, I recognized some Raza who I had met earlier in the year at a Chicano Youth Conference in San Jose.

The hearings began with the representatives listening to a series of incidents of harassment by the migra in Northern California. Then a few cases were heard concerning police abuse in Stockton and Oakland and then the mass harassment of the Raza on Story and King in San Jose. The hearing went on with all the representatives taking notes. Then Gil got up and introduced himself and explained what the GI Forum was doing to try to combat police abuse. He said that they had flown me up so that I could give testimony, so that I could give a firsthand account of the harassment the Raza were receiving at the hands of law enforcement.

I do have to admit that all the government representatives seemed to be startled in that they had just heard testimony, and they had reassured everyone that they would investigate. Yet out of nowhere, I popped up as an actual case. It was kind of a weird feeling because my presence was causing a bit of a commotion. I introduced myself, explained my case, and then I circulated the magazines to all the government representatives. What took me by surprise is that everyone in the audience wanted a magazine too. The reason it surprised me is because San Jose was the home base for *Lowrider Magazine.* I gave out all the magazines but there weren't enough. Then, as I continued, I further explained that not only had I been a witness to an incident of police brutality and I had photographed the event, but that I in turn got hit on the head and I had ended up being the one who was charged with a crime. If it hadn't been for the fact that I could have gone to prison, the charges would have been kind of funny in that I was charged with assaulting two officers. I explained that the charges were assault with a deadly weapon and assault and battery on a peace officer. Everyone, including the representatives, almost fell off their seats when I explained that the deadly weapon was my Olympus 35-millimeter camera. It was funny except for the fact that I had ended up in a hospital.

The reason my presence had caused a bit of a commotion is that, in fact, nobody knew I was going to be there. More important, everyone had been skeptical all along, thinking that the government representatives were just there going through the motions, and that as soon as the hearing was over, they would pat everyone on the back, they would say how much they like to eat tacos, and then they would pack their bags, board the plane, and go back to where they came from. Another successful mission. Another publicity stunt for the administration. Since they said they were committed to justice, they had compromised themselves when my case came up. They heard me out, and then I pulled out the photographs that blew away the government officials. They were convinced. They said they would definitely investigate the matter. I felt bad. All the Raza had come to complain about the harassment that they were going through in San Jose and other communities up there, and my case "had stolen the show." The reason I felt bad is that the representatives seemed as though they were just taking notes so they didn't look disrespectful. When I heard about the cases in San Jose and Stockton and the abuse by the migra, I felt that the officials were just saying they were going to investigate so that they wouldn't get jammed. When I presented my case, I felt that the representatives had been compromised. They assured me that all their outfits, including the White House, would look into the matter. As the hearing came to a close, as I was leaving, one of the representatives asked if I could leave them the photographs. I hesitated, but Gil nodded that it would be OK. I gave them my work address, my home address, my dog's address, his next of kin. I told them that the photographs were very important and very valuable. Besides, I said, "They're pertinent to my case." They assured me that within one week, I would receive them in the mail. I know that everyone makes fun of the ineptness of the Postal Service, but it's not completely fair to blame them every time something comes late or never shows up. I haven't lost hope in the Postal Service. To this day, I'm still waiting for the photographs, but I don't think it's the fault of the Postal Service. There was probably foul play involved, like the FBI, the CIA, or the infamous UIA (a top secret organization that operates underwater). Even though I never received the photographs, events continued to unfold. As soon as the hearing ended, everyone was glad I testified. I was kind of glad too, although I wasn't convinced the officials were really going to do something. Besides, I thought the White House had better things to do like plan wars or save hostages (the embassy had just been taken over that weekend in Iran). I thought the only thing that would come out of it is that my case and my photographs would end up in a dusty file, and maybe even the FBI would borrow them.

After we left the hearing, we went back to Gil's house, and from there he arranged for a live, over-the-phone interview with Radio CASA. I think that's what it was called. All I remember is that it was a popular radio station for the Raza in the San Jose area. I felt good about the interview because I knew that the Raza from San Jose were behind me, but I thought that it might not matter because the sheriffs and my trial were in Los Angeles. It didn't matter. It was a good feeling to know that the Raza were there, solidly behind me. As for the "secret hearings," I felt it was a mission accomplished.

Later that night, I flew back to L.A., thinking that the plane was sabotaged. I thought, "They wouldn't bomb one plane just because of me, would they?" With that thought, I was never afraid to fly. I figured I couldn't get pulled over in midflight. When I got back, I was full of energy. Even though I didn't place much hope in the government representatives, I still felt more confident than ever in that, based on their reactions, I figured if my case ever did reach trial, the jury would laugh it out of court. There was no way I could lose, but if I did lose, I wouldn't be the first innocent person to go to prison. Still, there was no way I could lose.

On Tuesday morning, I talked to both lawyers who were representing me. I told them about what I had said and done and all that stuff. At Miguel's office, I told him I was glad I had left the negatives there because I gave the government officials the photographs. When I talked to Antonio later that afternoon, he not only said that it was good what I had done, but also that he had testified before the L.A. County Board of Supervisors at a hearing concerning brutality on the part of members of the sheriff's department.

All of a sudden, after nine months of foot-dragging and endless court appearances, it seemed as though the ball was finally rolling. He said that he was positive that the next day, on the date of my next court appearance, the charges would definitely be dropped. I had heard that before about twenty times, so I wasn't exactly convinced, though it did seem like something was finally beginning to happen.

The following morning, because I was a little anxious, I went to the courthouse earlier than my scheduled court appearance. I was a little edgy, so I called Antonio's office. I was told he had already left and that I should read the Metro section of that morning's *L.A. Times,* that I was in it. When I got off the phone, I rushed over to a newsstand and bought a copy of the *Times.* I sat down and read the article concerning the "alleged" brutality on the part of the sheriff's department. I was hypnotized in a way, in that I didn't know if the publicity was good. Antonio had reassured me that the charges against me were going to be dropped that morning, but I got kind of scared because I wasn't sure if someone from the prosecution or the sheriff's department had read the article. I already knew that they didn't like Antonio because I had overheard their conversations in court before. And now, with Antonio testifying and the story coming out in the *Times,* for sure I thought that if they had ever thought about dropping the charges, they wouldn't now.

I figured if they had read the story, now they would fight me all the way. If anything, to use me as an example. I went inside and sat in the courtroom thinking, "It's all a matter of timing." I kept wondering whether the prosecution attorney had read the paper. I thought, "Maybe she reads the *Herald.*" As I sat there, a couple of people who looked like lawyers walked in with the *Times* in their hands. They were talking about my case. I wasn't sure if they were cops or if they were lawyers. If they were lawyers, they didn't look like public defenders. I figured they were prosecution attorneys. The only thing I was sure of is that neither one of them was the one trying to prosecute me. I was praying, hoping they would drink their coffee somewhere else. Since they were mumbling, I figured they were there to tell the prosecution attorney that Antonio had testified and that the story had come out in the paper. They mumbled some more and walked out the back from where the judge usually makes his entrance. I breathed a little easier. After what seemed like hours, the prosecution attorney walked in. She didn't look at me. My palms started to sweat (as though they weren't already sweating). From the way she looked, I couldn't tell if she had read the paper yet. By this time, other people were in the courtroom, including the judge. I overheard the conversation of the prosecution. She was saying something to the effect that the charges were indeed going to be dropped. I breathed a momentary sigh of relief. I was sure she hadn't read the story.

Just then, I heard one of the ones who was huddled around her say, "You can't drop it. Haven't you read today's *Times?*" All I heard was a surprised "no," as she was taken aback. Since Antonio was late, the judge motioned for the prosecution to step forward. She was too excited; she said, "wait," and then ran out the doors with a quarter in hand. My heart just about stopped. My mind began to race about a million miles a second. How can I explain what I was thinking? What I was hoping for was an earthquake or that the news rack would be empty or that the quarter would fall into the gutter. Lightning didn't strike, so she was back in a minute. She told the judge to wait as she hurriedly read the article. It was as though my future was being determined by fate. I thought, "If that guy hadn't opened up his mouth." Right about then, Antonio walked in. The first thing he said was that they had told him they were going to drop the charges. Then he said, "Did you read the article?" I said, "Yes, but so did she." I pointed to her as her eyes widened. I told him that she didn't know about the story until some guy told her a few minutes before. Antonio said not to worry. I wasn't worried. That wasn't the right word. I was on the verge of pushing the panic button. The judge motioned for Antonio and the prosecution attorney. They went into the judge's chambers. Who knows what they talked about, but after losing about a gallon of sweat, after about an hour, the doors to the judges chambers swung open, and out came my lawyer. He had a smile from ear to ear.

Victory came at 11:30 A.M., November 7, in East L.A.

We gave each other an abrazo—like carnales. The victory meant more to me than most people can imagine. The victory wasn't the dismissal, because I had already accepted the fact that I could win or lose, that I could walk away a free Chicano or I could end up doing time. That wasn't the victory. The victory was that I didn't give up, that I didn't break, that I didn't buckle under pressure. The victory was that I stuck with a lawyer who wasn't exactly my best friend. That was the real trial. Most of my friends, those who knew how I thought, those whom I respected had said, "Don't be stupid, get yourself a Jewish lawyer, or get yourself a lawyer from the Westside. If anything, get a Japanese lawyer, anything but a Mexican, especially him. If you do hire him, you might as well get your pen ready so you can write from prison." Those words were like piercing stab wounds, and the advice was coming from the hardest of the hard-core Chicanos. I could not accept that advice. In my mind, I said, "I'm Chicano. If I go to court, it will not be with a Jewish lawyer, a rich white lawyer, or a Japanese lawyer. It will be a fellow carnal who will defend me. I would gladly go to prison if I lost, just to know that a Mexicano, especially him, defended another Mexicano." In my mind, I also thought, "If every time we get in trouble, if every time something gets a little too heavy, do we always have to run to white lawyers?" What do we need Chicano lawyers for, to defend us for jaywalking?"

When my lawyer walked out of the judge's chambers with a smile from ear to ear, I returned the smile, but I wasn't happy just because I won. I felt victorious because it was he who walked out of the chambers and not someone named Smith or Jones.

It Was a Victory for the Raza—por la Raza

After the victory, I almost forgot something really important. I felt like talking to the prosecution attorney and asking her if she knew that she was trying to convict an innocent person. I wanted to know whether it made a difference to her if an innocent person went to prison. I wanted to ask her badly, but I figured, "Well, it's just her job. She's just trying to do her job, but still."

I went back inside anyway because now that I had won, they no longer had a use for my deadly weapon. My Olympus camera had been in their possession for nine months. I asked the judge, "Can I have my camera back now?" He directed me to the bailiff or someone who told me I could pick up the camera at the Third Street station across the park. Antonio had to leave, so I went by myself. I took my written order to the station where they had been holding my camera as evidence. After going through a couple of bureaucratic changes, they came up with my camera. I couldn't believe that the Olympus had been a deadly weapon. To my surprise, the camera was not broken or damaged. It was in good order. The flash was still mounted and charged. But, not to my surprise, the real evidence, the film, was gone.

End of Round One.

11 / The Nine Months: 1979—Open Season on Chicanos

Between the time of the incident in March and the dismissal in November 1979, a lot happened. Probably the three biggest things, streetwise, that happened in 1979 were the closure of Whittier Boulevard, the Lowrider Super Show, and the escalating gang violence in Southern California. While all of this was going on, I had my case to worry about. I didn't know from one day to the next the status of my case. Everyone kept telling me "they" were going to drop my charges a week or two weeks after the incident. When "they" didn't, I began to worry. Because of the movie *Warriors*, *Boulevard Nights*, and one they didn't release on the West Coast, *Gang* (later changed to *Walk Proud*), a lot of publicity surrounded gangs, lowriding, and cruising. It was a mad scramble to see who could get the definitive story, the inside look on "La Vida Loca." Distortions were the order of the day. To add to the sensationalism, every Monday in the *L.A. Times* or the *Herald Examiner,* the L.A. area section resembled a Mexican death count. That year, there was an average of one gang killing per day. The situation was at a crisis point in terms of the media. The casualty list was not restricted to deaths but also included countless critical injuries. Although before, gang violence was seen as indigenous to East L.A., now it was seen as spreading to the San Gabriel and San Fernando Valleys, to central L.A., south L.A., the harbor area, southeast L.A. County, and Orange County. Stories were reporting that, whereas before the gang violence was centered in Mexican neighborhoods, now it was reaching the respectable suburban neighborhoods that had little to do with urban problems. Another element emphasized was that the gangs were not just indigenous to L.A. but that now immigrants were joining or forming gangs for self-protection. Whether the efforts of "The Coalition to End Barrio Warfare" were working or not was another story, but it was the only group that was sincerely and honestly working to curb if not end the violence that was claiming innocent lives. That year, over 500 gang killings were recorded throughout the state (not including the prison gangs). Almost all the killings were Raza against Raza. Very few were interracial except for those that occurred in the prisons.

Although this was happening throughout Los Angeles, East L.A., Southern California, and the entire state, the media seemed to isolate the problem to Whittier Boulevard, between Atlantic Boulevard and Eastern

Avenue, on Friday, Saturday, and Sunday nights. The sheriff's department, with the aid of the merchants and other groups, began a campaign to shut down Whittier Boulevard on weekends, on the pretext that there was too much gang violence on Whittier Boulevard. They did not propose any workable solutions to eliminate or help curb the violence. The concern was solely to shift the violence away from the Boulevard. Whether in collusion or not, what resulted was the highlighting of gang violence in the media. Somehow, whether or not the crime occurred on the Boulevard, all gang violence in East L.A., all incidents of crime committed by a gang member anywhere was directly or indirectly associated with the efforts to shut down Whittier Boulevard.

Aside from the media reporting or sensationalizing gang violence, the three movies earlier mentioned also did their damage. But it was not solely the movies. It was also television. Getting lowrider vehicles into TV programs or TV movies seemed to be a big thing. Most programs that featured lowrider vehicles used them in association with the commission of a crime. They would show someone committing a robbery in a ten thousand dollar brightly colored customized car. What a getaway vehicle! This type of bad media image caused a bit of a controversy on the streets and elsewhere. Many of the car clubs protested that they shouldn't be portrayed as gang bangers because they didn't participate in crime. They didn't want to get harassed unjustly by the false images being portrayed. Whatever the case, gang murders, cruising, and lowriding were bunched in together and were at the top of the news in 1979. What this meant on the streets was increased tension and increased harassment by the police.

I wasn't cruising in the sixties, fifties, forties, or before, but I think cruising peaked in the summer of 1979. A lot of it probably had to do with *Lowrider* and *Q-VO* magazines and all the media attention cruising received during that year. Also, the summer of 1979 climaxed with the closure of Whittier Boulevard on August 31, but that event was upstaged by the two biggest car shows ever put on anywhere at the end of that summer. *Lowrider Magazine* put on the "Supershow" at the L.A. Convention Center and Show + Kustom put on a pretty big show at the old Great Western in the City of Commerce. A lot of people went to those shows. So at the same time we were getting all the negative publicity, the interest in lowriding was growing in leaps and bounds. Everyone who was into lowriding knew all about the bad publicity and saw it as such, just bad publicity.

The bad publicity shouldn't have resulted in more harassment, but it did. Maybe I was imagining things, but it seemed like the Raza, and I in particular because of my pending trial, were getting harassed a little too much. Between March and November, I was arrested or stopped somewhere between twenty and thirty times, and that wasn't counting all the times I was hassled at parks or the boulevards.

What I'm talking about was getting arrested or stopped for phony warrants. My name isn't the most original, so I ended up in jail a bunch of times only to find that the real person they were looking for, with my name, didn't even remotely resemble me except for the fact that we were both Mexican. It got to the point that I couldn't be in East L.A. after dark. At the time, I moved from the East L.A. College area to Monterey Park, near Rosemead. It was a good place to be while awaiting trial except that the offices of *Lowrider* were in the heart of East L.A. on Whittier Boulevard, a couple of blocks east of Atlantic. To top it off, sheriffs hung out in front of the office at Zorba's hamburger stand. Getting to and from work was like an obstacle course everyday. I thought to myself, "Maybe they don't even know me or even care who I am. Maybe I'm just paranoid." I had definitely been made paranoid, but when I began to get pulled over every time I got in my car, I figured it was either a big coincidence or it was scare tactics. Of all the days, I hated Friday afternoons because Friday night is when the barricades went up. And when they went up, that meant that the Boulevard was crawling with sheriffs. We were only two blocks away from Atlantic Boulevard, from the barricades, so anyone near the area was not safe.

When I look back at those nine months, I can't believe that I was stopped all those times. Some of the situations were pretty tense, while other times, they were practically funny. One time, driving east on Whittier Boulevard in a '54 Chevy Panel, I was held for over an hour. For whatever reasons, I knew they weren't going to arrest me because I had documents that said I had no warrants. Anyway, after that hour, after I was cleared, and after they gave back my license, I said, "Can you tell me the reason why I was stopped?" One of them responded, "We like your car." That was one of the times that I almost laughed because I figured at least they didn't act like they were going to kill me.

The time I got arrested in Venice was probably the time I was scared the most. The incident occurred sometime during the day. I had driven my Camaro from East L.A. to Venice, to the apartment on the beach that served as a "westside office" for *Lowrider Magazine.* That morning, the publisher's wife, Alicia Madrid, and his brother, Rudy Madrid, were at the apartment. After having a short meeting, Alicia and I were going to go back to the office in East L.A. But first we were going to drop Rudy off by the pavilion, and later we were going to the bank. We left the apartment, which was on the beach off of Pacific near Washington Boulevard. I drove north on Pacific toward Santa Monica. I hung a left on the street that leads straight to the pavilion. The street only goes about 100 yards and then it ends because of a beach walkway. Anyway, I drove the car as far as I could go, threw a U-turn, and stopped to let Rudy off. The car was in neutral at the time. As he was getting off, an undercover, unmarked car raced in front of us and cut us off as if we were going somewhere. Earlier, I had been telling the publisher, Sonny Madrid, that I had been getting harassed too much. He had shrugged it off as though it was nothing, and maybe it had been nothing up till then. This time, the officers jumped out of the car as though they were apprehending armed and dangerous criminals. There were two officers in the black and white and two officers in the undercover car. Actually, it was only the undercovers who came out at first. The black and white didn't appear till a little later. When the undercovers came at us, I knew they were cops, but they sure didn't act like it. They acted more like they were Starsky and Hutch. They started yelling, demanding answers to questions they hadn't even asked. The way they were acting, I didn't think this was going to be the usual harassment I had become accustomed to. This time, it was a couple of undercovers who obviously had apprehended the wrong suspects. The whole incident lasted about an hour. They questioned me; they questioned Alicia and Rudy. It wasn't too cool what they did to them. In a way, I was used to it because it was happening to me routinely. I felt bad because I think it was her first trip to L.A., and she was greeted as though she were a heroin courier, making a connection. I could write for days on how the police treated them, because afterward they were both pretty shook up.

When the officers took me to the side, they checked me for marks, tattoos, the works. They asked me a million questions. I didn't even have time to respond. They also wanted to know if I had stolen the car. The car was not in my name because I was buying it from Alicia. Even though we had proof, they acted like they didn't believe it. We were innocent of any and all charges they were thinking of. To top it off, Alicia had about four or six hundred dollars with her. They must have figured that Mexicans were not supposed to have that much money unless we were drug pushers. As a crowd gathered, things proceeded from bad to worse. Now the officers wanted to know my arrest record. I knew that I had a right to refuse to answer, but under the circumstances, I figured they were going to run a make on me anyway. I thought that maybe the assault charges hadn't registered on the computer because I hadn't been convicted. They started shouting, "When was the last time you were arrested?"

I responded, "I don't remember, but I think I was arrested on a warrant for a traffic ticket."

"Don't get smart, you know what I'm talking about."

Since they had already detained us for a long while, I figured they knew about the assault charges and they were just testing me.

"When was the last time you spent time in jail?"

After they began to be more belligerent, I figured I better tell them. Each time I had previously been stopped and arrested, I had told my lawyer and my boss. The latter had told me that the next time it happened, to joke around with them so that they wouldn't get so mad. So this time, I figured that maybe I should joke with them, although they didn't look like they were in a joking mood.

I told them. "Hey, if I tell you the charges, do you promise not to get mad?"

The guy nearly blew his top.

"What the fuck! What were you arrested for?" he shouted.

"You promise," I said.

"What the fuck were the charges!?" again he blew his top.

"I was arrested for assault with a deadly weapon. I paused, "and assault and battery on a peace officer."

If he had blown his top the first two times, this time he was steaming. I thought he was going to shoot me right there. I think he called his partner or one of the uniformed officers.

I told them, "Hey, I didn't do it."

They yelled some stuff that's not worth repeating.

"I'm serious, I'm innocent."

They said something to the effect of, "That's what they all say." They didn't say it in those words but that's what they meant. I responded, "If I was guilty, I'd be behind bars right now."

Again they yelled some other stuff.

"I haven't been convicted," I said. "Why do we have trials if you're going to act like I'm guilty?"

I don't think the strategy worked because it got them even more irritated. Meanwhile, the other cops were harassing Alicia and Rudy. I didn't know what was happening to them because I was busy dealing with the other officers. I didn't know how I was going to get out of this one. Finally, after a lot of hot air, they took me to my car and began searching it. I started shitting bricks because at that time, I carried duplicates of all my evidence with me. In my briefcase, I had the indictments, the court papers, my complaint, list of witnesses, and some color photographs. I thought I was done in. I thought I had made a stupid mistake carrying all the evidence in my case with me. Luckily, I also had the July issue of *Lowrider* on me. I was lucky in that it distracted their attention away from the documents I had, but unluckily that was the issue in which I explained what had happened to me on the Boulevard. There was a before and after picture of me. The after picture showed my face with the scar on my forehead, in black and white. When the undercover started leafing through the magazine, I didn't even remember that I had the evidence with me, all I knew is that the magazine had my face in it, and it carried the story I had written explaining the ordeal I was going through. It also mentioned police harassment and mass arrests that had taken place throughout the county. To my luck, Venice, where we were at, was the first area mentioned. I was praying that he didn't happen to come across the story. As he began leafing through it, I told him he could have the magazine. I didn't want him to spot the story or my picture. He kept leafing through it.

"Take it," I said, "I have plenty."

Finally, his eyes lit up as he saw my picture. "For sure, I've had it now," I thought.

He began reading the story. The headlines read "Roberto Rodríguez Awaiting Trial."

Since he was reading it, I said, "You see, I haven't been convicted yet."

The guy started boiling up again. He called his partner over. He said to me, "I'm going to take this to the station to make a copy of this." As his partner got there, I said, "Take it, you guys can have it." He kept reading. He showed it to his partner. "This is him," he said.

Around this time, the other officers, the black and whites, said, "He has a warrant for a minor traffic ticket." He turned to me and handed back my license.

At this point, Alicia started demanding an apology. The undercover took me to the side and said, "What does she mean she wants an apology?" At this point, I thought we were already off the hook, and knowing he was baiting me, I responded, "Ah, she didn't mean it. We don't need an apology."

"I didn't treat you wrong, did I?" he sarcastically responded.

"No," I said.

He turned to his partner and they continued reading the article.

Again I told them, "You can keep it."

Meanwhile, the uniformed officers who had been cool with me throughout this incident said, "You can go, but take care of that traffic warrant."

The undercover who had been interrogating me the whole time said, "No, we want him. We're going to take him in."

I guess the undercovers had seniority because I thought I was off the hook. To cut it short, I gave my keys to Alicia and Rudy and told them to follow me. I told them, "No matter what you do, don't lose me." I was handcuffed, put in the backseat, and then the undercover got in the backseat also. I didn't think they were going to kill me; I just thought I was going to wind up at the station with a bunch of bruised ribs. Right before I was put in the backseat, the guy said, "We're not rowdy like the sheriffs." If I hadn't been handcuffed and in that situation, I probably would have laughed. Anyway, as the unmarked car pulled away, whoever was driving my Camaro lost me almost immediately. I knew they weren't from L.A., but I didn't think they would lose me that fast. As it turned out, I was hassled but not beaten, and to my surprise, we went straight to the Venice station. I was handcuffed to a bench, and over me, the magazine was taped to the wall so that every cop could see that the undercovers had captured me. Every cop who went my was told, "That's him."

Since the original incident in March, I had mentally debated whether or not it was wise to have a lot of publicity. Since I knew I was out on the streets all the time, I thought it was a bad idea because I was stopped a lot. After seeing cop after cop being told that it was me in the photograph, I didn't need any more convincing. I got bailed out after a couple of hours. I didn't have to go through the whole process, but the undercover insisted that I be booked and fingerprinted. After I got out, I felt glad that nothing had happened to me, but to my surprise, I found out that Alicia and Rudy had also been harassed. They had taken it pretty bad. They told me that they had lost me because the unmarked car had made a left hand turn from the right hand lane. I wasn't shaken up by the incident, but it did give me a lot to think about. It was the first time I had been arrested while someone was with me. It showed me a little of what to expect for any of my future passengers. More important, it gave me something to think about in regard to publicity. I had to wonder if the story, "confiscated" by the undercovers, was going to be circulated. If I had been naive before, this kind of straightened me out. I knew that cops already looked at our magazine, maybe not all of them, but I knew they studied it. I couldn't give up just because of that. I just had to be extra careful. I wasn't doing anything wrong. In fact, the more they tried to intimidate me, the more determined I was to win. I was going to file a complaint, but then I figured, if I filed a complaint every time I was harassed, half the police departments in the county would be served notices. This time it was Venice, but the day before it was another part of the city or another part of the county. Besides, I figured that they would probably say that harassment from Venice undercovers had nothing to do with sheriffs, that it had nothing to do with East L.A. sheriffs.

At the time, I thought I was playing my case low-keyed, but after the incident I figured I even had to be cooler about it. No more pictures, no more stories until my case was won, until final victory.

12 / The Lawsuit: Round Two

Almost right from the moment that I was hit by the riot stick, I knew that if I wasn't killed, I would file criminal charges against the sheriffs who took part in the assault. When I ended up in the jail ward of the county hospital, I couldn't believe what was happening. I had gone into physical shock at the first hospital I was taken to, Santa Marta's. There I was treated but was told the hospital wasn't equipped to handle that type of an emergency. I was shaking uncontrollably because I had been in fear for my life.

I was shocked that the sheriffs even took me to the hospital. When I found out they couldn't treat me there, I asked if I could make a phone call. The sheriffs said "yes." Again, I was surprised. I thought, "Maybe they're not going to kill me after all. Maybe they're just going to work me over again." I ended up changing my mind. I told the sheriffs I didn't want to call until I got to another hospital. At the time, I thought that if I explained over the phone what happened, the sheriffs might work me over after we left Santa Marta's, and then when we got to the county, they would claim that the new injuries were part of the original beating. Maybe I should have called from Santa Marta's, but I was still in a daze, and I was still afraid they were going to kill me.

All I remember is that by the time I got to General Hospital, I was completely drenched in blood. I was led up to the thirteenth floor where I was seen by a doctor. I didn't know if the doctors worked for the county or the police department, so when the doctor asked me what had happened, I didn't respond. I told him later that I had tripped while getting arrested. He knew I wasn't telling the truth, but I wasn't about to say what really happened until I had been released and had talked to a lawyer. I was there Friday night, Saturday night, and Sunday morning and afternoon. I was finally released about a couple of hours before sundown.

Throughout all this time, it was hard to keep quiet. It was hard holding back. For some reason, I knew that if I said anything, even to the other prisoners, somehow it would get me in trouble. The doctor constantly asked me, "What really happened?" When one of the nurses talked to me as though I was under the influence of PCP, I told her that I didn't even smoke or drink. She just sneered, saying that's what everyone says. She was getting me a little irritated because she was making wild accusations and assuming a lot. I felt like telling her what really happened, but I figured she was just talking that way so that I would spill the beans. I came close, but I resolved not to say a word until I was released. Some of the custodians and other workers also asked. They looked honest, but I was still paranoid. I figured there were microphones that recorded all conversations because we were in a jail.

When I was there the first night, I tried to rest, get some sleep, and forget about the incident. It was like a nightmare that wouldn't go away. I didn't make a phone call till about 5:00 A.M. At that time, I looked in the mirror, and I couldn't believe what I saw. My face was disfigured. I bore no resemblance to the way I looked a few hours prior. I don't think I can adequately describe how I looked except to say that my eyes were so swollen I could barely see. I was black and blue all over, and there was a crosslike gash on my forehead. Because of the way I looked, I didn't think I was getting out for quite a while. I figured they wouldn't want people to see how I looked. The worst part about it was that everyone else who was in the jail ward of the county hospital also had their heads cracked.

Things didn't get any better Saturday night. More people were brought in that night than had been brought in on Friday night. The ward was packed. Everyone had a story to tell. I could barely resist not telling what happened to me. I knew that if I told someone, somehow it would affect my getting out. I was scared and I was paranoid. I do not blame myself. I had heard about so-called suicides in L.A. jails. I figured something was going to happen, especially if I opened my mouth. Throughout Friday, Saturday, and Sunday, I kept quiet. It was hard, especially after I found out what the charges were. I kept asking everybody what the charges were, but nobody seemed to know. Finally, I was told that I had been charged with assault with a deadly weapon and assault and battery on a peace officer. I was accused of leading a riot. I couldn't believe the charges. I was dumbfounded. I thought to myself, "What weapon?" The first thing I thought was that all the stories about cops planting weapons were true. I had always thought that one day, something like that would happen. Now, here I was, locked up, trying to figure out what weapon had been planted. I figured they had planted either a gun or a knife. Either way, I figured I was in trouble. I had heard of a lot of cases of people going to prison on false charges. It was like a nightmare in that I knew it had happened, but I couldn't believe I was actually in the position to go to prison for quite a while.

I had a lot of time to think. All the while I was in there, I knew that my family was trying to get me out, but I didn't know how long I was going to stay in. The last thing I wanted to do was to be in there still when Monday rolled around. I wasn't too sure, but I knew there was a law that said the police could hold a person for up to 72 hours without being charged, and that didn't include weekends. I figured I was probably going to be there till about Wednesday. At that time, I was still in a daze, so I wasn't too sure of anything. I thought I'd be out about an hour after I had made my phone call.

Although it seemed like forever, when I was finally released on Sunday, I was actually surprised because I could have easily been out early Saturday morning. As I recall, I remember the people in the jail ward claiming that the computer had broken down. The reason I was not released when I should have been is because the county came up with two false warrants on top of the bail. Even to this day, I have not been repaid the money for the phony warrants that were supposedly mine. It turned out that the warrants belonged to someone with the same name but who did not even remotely resemble me.

Despite all the delays, I did end up leaving without spending Sunday night at the county. My first thoughts as I was released was to pick up my car, get photographed, contact a lawyer, and file a complaint. I didn't just want to file a complaint; I wanted to file criminal charges against the guilty sheriffs. As I was leaving, I asked what became of my camera. First they said I didn't have a camera. Then when I insisted, they checked their records, and I was told they were keeping my camera as evidence. I was puzzled. I responded, "Evidence! What evidence?!" The admitting officer responded by saying something to the effect that the camera was the deadly weapon. I almost cracked up in front of him. While I had been locked up, I kept wondering over and over what the deadly weapon could possibly be. The thought that it could be my camera did in fact cross my mind, but I dismissed it as very unlikely. I had been scared all along that I might end up going to prison, but after learning that the camera was the deadly weapon, I shook my head and couldn't believe it. Here I had been expecting a gun, a knife, or even a crowbar, but my Olympus camera ended up being the deadly weapon. When I received the indictment against me, I learned that the sheriffs claimed that I was leading a riot and had attacked two sheriffs with my camera. What a joke. It was right out of the movies: false arrest, police brutality, false imprisonment, phony charges, phony evidence (plus the two phony warrants). The thing that didn't make any sense is that a camera doesn't make for a good deadly weapon.

From a philosophical point of view, the camera was a deadly weapon. It is the modern version of "The pen is mightier than the sword." The camera was obviously a threat. It was used not in the commission of a crime but rather as a tool that would have recorded a vicious attack and abuse of police authority. When I was released and I had learned that my camera would be held as evidence, I knew that my case would have ramifications beyond just these charges. I figured my case involved the media, the suppression of evidence, the First Amendment, etc. I was confident I could win my case and that I would easily win the lawsuit that I would file. It didn't turn out as I thought it would. Most people told me not to worry. Everyone said that the charges would be dropped by the time I went to court. I went to court a week later, but they didn't drop the charges. I waited for the second court appearance, the third, and so on. Nothing happened. The charges were not dropped like everyone had said they would be. It wasn't until nine months from the date of the incident that they finally dropped the charges. A lot happened in between, but the main thing was that I learned a little about the justice system.

I didn't wait till I won my case to file a lawsuit. I remember the first thing I told the lawyer who defended me was that I wanted to file a lawsuit against the guilty sheriffs. The procedure, I was told, was that I had to file a complaint within 100 days of the incident. Actually, I didn't want to file a complaint, I wanted to file criminal charges against the sheriffs. I know I'm no lawyer, but till this day, I don't understand why charges were never filed against those sheriffs. That is what I wanted. To me, the lawsuit was secondary. The main thing I wanted to see was justice. They had committed a crime, I had been charged, and they were probably never even reprimanded. Since charges couldn't be filed against the sheriffs, the least I could do was sue them. When I filed the lawsuit, I didn't expect it to take this long. I had heard that the wheels of justice were slow and I kind of knew that lawsuits took a long time, but to actually wait it out is longer than I had imagined.

Probably the biggest factor in writing this was due to the fact that I had planned to write about the incident after I had won my lawsuit. But as of this writing, it has been five years since the incident. It may be another few years before it goes to trial. It's beyond ridiculous. You would think that justice should take place immediately, not after you've aged ten years.

For different reasons, I wanted to drop the lawsuit about a hundred times. Many times I didn't want to be bothered by it, viewing it as more of a headache than anything else. Up to this point, five years have been a long time to wait. It has been a long time to reflect, and it has been a long time to think about a lot of things. In a way, it seems like an eternity, and at other times, it seems like it happened yesterday. Despite the many times I thought about dropping the lawsuit, I am still pursuing it.

13 / After the Dismissal: Let Me See Your Arms

In November, when the charges were dismissed, I don't know how long I got to celebrate, but it seemed like right after I won, the next words I heard were, "Can I see your license?"

For some naive reason, I thought that winning my case meant the end of the harassment I had been going through. I wasn't getting arrested all the time, but I was getting pulled over, it seemed, every time I got behind the wheel of my car. Maybe it was my imagination. I wasn't 100 percent positive that the sheriffs were after me. I wasn't aware of a written order saying, "Get that guy." I had figured that when we went to trial, my lawyer would have requested that they open up their files on me under the Freedom of Information Act. But then I figured, if they wanted to make life difficult for me, they wouldn't put it in writing.

To this day, I could say that it's possible that all the arrests and all the times I got pulled over might have been a coincidence and that it's possible that there indeed was no conspiracy to get me. On the other hand, it may not have been a centrally directed vendetta, but, since the case had been in the news and my face was in the magazine, maybe there was an unauthorized campaign to make life difficult for me. Of one thing I am sure, I did get paranoid, but not because I was making everything up in my head.

A couple of days after I won my case, I was driving eastbound on Whittier Boulevard in East L.A. I passed the K-Mart area OK. When I passed Saybrook Street, right before Hay Street, a sheriff passed me, going in the opposite direction. As he passed me, he gave me a look as though he recognized me or something. Since I had been stopped enough times within the past nine months to last me a lifetime, I knew he was going to pull me over when he slowed down and attempted to make a U-turn. As soon as I realized he was going to come after me, I threw a left turn on Hay. He was momentarily delayed because of an oncoming car. Then, as the car passed, he threw the U-turn and tried to also make a left. After I threw the left on Hay Street, I threw another quick left into the alley and hung a right on Saybrook. I parked my car, jumped out, and ran into one of the houses. I was practically out of breath. At the same time, a couple of the people in the house said, "What's the matter?"

"Some sheriff's after me. I was going down Whittier right here," I said. "When he saw me, he threw a U and followed me."

"Those . . ."

I didn't let them finish. "I'm not sure they followed me. Maybe I'm just paranoid."

"I thought you won your case?"

"I did," I said. "But just then, as I was looking out the window, the black and white was cruising by at about five miles per hour. He stopped by my car. I was just about to run out the back like I used to when I was a kid, but then I stopped. I was thinking, "Wait a minute. Why am I running? I haven't done anything. I'm not a criminal." Yeah, I wasn't a criminal, but for some reason, I felt like I was on someone's most wanted list. I was going to go out to the front and see what the sheriff wanted, but before I could, he left.

Just a couple of nights before, I had celebrated my victory with a lot of my neighbors and partners I had grown up with at this same house. Now, that incident gave me something to think about. In my mind, I thought that if I got hassled one more time on the streets, I was going to leave the state.

I must have wanted to leave the state pretty bad because it seemed like no sooner had I thought that than I was once again behind bars. Luckily, most of the time I was pulled over, I was not arrested, but each time, I had to deal with a wasted hour. Each time, it was the same routine. First it was, "Let me see your license." Then, after about a nervous ten or fifteen minutes, it was, "Can you step out of your car?" If it was at night, it was nervous city, especially if a second unit arrived on the scene. Next, it was, "Let's see your arms." They would check me for marks or tattoos. After that, it was, "So when was the last time you were arrested?" Luckily, I had been arrested so many times on Mickey Mouse charges or false charges that I would say, "About a month ago." Then they would say, "For what?" "For some parking ticket I forgot to pay." After that, they would say, "Do you have any outstanding warrants?" I would respond, "None that I know of."

Anyway, that was the line of questioning every time. Unfortunately, when you're innocent, even a polite interrogation is a bother. I ended up going to a bunch of police stations just to check on some possible warrants. Sure, you could say I have a common name, but why did the clowns with my name have to be criminals? A couple of times, after getting arrested on someone else's warrants, I had to carry court papers showing that I was innocent of any and all charges. If it had been happening to someone else, it may have been no big thing to me, but when it was happening to me, I was in fear for my life. I can look back on those days and almost laugh, but when I was going through it, every time I saw a black and white, especially behind me, I thought I was done for, and most of the time, I was in fact pulled over. After my dismissal, I think I was pulled over at least once a day, sometimes even twice.

The first time I ended up in jail after the dismissal, I told the owner of the magazine to make arrangements for me to leave the state. He agreed. He said that as soon as it was possible, I would be going to Arizona. I was relieved. I was ready to go at a moment's notice. It would have been cool if I could have gone at the moment because the next month and a half was like a recurring nightmare. One day, as I was being followed, I pulled over to the side, not to evade the cop, but just so I could avoid being hassled. Of course, I was doing nothing wrong. I wasn't carrying a cannon, nor did I have a 5 million dollar heroin shipment. I just didn't want a cop on my tail. As I pulled over to the side, he pulled over with his lights on. I turned the inside light on and put my hands clearly on the steering wheel. I didn't want any "accidents" to happen. He approached the car carefully. In any case, it didn't turn out to be a big thing. I just told him I didn't like cops following me or something like that. I told him I had no warrants. I think that was one of the few times I wasn't hassled. I think the whole exchange took less than five minutes.

In between the time I won my case and when I left for Arizona, I was involved in two other incidents that were not routine. The sheriffs who had been involved in the original incident were from the Special Enforcement Bureau, meaning they were not necessarily from East L.A. In fact, I don't think any of them regularly worked out of the East L.A. sheriff's station. Because of that, I didn't run into any of them again, although I saw one sheriff who I do remember seeing on the Boulevard that night about a couple of weeks after I won. When he saw me, and I recognized him, I knew he wanted to stop me, but he had to deal with the situation at hand. What happened was that I was talking to a partner of mine at a park in East L.A. along with a couple of other individuals from two different neighborhoods. Next thing you know, a couple of other dudes drove by. They got out and started something with one of the dudes we were talking to. As they started to get into it, a sheriff's car pulled up. As the officers ran out of their cars to break up the commotion, one of them momentarily stopped as though he recognized me. The other sheriff kept running since there was a weapon involved. When he got there, he went to the individuals who had driven by. The other sheriff, knowing that the other guy might get away, looked at me as if to say, "I'll be back." Normally, I probably would have taken off except that they both had their hands full. I was sure they would have no time to deal with me, and I was right. Although one fight was stopped, another one started up. The sheriffs ended taking a couple of them away.

The other incident that I mentioned took place a few months earlier, when I bought my Camaro. I no longer had a use for my old car so I ended up giving it to my friend's sister, whose husband was a mechanic. Anyway, a few days before I left for Arizona, she told me that she had been using it but that she was afraid to drive it because the car was registered in my name. It wasn't like it was a big incident except that it got me thinking. I was already aware that other people could be hassled just because they were in the same car with me. That was the last thing I wanted. I figured that I had fought against the sheriff's department fair and square and that I had won my case. If there was going to be any negative stuff, it should be directed against me, not my friends or my passengers. That's what was hard because at the time I really thought they were going to do me in. I wanted someone to always be around me, as a witness. But after I saw how they had mistreated some friends of mine, plus the publisher's wife and brother, because of me, I thought it would be better that I get hassled alone than to put someone else through it. When my friend told me she wanted to get rid of the car because she didn't want anything to happen to her, I felt bad.

I ended up leaving for Arizona in the middle of December, which was not soon enough because I was mentally exhausted. I had been stopped so many times, they no longer even asked me for my license. All during this time, I had about three or four tickets that had turned to warrants. I couldn't keep track because they were pulling me over even in my sleep, faster than I could pay for them. From the time of the incident in March till I left in December, I think I went down to my parents' house in Whittier about four or five times. The reason the sheriffs thought I lived in Whittier was because that's what it said on my license. I wasn't about to correct them. During this time, cops kept going down to my parents' house trying to serve me warrants. I didn't know how to deal with all the ticket warrants. Every time I got arrested for one of them, I would say, "Is this the only warrant I have?" They would say yes, I would pay the fine, I would be released, and the next time I got stopped, I had another warrant. Half the time, I had already paid for the warrants, but they hadn't registered in the computer, or they actually belonged to someone else. A lot of times, I felt like saying, "Can you run a make to see if I have any more warrants or more tickets?" It got so bad that I used to have to save all the receipts from the paid tickets and warrants and would carry them in the car. When I would get stopped and they would search my car, they would come across all the paid warrants and get all belligerent. They thought that if I had that many, maybe I had more. There was no way I could win. You know how people carry dimes to call from jail, I used to carry about $130, enough to cover bail money for two warrants.

All this warrant stuff reminded me of when I was in college, when we were protesting the lack of Raza at UCLA. A partner of mine, Eddie, had told me that any time you get involved, you should always take care of your warrants (but he didn't say I should have taken care of all of the Rodríguezes' warrants in Southern California). When I started getting hassled, I remembered that and tried to take care of them. I often wanted to go to the sheriff's station and ask them if I had any outstanding warrants or tickets, but I never went because I figured that if they did find some warrants, they would keep me there. That's about the time I figured that the reason people hate cops is that they only run into them in negative situations. I wondered why they didn't develop a system where you could ask members of law enforcement whether you had any tickets or warrants without the fear of getting arrested while you're going to work or home, as if getting a ticket for making a wrong turn was the equivalent of armed robbery.

I do remember something else that happened on November 24 or 25, whatever day was Thanksgiving day in 1979. Since I hadn't seen my family in months, I wanted to see them for Thanksgiving, not because I was into that holiday but rather just because I knew my whole family would be together. The way I figured it, if the cops actually wanted to arrest me, they would probably come looking for me on Thanksgiving since they had been coming to the house and hadn't found me home. In my mind, I had a mission impossible on my hands. How was I going to get from East L.A. to Whittier without getting arrested that Thanksgiving? The Sherlock Holmes that I am, I convinced my partner Larry to switch cars for a day. I let him use my Camaro and I borrowed his '64. The plan was that I would go to my house from around 3:00 P.M. to about 7:00 P.M., and then I would go to his house and eat dinner. It sounded like a good plan because he and his family were from up north and they had no family in Los Angeles. Besides, I was going to baptize "gordo," one of his sons. I said, "Don't start the dinner without me." I think we were in the magazine's office when we agreed to this plan. Since where I grew up was only a few blocks away, I went there first to where all my friends were and got out and joined everyone in the celebration. It was only about 11:00 A.M. or maybe it was a little after noon already. All I know is that it was early to be drinking, but who cared. A lot of us hadn't gotten together since Easter or Christmas. In the beginning, there were only about five or six of us drinking, but by sundown, there was about twenty or thirty of us having a great Thanksgiving. It wasn't even dark. We hadn't even had dinner and we had already celebrated enough for a whole weekend. Everyone wanted me to take pictures. I wanted to but I kept thinking that if I put them in the magazine, they would get hassled because they were my partners. Anyway, they thought I had a firme '64. I told them it wasn't mine and why I had it. I told them I was going to see my familia. Since where I was at was like my familia, the parents at that house wanted me to eat with them. Of course, I was going to eat at my parents' house and at my partner's house, but I couldn't refuse. I had drunk so much that I had to get something into my stomach so that I would be able to drive away without driving on the wrong side of the street. I was at my friend's house, whose sister I had given my car to. They tried to tell me to stay, but the more I drank, the more I said I had to see my familia. I kept saying how it wasn't right that I had to sneak around in a friend's car to visit my own familia. I stayed there a few more hours. Finally, I went across the street to talk to the familia of my friend's in-laws, my partner's family. There, drunk as I was, I pleaded my case regarding how wrong the sheriffs had been in doing what they did, in putting me through what I was going through. I left the house and said that, no matter my condition, I had to go. Well, I didn't get too far before I realized that a clean '64 attracts more attention than a Camaro. As I was weaving, I figured that I couldn't go to my parents house. I decided to go straight to my partner's house, via the Santa Ana Freeway. I don't know how, but I got to Anaheim. Since I was going to a dinner, I didn't want to go empty handed so I stopped off at a liquor store and bought two one-gallon bottles of wine. When I got to the house, they were cracking up because I walked in staggering with two big bottles of wine. I told them what had happened and how I didn't get a chance to visit my familia. I told them not to worry about the '64 because I had only hit one car.

Now, five years later, everything seems funny, but it didn't then. When I finally left Los Angeles, on the one hand, I wanted to leave real bad because I had to get away from the cops, but on the other hand, I felt bad about leaving because I felt I was being forced to leave. Besides, I liked someone, and I didn't want to leave her. I also liked someone else a lot who had been there when I needed her, when I was going to court, when I thought I was going to prison. I hated to leave, but I figured, for my sanity, I had no choice. Whether or not there was a concerted effort to get me, I didn't really care. All I knew was that planned, coincidence, or whatever, I was glad I was leaving. I wasn't quite sure for how long, but I was leaving.

14 / Leaving L.A.:
To Where They Treat
You Human

Leaving Los Angeles was probably the best thing that ever happened to me. At the time, I felt I had to leave. If I had been seeing a psychologist, the psychologist probably would have said that I was paranoid. Every time I saw a black and white, I thought I was going to be pulled over. Since I figured cops didn't like me or the magazine, I figured one of them was going to finish the job. Maybe they weren't after me, and maybe they weren't going to finish the job, but by the time I left for Arizona, I felt I had been stopped more times than the Jesse James gang. I was never arrested for any legitimate reason. I left in a paranoid state because there were too many coincidences, too many close calls; and, in general, it was too much of a strain wondering every night whether I was going to be killed. It was a fear I wouldn't wish on a mass murderer. On second thought, a mass murderer yes, but an innocent person no.

Reality merged with paranoia in that I wasn't irrationally afraid of cops; the incident and the ensuing harassment are proof of that. The paranoia came in when I overreacted. I hated it when people would tell me to be careful. That would trigger automatic fear in that, to myself, I would ask, "why are you saying to be careful?" The reason those words would trigger fear is that before the incident, someone I knew had kept telling me over and over to be careful. I thought it was kind of weird because I turned to that person and said, "Why are you telling me to be careful, you're the one who's leaving?" I remember that when I got hit by the riot stick, before I hit the ground, those words "be careful" were ringing in my ears.

After the dismissal, when I was still getting pulled over, I started getting real anxious to leave. I thought it was only a matter of time before my luck ran out. I had already been told that if I won my case, I would be going out of state, and if I lost, I would be *Lowrider Magazine's* "reporter from the inside." It was a joke because everyone knew I would win, although we didn't know when. When the charges were dropped in November, I was surprised because I was already prepared for the trial. Whatever the reason, I didn't end up leaving till the middle of December. From December 1979 till a few years later, I was gone from L.A. and had the time of my life. I was always in conflict with the owner about almost everything, so if I hadn't left L.A., I probably would have quit. I had wanted to quit all the time; in fact, I thought that after my trial, I would split the country. I stayed in the country because I figured I had to wait until the lawsuit was finally settled. Staying in the country didn't mean staying in L.A., so when I finally did leave, it was to Phoenix. In a way, it was just what the doctor ordered. I stayed in Phoenix for a couple of weeks. It was so different from L.A. that I knew it was the place for me to be. The Raza there, from the streets to the colleges, were really uniting. In a way, I began to recover my sanity. Two weeks went by like a couple of days, because before I knew it, it was near Christmas time. I returned to L.A. to visit my parents because I had seen my family only about four times that year. I was there for Christmas, but I left for Phoenix for New Year's. During my four-day stay in L.A., I got a couple of tickets, and I got arrested and pulled over a couple of extra times. Of course, it was more Mickey Mouse stuff. Did you ever hear of a rich person having to spend a night in jail because he or she was mistaken for someone else, or because he or she forgot to pay a parking ticket?

I was back in Phoenix before I opened up my presents. I should have opened them sooner because some practical joker gave me my own set of handcuffs. I was back in Phoenix in time for a New Year's party, and I was convinced to stay. I would rather have been in Phoenix than L.A. anyway, but for me it wasn't a matter of choice. It was the strangest feeling knowing that although I didn't want to be in L.A., I couldn't be in L.A. That was the first time I felt I was in exile. It didn't matter because that was the first party I had been to at which I felt good, where I was relaxed. I didn't drink that night. At least I didn't at first until I felt really confident. I felt as though I didn't have to watch my back, and most of all, I didn't have to worry about being pulled over, arrested, and shot. I had a dime that night, a common practice I had heard about but did not know the importance of until I had to make a call from jail. After that, I always carried two dimes with me, in case the first one was confiscated as part of the personal belongings. That night, in Phoenix, I didn't feel I needed it, and I didn't. In fact, outside of L.A., to this day, I never needed to use a dime again.

Welcome to Albuquerque: For a couple of years, I was in a different town almost every week. I think I remember having only two bad experiences the whole time I was out of state. One was some lightweight stuff in Arizona and the other one was when I arrived in Albuquerque. What happened in Albuquerque was kind of funny because I had driven for a car show from L.A. to Phoenix to San Antonio in the magazine's '62 Chevy. It was the first time I had been in San Antonio, but because of some difficulties, I didn't want to go to the car show there. Instead, I wanted to go to Nuevo Mexico. I ended up going back to Phoenix, where I picked up my car. When I got to Albuquerque, I was greeted by an officer from the Albuquerque Police Department. I was looking for a park where I had been told the Raza hung out. As I was looking for the park, I got pulled over. It was nothing, but I thought, "Ah, shit! I hope their computer doesn't have my record." I didn't even have a real record, but I thought maybe they still had the records for the phony assault charges. Luckily, the cop was cool. Maybe he just pulled me over because I had California license plates. Anyway, it turned out to be cool. Later that day, after meeting some people, I was taken to a "Latin Pride" car club get-together. I had been there only a few minutes when someone recognized me. It was funny because the magazine was happening there. The lowriding scene was alive and kicking, and they were aware of the closure of Whittier and my case. I must have been naive, but I thought it was funny. It didn't matter because I met some Raza there that I'll never forget. I think if I had a choice, that's probably where I would be, even today. The Raza there are real hospitable.

The lightweight incident that happened in Arizona is that some highrider bozo tried to race me in the magazine's '62 Chevy. I ignored the clown but he wouldn't stop revving up his engine. Finally, I dropped the lifts on him, first the front, then the back. The clown got so mad he raced as fast as he could to the corner, which had a red light. He must have been furious. I cruised up to the intersection at about 15 miles per hour, and again I dropped the front as I stopped. The clown spat at the '62 in frustration because I had unintentionally made him look like a jerk. A block down, I got pulled over, but I didn't get a ticket or anything because the cop just tripped on the car. I guess he hadn't seen a paint job like the one the '62 had. All in all, I did meet a few cops wherever I went, but only in L.A. did they treat me as though I was guilty first.

Outside of L.A., I was doing everything I ever wanted to do. I was breathing fresh air, I wasn't getting arrested, and I was meeting a lot of cool Raza. Once in a while, I'd pop back to L.A. for a couple of days, look at the gray sky, and be convinced I didn't belong there.

As I mentioned, there were some difficulties preventing me from going to the San Antonio car show. When I was in Phoenix, I had been told that I was to drive the '62 to San Antonio. The problem was that one of the fender wells had to be painted over. If you've ever seen that '62 (it used to belong to some guy named Julio from Lifestyle car club in L.A.), you'd know that the paint job would be hard to match, all the different shades of green and blue. The car was supposed to be ready the night before, but it wasn't. I didn't blame the guy. He had been asked to perform a miracle. The car wasn't ready until close to midnight. The reason there was a rush on the car was because the '62 was supposed to cruise the streets of San Antonio to promote the big upcoming car show. When I picked up the car, I couldn't see myself driving it with a fresh paint job. I drove it home and tried to sleep, but I couldn't. I got up and got ready. I had no spare tire, but I had no choice. I filled the gas tank, but that turned out to be another problem, fumes. Not only that, the gas gauge didn't register. Just knowing that I was going to travel over a thousand miles through the desert with a broken gas gauge added to my nervousness.

I took off and ended up in Tucson a few hours later. I was going to stop a while and sleep except I felt I should go on. About an hour or two outside of Tucson, I became hopelessly drowsy and pulled off the road at a rest area. Since it was freezing cold, I rolled the windows up and knocked out. When I awoke in the morning, I had a tremendous headache. In fact, every inch of my body was buzzing, almost vibrating. I thought maybe I should eat but changed my mind and decided to wait till I got to El Paso. When I got there, my body was completely buzzing. I kind of thought it was the end for me. I felt like I had electricity coming out of me, like I had gotten heavy doses of electricity. Every step I took brought on excruciating pain. I got to a phone booth and made a phone call to San Antonio. I told them to fly someone in to El Paso to drive in the '62, because I couldn't. There was a big party going on in San Antonio, a grand opening for a new hydraulics shop, which was why I couldn't connect directly with the owner. I needed a phone number of someone in El Paso. After a few phone calls to L.A., San Jose, and San Antonio, after a seeming eternity, I connected with Benny, the president of the Imperials Car Club of El Paso. When I got to his house, I was a virtual zombie. I remember a Laker championship being on TV, and people were all into the game. I would have gotten into the game too, but in my condition, I knocked out like a light. About ten hours later, there was no change in my condition. I felt like a light bulb, as though I was radiating electricity. My whole body was affected. I remember Benny and his friends wanted to use the '62, so reluctantly I went with them. We went cruising through the streets of El Paso and then went to a pretty heavy night club, although I was in no condition to enjoy it. A couple of hours later, I was back and slept another sixteen hours. When I awoke, there was still no change. Benny offered to drive the '62 into San Antonio if no one else came in. After eating and resting a few hours, I decided to continue the journey to San Antonio, but I couldn't leave yet. The right front tire was completely bald, and I was out of money. Benny lent me some money, about forty or fifty bucks, and not knowing what to expect, I left for San Antonio, about 600 miles away. I don't know how much later, but I arrived in San Antonio in the middle of the night. With my body still buzzing, I drove to a Holiday Inn, dropped the lifts at the entrance, got a room, and knocked out.

I think that was one of the worst things that ever happened to me, after the L.A. incident, and I didn't know how to explain it. That's why I didn't want to stay in San Antonio. I wanted to go back to where I was calm. In the next few years, a few incidents like that happened to me, incidents I hope never happen again.

In these past few years, after leaving L.A., I can say that I have learned a lot despite these few incidents. Probably the most important years of my life were the ones I spent going from varrio to varrio in every city of Aztlán—that was real important. That's why I should write more about El Paso or San Antonio, about Houston and Northern California. When I was traveling to those places, I knew I was doing something that few people had ever done. I wasn't just visiting; we were connecting varrios that had never heard of other varrios. Throughout all this, I kept thinking that it was too bad that I wasn't doing it for *La Raza* magazine.

People who surveyed for the magazine said that for every one person that bought a copy of *Lowrider*, at least five people read it. That's a pretty big number because, from what I understand, the best selling magazines are read by three people for every copy bought. *Lowrider* was hotter than *Playboy*, and that's the truth. Since *Lowrider* was putting out about 100,000 magazines per month, with a 5 to 1 ratio, you could assume that at least a half-million people were reading the magazine monthly. Just from what I saw, I think that the estimates were way off. I knew of barrios and towns where one magazine would circulate through everyone's hands. Town after town, barrio after barrio, everyone was up with the latest issue. Also, from what I saw, I think that what caused the big interest was that the controversy over Whittier Boulevard affected everyone. Everywhere you went, the Raza had somewhere to cruise. They were also going through the same problems with the cops and the media. I think every boulevard, every cruising spot in the Southwest, was either shut down or was planned to be shut down. That's what made Whittier Boulevard important, because the closures had begun there.

Probably the most important reason the Raza liked the magazine is they knew that eventually they might come out in the magazine. In the beginning, the magazine wasn't into idolizing Hollywood or famous people. The magazine was about the Raza, the streets. That's why many people hated it. They would say, "How come you put all those bums in the magazine. They don't even own a car!" Others would say, "Why do you put people like that in the magazine? They're a bad example." Still, others would say, "Why don't you put Raza who own businesses or movie stars?" The people who were saying those things were missing the whole point. The magazine wasn't about movie stars or disco ducks. It was about pride. It was about the streets, the Raza, the plebe. Those who objected to the magazine for those reasons couldn't get it through their heads that the magazine wasn't like *Nuestro* or *Caminos* or any other magazine. In fact, there never was a magazine like it for any ethnic group.

The reason the Raza backed up the magazine is because it was a magazine in which everyone could appear. You didn't have to be or act white, you didn't have to shake hands with the President, you didn't have to kiss anyone's butt, you didn't have to reject your own Raza, you didn't have to earn $100,000 a year, and you didn't even have to own a fancy car. Probably 95 percent of the readers of *Lowrider* didn't own a fancy lowrider.

The majority didn't even own a lowrider. Only in L.A., in some areas, were people preoccupied with the Hollywood scene. Most people didn't care about reading about some up-and-coming movie star baboso who sold out his race because he was a struggling actor. Nobody wanted to see Hollywood phonies. Nobody wanted to see Chicanos play sleepy Mexicans on the screen and then act as though they were famous. The biggest letdown came when the magazine began covering the Chicano Hollywood scene. I tell you, only a few stargazers were into that scene. The magazine had been a success for the opposite reason. The magazine succeeded because it was about the streets, not about glorifying things that were glitter. Everywhere I went, people dug the magazine because they recognized someone or they knew someone who had appeared in it. When the Hollywood stuff started coming in, people were practically repulsed. They couldn't see how a righteous street magazine could turn Hollywood. The magazine was supposed to represent pride, pure pride. The people were proud that the magazine wasn't pretentious. It was about people, real people. That's where it derived its strength. That's why the magazine was welcomed with open arms in every barrio in the Southwest. People dug it. Sure, everyone had a complaint here and there, but the main thing was, "How come you don't put our barrio in your libro?" In three or four years, there were probably over a million faces that appeared, probably more than all other magazines combined. The reason for this was that other magazines focused on the newsmakers, the performer, or the stage. *Lowrider* focused on the audience.

For that reason, I was able to go from barrio to barrio and get total support. If I hadn't worked for the magazine, I may have gotten that support anyway, but I do know that because of the magazine I was welcomed into many places with open arms. I didn't have to worry about a lot of things. At the time, worry was the last thing I needed.

When I was going to all the different cities in the different states, I didn't worry as I had in L.A., but the case was always on my mind. I was getting support and finding out that the Raza were in full support of my case, yet it did not take care of the fear that I had in L.A. Being out of L.A. was like being in paradise, but I knew that it was artificial. I knew paradise could exist for me only if I stayed out of L.A. After seeing the rest of the Southwest and Mexico, I didn't want to return to L.A., but that wasn't the point. I liked seeing a blue sky rather than a gray one. I liked the calm and the unity of the Raza throughout the Southwest better than the urban madness of L.A. I liked not being chased by cops better than having to constantly look in the rear view mirror. On a scale from 1 to 100, L.A. was probably a 1 in relation to how good it was for my health. L.A. is probably the worst place for Chicanos to live once you see how others live. Nonetheless, after living in paradise for a couple of years, I returned to L.A. for a couple of reasons. The main reason was personal. No matter how much I liked Nuevo Mexico or San Antonio or Phoenix, I had to return to L.A. because I didn't like the idea of being forced to live away from L.A. The biggest sacrifice I ever made was voluntarily leaving the paradise of San Antonio where they had even elected a Chicano Mayor to return to the gray skies of L.A. I came back around June or July 1981, but luckily for my sake, I didn't return to the East Side. I moved into an apartment (which the magazine rented) on the beach in Venice until I was given a new assignment by the magazine. When I came back from Texas, I really wasn't sure how long I was going to stay in L.A., a month maybe. I didn't figure on staying any longer. I thought I just might split to Mexico or I would go to Colorado or Chicago, places where I hadn't gone for the magazine.

After the editorial that appeared in the July 1981 issue, when I decided to quit, I lost interest in any future dealings with the magazine. The only concern I had thereafter was quitting and getting my last check. It turned out that my last stories didn't come out till the September issue, so after I picked up my check, I was gone. Moneywise, it was a dumb decision because for the last few years I had been living like a king, but that didn't matter. What mattered now was that I had to deal with living in L.A. again, if I chose to stay.

Emotionally, I know the decision to stay in L.A. was the wrong one. All that had been done in the preceding few years was undone by returning to L.A. Luckily, I haven't been arrested since I've been back, but I did get pulled over a few times. Of course, I never did anything wrong. Just being here made me nervous again, especially when I was in East L.A., and I saw a sheriff. It took me a while to even be in East L.A. at night, but now it's cool. I probably will end up moving away somewhere, and wherever it is, it'll be where people are treated as humans by the police and where you can see a blue sky all year round and breath decent air.

15 / The Closure of Whittier Boulevard: You Can Close the Boulevard, but You Can't Stop the Cruising

When historians take out their note pads and write the history of East L.A., only the death of Rubén Salazar will overshadow the illegal closure of Whittier Boulevard. When the closure becomes a part of history, people will remember August 31, 1979, the way people remember August 29, 1970.

August 31, 1979, is the day the barricades first went up on Whittier Boulevard in East L.A. It was an unprecedented act which continues in effect to this day. Since August 31, 1979, it has been against the law to drive or cruise down Whittier Boulevard on Friday, Saturday, and Sunday nights between 9:30 P.M. and 5:00 A.M. Those who were or are against cruising on Whittier probably think the closure is good. The significance of the closure is not that the Boulevard was closed, nor why, but rather how it was closed and who was behind the closure.

Cruising did generate some problems. There were those who wanted the Boulevard closed, but what did they actually hope to accomplish by the closing of Whittier Boulevard? Were they interested in ending gang violence or did they think they could stop the cruising?

Those interested in shutting down the Boulevard succeeded, but that didn't solve any problems. Not one. Gang violence, which supposedly was their prime concern, peaked in '79, '80, and '81. The year 1980 was one in which the Boulevard was shut down for 52 weekends, and gang murders peaked in L.A. County. Violence was unparalleled in the history of L.A. as well as in the history of the United States. How is it that cruising was responsible for gang murders? Whittier Boulevard had nothing to do with the problem. Gang violence was the major problem, but the closing of the Boulevard was not a solution. If a murder was committed at a party, would you ban parties? When violence occurred at Magic Mountain, no one began a campaign to shut down Magic Mountain. Similar incidents occurred at Knott's Berry Farm and Disneyland. The rip-off artist who specializes in oldies concerts, with a guaranteed gang fight at each one of them, always makes a lot of money. A lot of blood is spilled, but does anyone outlaw his concerts?

The closing of the Boulevard did not save one life. If a murder occurred on Hubbard, one block away, parallel to Whittier Boulevard, would it be OK because it didn't occur on Whittier Boulevard? Those supposedly concerned with the violence didn't really have a solution in mind and knew full well that the cruising could never be stopped. The closure only gave the sheriffs more authority than they already had. Most people who have never been in East L.A. at night do not realize the significance. With the Boulevard shut down, everyone driving in the vicinity becomes a potential violator, a suspect. According to the sheriffs, their concern wasn't closing Whittier Boulevard; it was eliminating cruising altogether. That meant they had given themselves the authority to arrest anyone they suspected of cruising anywhere in East L.A. The ramifications are unthinkable. When the Boulevard was first shut down, the question in everyone's mind was "After dark, can anyone come into or leave East L.A. without getting arrested?" Of course this sounds like an exaggeration, but it isn't. If ten thousand people were out cruising Whittier Boulevard, not everyone would be arrested, but the sheriffs had the newly granted authority to stop anyone they suspected of cruising.

For some people, that still doesn't sound an alarm. The idea that the sheriffs can exercise unlimited power is not real if you stay home 24 hours a day. People, because of the media, view cruising as a criminal activity, so any efforts to stop the cruising is seen as good. The problem is isolating the criminal elements from those out to have a good time. Nobody I ever met promotes or condones crime. Nobody I ever met went to the Boulevard to kill or be killed. Probably less than 1 percent of those who went to the Boulevard went to look for trouble. Because the sheriffs could not deal with that 1 percent, the other 99 percent had to pay the price.

Government is supposed to work by checks and balances, meaning that if one is dissatisfied with those who represent or serve the people, one is supposed to have a recourse. In other words, if the sheriffs could not deal with the situation and were abusing their power, the people should be able to do something about it. According to the sheriffs, the problem on the Boulevard was caused by the gangs. But what about the people who think the sheriffs are part of the problem, that they abuse their self-appointed power? Who asked the sheriffs to patrol East L.A. anyway? The sheriffs in East L.A. are like an occupying army. Their sole function is to enforce the laws that were not agreed to by the people. They don't serve and protect. They are not even Mexican, nor are they from East L.A. The worst aspect of an occupying army is when they replace their troops with indigenous troops. The idea is to train them to oppress their own people. What has happened in East L.A. is that the situation has eroded so badly that people don't even know when their Constitutional rights have been taken away. First, one right is taken away. A few people complain. The commotion dies down. Then the loss of that

94

right is taken for granted. Next a second right is taken away. A few people complain. The commotion dies down. Now the loss of that right is taken for granted, too.

In East L.A., the right to vote and the right to representation have never existed. East L.A. has no representation of any kind. The freedom of assembly and the freedom to travel has also been recently taken away. How many more rights must be taken away before people do something about it?

When the Boulevard was shut down, it sent shockwaves throughout the country. Boulevards and parks throughout the country were shut down like a series of dominoes. In the L.A. area, wherever Raza gathered, every boulevard or park was shut down, and cruising became a criminal act. The gathering of Raza anywhere practically became outlawed. Worse, it spread from city to city across California, Arizona, New Mexico, Colorado, Texas, and even Nevada. Even though cruising is pretty heavy in the Mexican border region, reports of closures in Mexico were not reported. Throughout the Southwest, boulevard after boulevard began to be shut down, and that was followed shortly by the closing of parks, from Denver to San Antonio, from San Diego to Albuquerque, and from San Jose to Tucson. It was the same everywhere, but East L.A. was unique because nobody did anything about it. In San Diego, the Lowrider Council and the Committee on Chicano Rights filed a lawsuit to prevent the closure of Highland Avenue in National City. In Phoenix, quick action by the lowriding community prevented the closure of Central Avenue. In Albuquerque, the Raza took on a different approach. They negotiated with the police department. Over there, relations were much better, so negotiations were possible. In San Francisco, in the Mission District, the Raza filed a lawsuit against the city to reopen the Boulevard. Ironically, Whittier Boulevard was the first boulevard shut down, and today, five years later, Whittier Boulevard remains the only boulevard in the country that sees barricades go up every weekend.

Everywhere authorities sought to curb the rights of the Raza, the plebe fought back and won. Why it didn't happen in Los Angeles is a mystery. I remember that when the Boulevard was shut down, the first thing we did was call the American Civil Liberties Union. They are supposed to be the ones who defend the rights of people. The answer was a flat "no." The champion of Civil Rights was so busy that they couldn't take the time to defend the Raza. Another lesson was learned. At the time, I was still fighting my case. My charges weren't dropped till three months later. Since I was concerned with my legal defense, and the ACLU had turned down the request, a lot of us spent a lot of time thinking about creating a mass movement to reopen the Boulevard. We figured that through my trial the real evidence would surface. That is, the abuse inflicted by the sheriff's department would be exposed, triggering a better coverage on the part of the media. But since the escalating violence in the streets was equally matched by the sheriffs, it probably wouldn't have been a good idea to reopen the Boulevard at that point. Maybe when all the sensationalism died down, we could legally challenge the anticruising ordinance. It was a battle if not a war, and the sheriffs had definitely won. If the Boulevard was reopened through legal action, they probably would have retaliated by cracking a lot of heads. It would have been easy to win an injunction against the closure, but those who would suffer the consequences were those who would go out to cruise and get their heads busted.

I think that failing to legally pursue the matter was a result of nobody wanting to see anyone's head cracked. At the time, the sheriffs were getting crazy on the Boulevard, so nobody wanted to see other young Raza fall victim to a riot stick.

From the outset, the reopening of the Boulevard would have been useless unless the Raza controlled the sheriff's department. The only way that could happen is if East L.A. became a city.

Today, five years later, the Boulevard remains closed. The Raza are still politically powerless, but the plebe are still cruising. "You can close the Boulevard, but you can't stop the cruising." No barricade can stop a tradition. As of this writing, the Raza don't cruise from Atlantic to Eastern, but they do cruise Whittier, east of Atlantic Boulevard to Garfield Boulevard. It's not the same, but it continues. When they close that part of the Boulevard, the Raza cruise Hubbard or Atlantic. Maybe in a year, Olympic Boulevard will be the big street, or maybe it'll be Beverly or Floral. Nobody likes gang bangers, but cruising is not gang banging. You can lock up gang bangers but you can't imprison lowriding. You can't imprison a tradition. When the Boulevard was first shut down, people were wondering, "How long can they close the Boulevard?" People thought a few months, a year, a few years; some people even said ten years. The sheriffs said it would remain closed as long as lowriders and cruisers continue to come to the area. Apparently, according to their own accounts, the Boulevard is going to remain closed forever. That's how long a tradition lasts. That's how long people will continue to wait to come down the Boulevard.

I doubt that the Boulevard remains closed for ten years, but neither should it be reopened without guarantees that people will not get their heads cracked. When I first started this section, I mentioned that August 31, 1979, was the second most important date in East L.A. history. When the Boulevard is reopened, that day should be the most important day for not only East L.A. but for all Raza throughout the country. But it shouldn't be done through the courts. Whittier Boulevard should be reopened by the will of the people. The only time the people will be heard is when we truly control our own destinies. When East L.A. exercises the right to vote and the right to representation, only then should the Boulevard be opened, if the Raza want it reopened. When we patrol our own streets, when we are able to curb or eliminate the violence, then we will have no need to hand over our security to those who abuse their self-appointed authority. It's a monumental task, but it is not impossible. Remember, a lot of Raza, though they may live in Phoenix or El Paso, still have their heart in East L.A. The worst thing that could happen is for East L.A. to become a city due to a crisis. We don't need five-year-olds getting killed to trigger a movement. Enough rights have been taken away for us not to rebel to the intolerable situation. Have we grown accustomed to not having any rights? What will it take? A crisis? A martyr? More of our rights taken away? East L.A. is but a hundred thousand people, but also it is more. It is the heart and soul of a people. It is where millions have grown up. It is where people have left their hearts and where a lot of people still call home.

16 / East L.A.:
A State Of Siege

By the time I left for Arizona in the middle of December, I had won my case, but I had left something just as important unresolved. Abuse and harassment by sheriffs had scaled to new heights after the incident. It all had culminated with the successful drive, led by the sheriff's department, to shut down Whittier Boulevard. On August 31, 1979, barricades went up on Whittier Boulevard, from Atlantic Boulevard to Eastern. On every street north and south of the Boulevard, barricades and posted signs went up. On Atlantic and Eastern, signs went up saying, "Road Closed Fri., Sat., Sun.—9:30 P.M. to 5:00 A.M." When the barricades went up, it was as though we couldn't believe we were in the United States. The place resembled a war zone. It reminded me of Ireland or Lebanon. Actually, it seemed more like a Latin American country where the military authorities had declared a state of siege.

After waging a war on the streets and a clean-cut image in the media, the sheriffs, the self-appointed guardians of East L.A., had not only succeeded in closing down a street. They had rendered a community powerless. That was my only reason for not wanting to leave L.A. Different circumstances had brought on the situation. Before the magazine, the media more or less ignored the cruising, but when it did cover it, it portrayed Whittier as a haven for criminals and criminal activity. Before that, no magazine showed the other side of the story. When the magazine showed a different side to cruising and lowriding, it seemed to have become the arch enemy of the conservative establishment. For whatever reasons, the magazine became the defender of the Raza on the streets. The magazine obviously didn't start the cruising, but it became an important element in the battle over the shutdown of Whittier Boulevard. The controversy over Whittier Boulevard would probably have taken place regardless of whether 538 people had been arrested on the weekend when *Boulevard Nights* had premiered. The incident simply brought the media into East L.A. People had been lowriding for years, but then suddenly the media discovered Whittier Boulevard. The following weekend, every radio, TV, and newspaper was on the Boulevard to see what was happening. What did they report? They reported the sheriffs' efforts at trying to control the gang violence and the outsiders. Of course, they didn't talk about police abuse. The media didn't see any, so it didn't exist. As soon as the media physically left Whittier, it was back to normal. The state of siege continued. The barricades remained, and the harassment did not let up. During this time, the threatened closure of

Whittier Boulevard and my pending trial was hand in hand. I was fighting my case, and at the same time, we were fighting against the proposed shut down. On August 31, they won. I felt personally responsible. I felt the magazine had not done enough.

When I won my case on November 7, we had still not won the major battle, the battle over Whittier Boulevard to curb, if not end, the sheriff's department's state of siege on the young Raza, on the lowriding plebe who were constantly being singled out and harassed. The charges against me were dropped nine months after they were filed, preventing the testimony of the pervasive abuse and harassment by the sheriffs in East L.A. The trial would have exposed all that. I felt bad that we didn't get a chance to expose the police violence. They had gotten off the hook for the time being, but with my lawsuit, I knew their time would come in court. The only problem is that lawsuits take on the average about seven years, a long time to wait.

Without much of a choice, I moved to Arizona, leaving the battle unfinished. I felt that one day Whittier Boulevard would be reopened, somehow.

It was with those thoughts that I left for Arizona. I wasn't sure what to expect. I had been out of L.A. before, but this time I wasn't exactly going because I wanted to.

While in Arizona, I learned about East L.A. I also learned about East L.A. in Texas, in New Mexico, and in Northern California. Even though I had lived in and around East L.A. all my life, I didn't really understand East L.A. until I was out of the area.

East L.A. is probably the most unique urban area in the country. Geographically, it is a couple of miles east of downtown. It is bordered by Indiana on the west to around Garfield, adjacent to Montebello, on the east. The exact borders are not as important as the fact that East L.A. is in the heart of the biggest concentration of Raza outside of Mexico City. There are literally hundreds of barrios within this concentration around downtown and east and southeast of downtown. There are well over a million Mexicanos and Latinos in this area alone, and there may even be more because this is where the Raza lives, with or without papers. Fifteen years ago, the majority of the Raza was concentrated in the eastern part of the county. Today, the Raza is also in downtown itself, the Pico-Union area, central L.A. extending westward all the way into Hollywood and beyond.

Politically, everyone has the right to representation and the right to vote if they are U.S. citizens. Off the top, that eliminates a lot of Raza. Probably half the Raza are legal residents but not U.S. citizens. Legal permanent residents and Raza without papers do not have the right to representation. Politically, that is why Raza have little representation, but to add insult to injury, what makes East L.A. unique is that it is not part of Los Angeles, nor is it its own city like the surrounding cities of Montebello,

City of Commerce, or Alhambra. East L.A. is an unincorporated part of Los Angeles County. Big deal. What does that mean? Being unincorporated means that although East L.A. is only a couple of miles east of downtown, it has nothing to do with L.A. Politically, East L.A. has no voice as to what goes on in Los Angeles. In other words, the residents of East L.A. cannot vote for the mayor of Los Angeles, nor can the people have a representative in the Los Angeles City Council. Politically then, East L.A. has no representation in City Hall. Since East L.A. is not a part of Los Angeles and since it's not its own city, the only representative is the Supervisor for the Third District of Los Angeles County. In other words, in East L.A. there is no will of the people. There is no functioning democracy, not even for the citizens (as if the rest of the Raza were not people).

The most basic right in a democracy is the right to vote, the right to equal representation. You pay taxes on the premise that you are being represented. If you don't like your representative, you vote him or her out of office. Since about half the Raza either are legal residents or have no papers, our population is deprived of equal representation. In East L.A., over 100,000 Mexicanos are virtually subjects of the county, citizens and noncitizens alike. What this means is that if the people of East L.A. are dissatisfied with something, their only recourse is to pray to the Great White Father (whoever happens to be the Supervisor of the Third District). The people can also either jam the county Board of Supervisors' meeting or riot, which was done in the early seventies. Since the Supervisor has other concerns, with East L.A. being low on the list, true representation cannot come out of this situation, nor should it be expected. In effect, what you have is over 100,000 Mexicanos in a colonial situation. East L.A. is like a giant urban reservation. They have no mayor to elect, nor any city council to take their grievances to. As of this writing, it is 1984, you would figure someone would stand up and say, "Hey, wait a minute! It's not supposed to be this way. We're supposed to have representation, aren't we?" We read in the history books that that was why the United States revolted against England. Wasn't their slogan, "No taxation without representation"?

Actually, people have revolted against this situation. Three times, people tried to make East L.A. a city, and each time the effort has failed. People had different reasons why they wanted to see East L.A. become a city. The last time, La Raza Unida Party led a campaign that almost succeeded. You may be wondering, "Who wouldn't want East L.A. to become a city?" Ironically, when you scare people and when blackmail is used, people will surrender their right to representation. The reason East L.A. failed to become a city is that the opposition pointed out that East L.A.'s tax base was too small to meet the expenses of the proposed city. The reason is because the industrial belt, the southeastern part of East L.A., had broken away to become City of Commerce. The residents had been told that to become a city would mean unbearable taxes. You know the result. The residents weren't given a choice between representation versus no representation or a Mexican representative versus a white representative. No, the residents or rather the citizens were given a choice between representation and higher taxes versus continuing with the "no representation." In reality, the residents were given no choice. Well, if you know anything about East L.A., it's still unincorporated, and the taxes? What do you think?

There's more to be said about this situation, however, the thing to be learned about this is timing. If the election regarding cityhood had been held in September of 1970, East L.A. would today be a city. East L.A. in 1970 was ready to explode. Rubén Salazar had not only been killed, but the guilty sheriffs had been let off the hook. A true state of siege existed after the infamous August 29th Moratorium against the Vietnam war. Sheriffs patrolled the streets day and night. Who told the sheriffs to patrol the streets of East L.A.? Who hired them? Who elected them? Who gave the sheriffs the right to exercise their authority? Not the residents. Not City Hall. Not the representatives of East L.A.

A situation existed in 1979 in which the sheriffs derived their power not from the people, but from the headquarters of the L.A. County Sheriff's Department. If that was unacceptable in 1970, in 1979, it was still unacceptable. The difference between 1970 and 1979 is that those who lived in East L.A. in 1970 had moved out to Pico Rivera, to Whittier, to El Monte, to Baldwin Park, to La Puente, to Santa Fe Springs, to other parts of the county, and even to other parts of the country. In 1979, when the sheriffs decided to close the Boulevard, it was not done by the consent of a democratically held election. It was done in a colonial manner. The Great White Father knows best.

When I was growing up in East L.A., and later, when the incident happened, I knew all about inequality and police abuse, but it was not until I moved out of the state did things become clear. They say when you're in the middle of something, you don't really get to see what's around you. As much as I knew what was around me, I really didn't know the significance of Whittier Boulevard and East L.A. in relation to the Raza throughout the Southwest, throughout Aztlán.

East L.A. is bordered by Boyle Heights, City of Commerce, Montebello, and Monterey Park and has a population of over 100,000. If it were a city, it would be one of the biggest in Southern California. Anaheim, Long Beach, Los Angeles, and San Diego would be bigger. Obviously, it is nowhere near the size of Los Angeles or San Diego, but certainly it would be bigger than a lot of big name cities up and down the state. East L.A. is close to 100 percent Raza. East L.A., although an integral part of Los Angeles is seldom seen in the media. The only time you hear about East L.A. is when there is a gang murder. To a lot of people, East L.A. is a mecca for criminals, the capital of crime, and a producer of an unlimited supply of prisoners to the state correctional system. East L.A. is tough.

There is a lot of crime, and there are drugs and hardened criminals influencing the youth, although, even by police estimates, not even 10 percent of the youth are involved with criminal gangs. Nonetheless, all of East L.A. is cloaked with an image of some kind of sin city. Nothing could be further from the truth. The media has distorted East L.A. because they would like to make people believe that every Mexican is a lazy drug-dealing cutthroat gang banger. The majority of the Raza who live in East L.A. are hard working, trying to make a better living for themselves and a better future for their children. It sounds like a typical barrio, like every Mexican barrio in the United States, and it is, except there is one very big exception. Los Angeles and specifically East L.A. is the gateway into the United States. Sociologists say that Los Angeles is like New York was at the turn of the century. The majority of people who move into East L.A. are from Mexico, but they do not stay forever in East L.A. Most people use East L.A. as a stepping stone. There's a saying that you don't move into East L.A., you move out of it. As a result, almost everyone in California if not the Southwest has lived or has family or friends who have lived in East L.A. Twenty years ago, El Paso might have been the principal gateway into the United States. Right now, Los Angeles has been the principal point of entry for a long time, and maybe in the future, San Diego or Chicago might become the gateways. Whatever happens in the future is another story, but for now Los Angeles is the heart of the Mexican people. Whatever happens in Los Angeles reverberates and happens elsewhere. To Chicanos, New York is meaningless. Nobody cares what happens there. Only white people follow New York or European trends. To Chicanos throughout the country, Los Angeles is the hub. It is the center of a people. The way whites like and hate New York, Chicanos also love or hate East L.A. Some people feel that all good or all bad comes from East L.A. When I moved to Arizona, I was aware of this relationship, but I didn't quite comprehend it completely. One thing I should add is that East L.A. must have the best and worst ambassadors in the world. Every time someone from East L.A. visits or moves out of the area, they always leave an impression for the next person to contend with. Upon moving to Phoenix, I tried to become low-keyed. I didn't come with the intention of painting the town with my last name. In my mind, Arizona was just sanctuary. It was a place to be, avoiding the heat from law enforcement. I wasn't a criminal, yet I was acting as though I were one or rather, I was being to forced to flee as though I were one. I had to be cool about everything I did. Because the magazine was widely read by the plebe, I couldn't really hide. A lot of people knew who I was. I tried not to talk about my case too much, but because Whittier Boulevard was always on everyone's mind, it was inescapable. In Phoenix, the Raza had Central Avenue, and they too had had to contend with its threatened closure. As I recall, I think the city failed in their efforts to shut down Central. Cruising Central in Phoenix kind of reminded me of cruising in the Mall in San Fernando. Although I didn't think the Mall was too rowdy, Central Avenue was even less. I'm sure there were fights here and there, but the atmosphere never approached the intensity of Whittier Boulevard. Everything was different in Arizona. Everything, you could say, was a lot better. I spent a lot of days and nights meeting people at the two main car washes, down Central, at the mountains and at Encanto Park. About 99 percent of everyone I met had heard about the closure of Whittier Boulevard. The reason they had heard about it was not just through the magazine, but because efforts had been made to shut down Central. One thing about Arizona is that there are a lot of people who live there who came from L.A. Many of them still have a lot of contact with Los Angeles. Everywhere you went, it was understood that Whittier Boulevard was the granddaddy of all the Boulevards. So it followed that when attempts were made to shut down Whittier, the lowriding plebe would have united and fought against it. At least that's what many Raza in Arizona thought should have happened. Even though it wasn't stated, Whittier Boulevard and East L.A. were seen as the heartbeat of the lowriding plebe. It was also not stated but known that there were racial motivations behind the crackdown on lowriders. If my eyes were opened in Arizona, I was shocked that New Mexico and Texas were going through the same thing. Everywhere in the Southwest, it was like a state of siege against boulevards and parks, wherever the Raza gathered. Again, they looked to people from East L.A. as the ones who should be leading the fight.

To my surprise, everyone I met thought that either East L.A. was part of the east side of Los Angeles or was a city in itself. I would try to tell people that East L.A. was unincorporated, that it was not a city or part of a city, and that if the Raza wanted to reopen the Boulevard, they couldn't petition a mayor or their city council because there was none. It was through this process of explaining that I realized how powerless we really were. Everywhere I went, everyone seemed to ask, "Why don't you guys make East L.A. into a city?" It sounded too easy, but it made sense. The more I was asked about Whittier Boulevard, the more people brought it up. They would say, "Here, when we were having problems, we caravanned to the city council." There, they could do it, but in East L.A., we had nowhere to go. Maybe my thoughts were getting distorted, being that I was out of Los Angeles, but my own feelings about leaving the battlefield made me determined to wage a battle, even if it was from Arizona, Denver, Albuquerque, San Antonio, or El Paso. I figured I knew everything about East L.A., and with the aid of the magazine, I could help wage a war not merely to reopen the Boulevard but also to make East L.A. a city. It would be a monumental task, and maybe it wouldn't succeed, or maybe the idea wouldn't even catch on. Nobody knows the future, so I figured, "You never know until you try." Maybe I was motivated by the encouragement of Raza I met throughout the Southwest.

The last time people attempted to make East L.A. a city, it was led by La Raza Unida Party and a lot of other people. What gave me the idea that we could succeed this time? The reason probably was because Raza everywhere thought it was a good idea, and this time it would come from the streets from the plebe who was not used to voting. The way I saw it, in 1974 when the election was held, probably most people 25 and under didn't vote. I figured that now anyone about 32 years and under probably had never been heard on the issue. It seemed pretty easy: "All you have to do is tap the 18- to 32-year-old vote, and you're in like flint!"

From outside Los Angeles, I began to write about the lack of political power in East L.A. The issue was not new, although a lot of people who lived in East L.A. in 1970 were no longer there in 1980. I don't remember where I was living at the time, but I got the OK from the publisher. So from there on, I wrote about the need to make East L.A. a city. I figured that maybe it would take from one to two years to get something going. I knew who I was working for. I knew he had other motivations. I too had a personal motivation. I wanted to move back to East L.A. I figured that the only way I could move back to East L.A. was if the sheriffs and whomever was policing the streets of East L.A. were accountable to the residents of East L.A. The only way the sheriffs would be held accountable was if the residents had some kind of representation, specifically through cityhood. At that time, I was having the time of my life, living and traveling all over the Southwest, but it was at a price. Although I liked the traveling, I really didn't like the idea of being forced to live away from L.A. Not that I really liked Los Angeles. I began to hate everything about Los Angeles: the smog, the freeways, the tension, the police. But despite all the negative aspects of Los Angeles and East L.A., I was determined to do something about the lack of political power for the Raza of East L.A.

Throughout all this, I had a recurring thought that maybe no one actually wanted to have the Boulevard reopened. I thought we should at least have a choice. If no one wanted it reopened, then it would be the will of the people. After I had won my case in November, I wrote one last article explaining the victory. After that, in almost every issue thereafter, I wrote an article about Whittier Boulevard and/or about East L.A. At that point, *Lowrider* was selling near or above 100,000 magazines per month. From what I saw through traveling, I was convinced that actually a million people were reading *Lowrider* every month. I was confident that, through the articles about East L.A., something would come of it. But how would I know it if I was in Phoenix or Albuquerque or somewhere else? Almost right from the beginning, we began to receive letters supporting the idea of cityhood for East L.A. One of the times I came back to Los Angeles, I met with some people from La Raza Unida Party. I figured they would probably be able to help out, but the real strength had to come from somewhere else. I knew where that would come from. I also knew that because of the conflicts I had with the publisher, I would sooner or later have to quit. I figured the best I could do was to keep writing about East L.A. until I had to quit.

When I actually did quit, I felt bad that I wouldn't be able to pursue the idea of cityhood for East L.A., at least not for a while. I think that through the incident, I discovered much about people. The drive to make East L.A. a city will probably surface again, but it will have to be done from within East L.A. I'll tell you one thing, if the guy running the magazine had been sincere, East L.A. might today be a city. The response to the articles was good although the question in everyone's mind was, "How?" Everyone knew why—so that people could have a voice in their daily lives. Actually, the stakes were even higher. People saw East L.A. as the heart of Los Angeles, the heart of the Mexican people. If East L.A. became a city, it would not only mean local control, it would become a symbol. East L.A. would become a symbol like Crystal City in Texas had been at one time. Crystal City, whose overwhelming majority has always been Raza, had been run by whites until La Raza Unida Party threw them out of office. If East L.A. could do that, it would be a symbol of immeasurable worth. If East L.A. became a city, economically things probably wouldn't change, but the psychological advantage of knowing that we had elected our own representatives would be enough to give people new pride and new hope. Who knows who would win or how the city would be structured. The importance of East L.A. becoming a city was not so much in its local outcome but in its significance to the rest of the Raza in the United States and in Mexico. There are a million reasons why it should be a city, and one day it may become a city. The problem will be to convince the Raza that people don't have to depend on "The Great White Father," that we don't have to give up our right to vote just to keep taxes down. The right to vote should never be compromised. The worst thing about it is that I hope it doesn't come about as a result of another crisis or another rash of police abuse. We can hope it will come about as a realization via righteous Chicano media.

Ten books could probably be written about East L.A., but here I can only reemphasize that East L.A. is more than just a big Mexican barrio. It has produced many warriors, and it has produced many dedicated Raza whose future is yet to be determined. Too much blood has been spilled in the streets of East L.A. for it to remain what it is today, a symbol of political powerlessness.

When I was in East L.A. night and day, police abuse was rampant. Today, I'm no longer there 24 hours a day. Maybe police abuse is no longer there, and maybe it is. The thing is, if it happens, who do you complain to? The sheriff's department? Do we need another crisis to happen? Why should we wait? Exercising your basic political rights should not depend on a crisis. All people who perform services should be held accountable. If you give up your right to representation, your rights begin to erode until you no longer have rights, and then you no longer complain. In 1979, the people in East L.A. were not used to having rights. First, there was no voting involved on the matter. Second, they closed the Boulevard, then other boulevards and streets. Then the park was closed. What was next? People had given the sheriffs the right to stop anyone at any given time for any reason. Who was identified as a lowrider or a cruiser? If you didn't wear a pendleton, were you cool? How about Levis and a white T-shirt? How about Stacy Adams or a Zoot Suit? If you were going to or from East L.A., were you a potential criminal? Can you imagine a more outrageous crime than getting arrested for being a potential cruiser, a possible violator? People are supposed to have the right to assembly and the freedom to travel. But apparently rights in East L.A. don't exist. The worst part about it is when people shrug off cruising as something insignificant. The biggest right has already been lost; now another one has been taken away. Today is 1984 and the Boulevard is still closed.

17 / The Media: Stay Away from the Boulevard

Like most people, I really wasn't too anxious to go to prison, especially since I was innocent. When the incident occurred, I didn't know I had been charged with anything until after I was in the hospital. Of course, there were about a million things on my mind, but my main concern was keeping quiet and getting out as soon as I could. I should have been able to leave the hospital by around sunrise but the sheriffs claimed that their computer had broken down and that I had warrants, which later turned out to belong to someone else.

For about the next 30 hours, all I could do was think. I felt worse than helpless because not only had I been threatened, but as each second ticked away, the temptation became greater and greater to complain, to start demanding my rights. Of course, I had rights, and I was aware of the Constitution and all that, but I also knew that no matter how many rights I had, on the streets I had none. In their custody, I knew I had the right to shut up, but the longer I stayed in their custody, the more I wanted to let them know what I thought. I even pretended that I wasn't mad and that the sheriffs had done nothing wrong. I just went along with their Mickey Mouse delays. Even though they knew I had a camera, while in their custody, I didn't tell them I worked for *Lowrider Magazine.*

While I was in the hospital, I kept quiet and thought, "Let them think I just happened to be some guy with a camera that just happened to be out there." In actuality, I wasn't just a witness. I had actually been taking pictures of the guy in the sarape in the middle of all the cars, before the sheriffs arrived. I didn't run to go witness an incident. I was already there. Throughout the nine months, especially when I was in the hospital, I knew that because I had a camera and because I worked for the magazine, I would win. That's what got me mad, because what if I didn't have a camera or what if I didn't work for a magazine? There was no question in my mind that I would win. I figured that in the United States, there is no right that is valued more than the First Amendment. Freedom of speech and freedom of the press are symbols of democracy. On Whittier Boulevard, I had witnessed some brutality on the part of the sheriffs, and in the jail ward of the hospital, everyone had a cracked head. What rights did they have? What Constitutional amendment was going to protect those without cameras?

While I was doing all this thinking, my main concern became, what was I going to do once I got out? From what I had been told by those who came in Saturday night, it had been worse that night than Friday night. One of the guards or someone who worked there said it was so badly crowded that they had run out of rooms. I knew from what I had seen that Friday night that it had been really bad, but I couldn't imagine how Saturday night could have been worse. I didn't know if the media had picked up on what was happening. What I did know is that the media were focusing more on the opening of *Boulevard Nights*, which was being picketed down the street in Montebello at the Garmar Theater. I figured that the Garmar was close enough to the cruising that some curious reporter might go down a few blocks to see what the real Boulevard was all about. In the movie, it was gang violence, but if a reporter had gone down a few blocks, the reporter would have witnessed a type of violence that was so routine that it wasn't even considered news. I was even mad, maybe unjustifiably, at the protesters because I thought they were missing the point. They were out protesting images, and down the block, young Raza were being subjected to a state of siege. And it wasn't just that weekend. The abuse and harassment by the sheriffs was nothing new. It didn't just come onto the scene with the opening of *Boulevard Nights*. Raza were being harassed week after week. Rights were routinely violated as though rights did not apply to the Raza. *Boulevard Nights* did do a lot of damage, a psychological damage, but the cameras and the protesters were on the wrong part of the Boulevard, where the physical damage was being done.

Not knowing whether the media had picked up on what happened was on my mind. I'm not 100 percent positive about what I was thinking in regards to the media, but I wasn't too enthusiastic about going in front of cameras because I had been threatened. Maybe nothing would have happened to me, but my thoughts were as distorted as my battered face. I couldn't think rationally. I wasn't thinking that I had rights or stuff like that. I figured, if they were serious about their threat, the last thing I wanted to do is put my face out in front of a camera. To me, it would have the same effect as a wanted poster.

I knew I had a good case on my hands. I knew I would win if my case ever went to trial, and I knew I could file a big lawsuit. The one thing I wasn't sure of is whether I would become a target. If I hadn't worked in the streets, I probably wouldn't have given it a second thought. All I would have had to do is make a big stink about it and stay indoors all the time. I couldn't do that because my job was to be out on the streets.

When I was released, I called a few stations, not about what happened to me but rather about what was happening on the Boulevard. When I got out, I was told that the Boulevard had been shut down on Friday night due to a riot. I also heard that for arrests, it had even been worse Saturday night. Sunday night was still to come, and the media were aware. Channel 7 found out what happened to me through a friend, and reporters wanted to do an interview. I was scared at the time because I didn't know if they were still after me. I said I couldn't until I checked with my lawyer. I didn't have a lawyer until Monday, and Antonio Rodríguez, the one who ended up defending me, thought it would be a good idea to do a big thing with the media. Normally, I would have thought that publicity would have been a good idea except that, in the back of my mind, I thought I was still in danger. I thought exposure in the media would seal my fate, if not my coffin. Nonetheless, Antonio and I agreed to have Channel 7 do something by Friday, the day of my first court appearance. Henry Alfaro showed up and did the interview. Later that evening, the interview aired.

What happened on the Friday and Saturday night after the incident did nothing to encourage me that I needed or wanted publicity. Of course, I might have been needlessly paranoid, but Friday night, I went to meet the Pharaohs Car Club of the South Bay. I had been out of the hospital only about five days, so the wound was still not healed. More important, I was still kind of scared. Since I was the only one who could go that night, I borrowed a camera and went. When I got there, all the Pharaoh cars were parked on one side of the street. I walked up and met everyone. Right away, someone said, "Hey, aren't you the one who came out on TV a little while ago?" How could I deny it since my forehead was still swollen, and the scar was still fresh? I talked about it a little bit, but I really didn't want to talk too much. As I started taking pictures, about 10 to 15 sheriff squad cars pulled up and parked on the opposite side of the street, facing the Pharaoh cars. The last thing I had figured is that the South Bay area was sheriff territory. So here I was with a camera in my hand and a whole bunch of sheriffs who didn't look like they had come to party. You could probably figure what went through my mind. I wanted to make myself thin. After a few tense moments, I continued taking a few more pictures. I was going to go inside and party and all that, but with all the black and whites across the street, I figured, to be safe, I better get back to the East Side. Since the Pharaohs knew what had happened to me, they thought it was cool. I felt bad because we promised we would give the event good coverage. As it turned out, I had to leave right away. Before I left, I asked the Pharaohs for a favor. I asked if one of them could follow me to make sure that I got on the freeway. That's how bad I was shaken up. I figured that if people I didn't even know had seen the interview, a few sheriffs probably had also seen it.

What happened the next night assured me that I was either crazy or that if I continued with the publicity I would end up going crazy. Saturday night was just a coincidence, but nonetheless, it did nothing to help my confidence. That night, I went to Van Nuys Boulevard in Pacoima, where I knew the Raza would be cruising. At that time, problems on the mall had convinced the varrios in the Pacoima area to start their own cruising. Since I knew a lot of the Raza from the area, they already knew what had happened to me, and they asked me if I would go take pictures of the cruising on Van Nuys Boulevard. I thought, "anything to stay away from East L.A." So I went that night to take a few pictures of the varrios of Pacoima. As I took pictures, everyone kept telling me they had seen me on TV and were backing me up. In a while, a bunch of black and whites pulled into the Jack-in-the-Box, and again, I caught myself with a camera in my hand. I couldn't believe what was happening in front of me. I wondered whether all the coincidences were in fact coincidences. I didn't see any provocation, but next thing you know, an altercation broke out and then all hell broke loose. Clubs started swinging, and bottles started flying. People started running in all directions. I was practically frozen, not knowing whether or not I should take pictures. As everyone was running, I heard someone call out my name. I didn't see anyone. Then, the door to a VW van opened. It was some Raza I knew from Pacoima. I couldn't believe it. It was like a movie. I jumped in. From the outside, you couldn't see inside the van, but from the van, you could see everything. It was like watching a riot from front row seats. I think we had to stay in the van for a half hour or an hour. It was kind of funny because some cops ran right by the van and stopped in front, but they couldn't see inside.

Anyway, I had spoken out in an interview Friday evening, and Friday and Saturday nights were like nightmares which I would like to have forgotten. Unfortunately, that weekend probably had a big effect on how I viewed the media. I thought the media was important, and maybe it would enable me to win easily, but not at the expense of my life or, at minimum, the loss of my sanity. By Sunday, I thought to myself, "I know I shouldn't have gone on TV." The events of that weekend ensured that I would not willingly put my face in the media, at least not for a while.

Close Calls, Now What?

From the hospital, while still in custody, my theory had been that publicity would do more harm than good, in that it might help me win the case, but it would also put me on the most wanted list, and I hadn't even committed a crime! If the sheriffs didn't have a real case against me, why aggravate the situation by making a big stink about it? Did I want more publicity? If I did, what would be the consequences? After the first weekend, I knew what they would be. The effect would be that every time I saw a black and white anywhere, particularly a sheriff, I would wonder whether they had seen my face on TV.

At the time, I knew my case was like a gold mine. I knew that if I wanted publicity I could get it easily. The nature of my case involved a camera. I had witnessed an incident of brutality, photographed it, and in turn had become a victim. The sheriffs, through their actions, had interfered in the performance of my duties. That was reason enough. Another reason I could have gotten publicity is because Antonio Rodríguez, the lawyer who represented me, was and is a well-known attorney. I knew I could get publicity, especially since the Boulevard was the center of controversy and the movie *Boulevard Nights* had just premiered.

The *East L.A. Tribune*

On the Thursday following the incident, my arrest came out in the crime report of the *East L.A. Tribune*. I didn't like what they wrote. It made it seem as though I was an outsider. Even though I lived in East L.A., I wasn't about to correct them and say, "Hey, I live on this street in East L.A." I let that ride. The other two things that bugged me was that it sounded like I had committed a crime. They didn't get my side of the story. I wanted to call and say, "Hey, don't you know I used to be a paper boy for the *East L.A. Tribune* and the *East L.A. Gazette*." I felt as though they were backing the wrong side, as if they should have been a little fairer, just because I used to throw their paper.

Aside from the *Tribune* mentioning my "crimes" and the Friday interview on Channel 7, I stayed clear of the media. The Boulevard was a hot item. It was actually at the top of the list in L.A. All week long, the media had been running stories about the incidents of March 23-25. The following weekend the media converged on the Boulevard the way reporters flock to a volcano ready to erupt. The media were giving it their own angle: "Stay away from the Boulevard." When I heard the media giving the sheriffs' version, I felt like doing something about it. The sheriffs were saying that they expected outsiders to converge on the Boulevard. All that week they were warning people to stay away. If it wasn't so stupid, what they were saying would have sounded funny. To say that outsiders were going to converge on the Boulevard, especially because of the movie *Boulevard Nights*, was asinine. They were saying that as though *Boulevard Nights* had created cruising and was attracting people to the Boulevard. The charge of outsiders was true of course, but it's like saying that Disneyland attracted outsiders. All events attract outsiders, except if they're white, they're called tourists.

If all events were off limits to outsiders, almost everyone who has ever staged an event would have gone broke. The fact that people were attracted to the Boulevard had little to do with the movie, and the fact that they were coming from outside of East L.A. did not automatically make them criminals nor suspects. Crime and violence, whether committed by residents or outsiders, is equally deplorable. The media should never have swallowed the sheriffs' version of the incidents of March 23-25. The weekend after the incident, while I was in the South Bay and Pacoima, the media were out in full force on the Boulevard. What was the media going to see? They sure weren't going to see any police abuse. The effect the media had was to prevent police abuse in front of the cameras. That's the good effect the media had, but the calm would only last while the cameras were there. The situation that weekend in East L.A. reminded me of the situation that occurs in Central American countries. Human rights don't exist, but when the cameras arrive, the government puts on a good face. They blame the violence on guerrillas and outside agitators. Despite overwhelming facts, the American public only sees a distorted view of reality. When the situation becomes so blatantly repressive, even the distortions fail to hide the truth. When that happens, the line they use is, "The situation is improving." Enough of that analogy, because it's a disservice to compare the two situations. However, I should say that the sheriffs were on record as saying they were not "opposed to cruising." What a relief! They were not opposed to cruising, but because they couldn't distinguish one Mexican from the next, everyone had to be treated equally (I guess they believe in equality). That's what led to the eventual closure of the Boulevard. They weren't interested in stopping the cruising. They were just interested in "preventing the gangs from converging on the Boulevard."

After the cameras left, it was business as usual. In fact, the sheriffs' war against the Boulevard intensified, culminating with the closure on August 31, 1979. Even then, their war did not end.

Channel 34

I don't remember how much time went by, but Antonio arranged for Channel 34 (Spanish language) to do an interview with me about the case at the Center for Law and Justice where he worked. In a way, I didn't want to do it, but for some reason, I thought the sheriffs didn't watch Channel 34, and maybe they don't. The guy interviewed me about the incident. It was nothing special, but as I realized later, that's how a lot of the Raza found out about the incident. I remember walking into a panadería on Brooklyn in East L.A., and someone, in Spanish, said, "Hey, aren't you the one who came out on TV today?" It wasn't like I could hide the fact either since I had a big scar on my forehead. Aside from that and *Lowrider Magazine,* nothing more came out in the media regarding my case until I won.

Because I worked for *Lowrider,* you would think that whatever appeared in it would be exactly what I wanted. Unfortunately, that wasn't the case. During the nine months that went by between the incident and the dismissal, my dealings with my own magazine were like dealings with the Twilight Zone. It was nothing intentional. It was just a lot of miscommunication. To me, *Lowrider* was my ace in the hole. Despite some of the things that went wrong, I think that limiting the story to the pages of *Lowrider* helped me win the case.

The case was reported for the first time in the May issue. Also included was my picture with the scar on my forehead. I was still paranoid in May about putting my face in the media, but the picture that went into the magazine showed me the way I looked three days after the incident. My face was so swollen that it didn't look anything like me. I figured, since that was the picture that would come out, the sheriffs probably wouldn't recognize me if I was standing right in front of them. That picture made a lot of impact graphically showing the extent of the injury. On another level, people believed I had started a new varrio. It was funny because a lot of people actually believed that. At first look, they thought I had actually tattooed a "T" on my forehead.

The next issue (June) asked for witnesses to step forward since a hundred people had probably witnessed the series of events. It was the July issue that really made the most impact. I was going to put an interview in that issue, which a friend had done, but for some reason, the publisher didn't like it. I ended up writing a letter, a plea to the readers explaining what I was doing that night, what actually happened, and asked for the support of the readers. That's probably how I learned how much influence the magazine had. After that article, everywhere I went, everyone had heard about the incident. It was kind of weird because I wrote it so that the Raza would back me up. At the time, I had been writing for maybe seven years, yet I had never written anything like that. It wasn't fiction, nor was it something I had analyzed. I just wrote it because before that I hadn't really written about what had happened that night. Many people told me that it was a good story. That's why I felt weird, because I would tell people it wasn't a story, that it had actually taken place, but they still liked the story.

At the time, the controversy over Whittier Boulevard was peaking so my case became associated with the attempts to close down Whittier Boulevard. Letter after letter not only supported my case but also were against the closure. That article, which appeared in the July issue, was also accompanied by two photographs. One was a picture someone had taken of me a week before the incident, and the other one was the same one that appeared in the May issue. I wasn't really scared at the time. Sometimes I was, and other times I wasn't. At times, I didn't even think about it. The article probably did me the most good of any article or any kind of publicity, yet it was that issue and that article that slapped me back to reality. That summer was when I got arrested in Venice, ended up in jail, and was handcuffed to a bench with the article about my case posted over my head. Each cop who went by was told not to forget who I was.

After that incident, I wasn't too anxious to have any kind of publicity at all, magazine or no magazine. Because of the incident, I didn't write about my case from July to December in any publication. Many people were telling me that I was doing everything wrong, that the reason I was getting hassled was because I wasn't making any noise. They may have been right, and maybe I should have made more noise, but at that time, I wasn't thinking rationally. My main thought was, if it happened once, it could happen again, but the second time I might not be visiting a hospital.

Remaining Silent

You would think that things like that don't happen anymore. If you believe police abuse doesn't exist, it's like believing there are no crooked politicians. There's a very fine line between abuse and proper use of force. I could probably cite a hundred cases of police brutality, but unless it happens to you, or unless you witness police abuse, you will probably go on thinking abuse doesn't exist, and if it does, that the bums deserved it. I've seen officers exercise their rights to self-defense, and I've seen proper use of force. That's not what abuse is. Police abuse is when an officer violates the law; police abuse is when an officer overreacts. Overreaction in itself is not malicious. There may be a fine line between proper use of force and overreaction, but blatant and malicious acts against citizens do not exist in a gray area. Outright police brutality does exist, and in some departments, it seems to be condoned in that a siege mentality prevails among many of the officers that are supposed to be there to serve and protect. Overreaction occurs due to street pressure and/or inadequate training. When officers overreact, people understand the officers might have acted out of fear or because they may have thought their lives were in danger. If someone gets hurt in the process, it's not excusable, but it can be understood. The victim should definitely have a recourse by filing a lawsuit. Those kinds of incidents are bound to happen in an urban setting, but police abuse is not overreaction. Police abuse exists, and it is intentional. Incidents of police brutality do take place and are triggered by many things. The percentage of "rotten apples" in police departments is probably the same as in the general population, probably less than 5 percent. There are some bigots who work in police departments, just as there are bigots at banks, gasoline stations, universities, etc. The difference between a bigoted teacher and a bigoted police officer is that we expect police officers to be the guardians of peace and justice. They are supposed to be perfect, and the problem is that nobody is perfect. Probably nobody disputes the fact that some officers do not belong in a uniform. The problem is that the nature of law enforcement is to protect their own. Officers have been known to kill, maim, cripple, and disfigure people, and they have been found actually to be guilty. But when have you heard of something happening to an officer? You've heard of officers getting complaints put in their files or getting slapped on the wrist for major crimes. A Mickey Mouse suspension is about the most severe form of punishment an officer receives. If someone came up to an officer and clubbed him on the head, that person would probably do a few years in prison (if he didn't get shot). Now, if an officer clubbed someone on the head, not only would nothing happen to the officer, but also the charges would be slapped on the victim. In other words, an officer can club people in the head, and it is not considered a crime. Part of the reason why that is allowed to happen is because a good guy-bad guy syndrome exists on the streets. That syndrome is perpetuated by the media. An officer is always justified in his actions, even if he's guilty of abuse, because he is the good guy.

The problem actually is a little more complex than laying the blame solely on law enforcement and the media. The problem is the role of police in relation to the community it is serving. Police should theoretically not only live in the community they serve but also should be there because the community wants them there. In some communities, police resemble occupation forces. Nobody knows who they are or where they come from. When you pay taxes and when you receive police protection, it is because you have entered an agreement. In East L.A., the people have made no agreement with anyone. If the people have a grievance against the sheriff's department, there is nothing that actually can be done. Police are not merely supposed to be responsive to the community, but they actually should be employed by the residents they serve. In other words, police are not supposed to be an autonomous body of individuals whose sole authority is derived from their own higher command structure. People can blame urbanization for this breakdown, but the situation in East L.A. is not a theory. The reason I had to elaborate on the role of the police and the sheriffs is because as of this writing, I have to worry whether there might be repercussions. Can you imagine how bad it is that I actually have to worry whether some sheriff might want some kind of revenge. On whose behalf would he be acting? If an innocent person has to worry about driving down Whittier Boulevard, then who are the police serving? Who are they protecting?

Between March and November 1979, I was worried about driving the streets of L.A. because I thought something would happen to me. How I used the media to win my case was actually determined by safety considerations and nothing else. After the July issue, I kept quiet until November 5 in San Jose, maybe because I felt safe over there. When my defense attorney appeared before the County Board of Supervisors on November 6 and then the *L.A. Times* on November 7, I didn't know that we were going to win that very day. Luckily, I did win that November 7th.

Right after I won, I made some phone calls to friends of mine in the media. When I appeared on the news, I felt pretty good because of the job the lawyer had done and because of the results. I felt the strategy, to avoid using the media, had paid off. When they reported the victory, I felt that that's what I wanted to hear. I didn't want them to report distortions. All along, the only thing I wanted was for the media to report a victory, nothing else.

December Issue of *Lowrider*

In the end, after I had won and the media had reported the case, there was one last thing to do. The November issue of *Lowrider* had already hit the streets so the story of the victory had to come out in the December issue. Even though the media had reported the victory, I figured that it was *Lowrider Magazine* and, more specifically, the readers who had stood by me to the end. It was the knowledge that Raza from Texas, Colorado, Nuevo México, Arizona, and all California had been backing me up that allowed me to feel strong. I felt I had a debt to the Raza and to the readers. To all the Raza who had sent letters of support, from soldiers in military bases in Germany to Japan, to my own partners in East L.A., from Raza who were locked up unjustly, to Raza I never knew, I felt I should explain. To this day, I thank all the Raza.

What came out in the December issue was the news of the dismissal and the announcement of the forthcoming lawsuit. I didn't want to write a long article, I just wanted to explain the series of events that led to the dismissal, and I wanted to let the Raza know that it had not been solely a personal victory. It was a victory for the Raza. Not only that, I was ready for round two, a lawsuit.

I was ready for round two, but I wasn't ready for round three. The harassment didn't end or decrease, rather it increased. When I finished writing the story, I sent it to San Jose, where the magazine was laid out and printed. When the magazine came out, not only did the story appear, but that same picture that appeared in May and July appeared once again. I couldn't believe my own eyes. I actually wanted to sue my own magazine. I couldn't believe they ran the same picture. I figured someone was either ignorant or someone wanted me killed. Probably, it was another case of paranoia in that those who were in charge of laying out the magazine must have been unaware of the harassment I had been going through, especially at that time when I was getting stopped at least once a day. Here I had written a short story, kind of low-keyed, but the picture wasn't too low-keyed. That was the same picture that had gotten me in trouble with the Venice police, and it was the last photograph I wanted to see in the December issue. I had wanted to walk quietly away, knowing that lawsuits take about seven years. I had thought that since my mug hadn't appeared since July, by now people, particularly the sheriffs, had forgotten how I looked. Maybe, I figured, they had seen my face, but at least it wasn't fresh in their minds. I was burned up, but what could I do? All it did was ensure that I would leave the state.

The *L.A. Times*

After I left, one other story did come out. Some writer did a story about the incident, about the nine-month wait, about the dismissal, and about the lawsuit. I could easily reread the story because it's on file, but just off the top, I think I remember that he also got the sheriffs' version. I didn't even know it had come out because at the time I had already moved to Arizona. When I returned to L.A. for the second time, someone told me that my story had come out in the *Times*. I think they told me as I was leaving for Phoenix because I didn't have time to check it out. I ended up going to Arizona State University in Tempe where I finally found the paper and the article. It was a pretty good story, except, for obvious reasons, I didn't like the sheriffs' version.

The *New Yorker*

A few months after I had been in Arizona, some writer for the *New Yorker* was doing a big thing about East L.A. He wanted to write about my case and the closure of Whittier Boulevard. I never really trusted the media so I said my lawyer had advised me not to say anything because it might affect my lawsuit. Nevertheless, I talked to him about cruising and Whittier Boulevard. The story ended up coming out in 1980, but I didn't even read the story until 1983. I should have read it in 1980. In fact, I shouldn't have even talked to the guy because the story turned out to be like all the rest. For some reason, whites in general and people from back East think we are a phenomenon. They think we're a big story. I remember even *National Geographic* tried to do a story on us. It was at a Fresno car show. I think that a reporter wanted to climb on top of our camper to get a better view of the Raza. When we didn't allow the reporter to climb up, he said, "But I'm from the *National Geographic*." And we said, "That's why you can't climb up here."

18 / East L.A. Revisited: The Heart of Aztlán

Although I grew up in East L.A. and have been around it all my life, I didn't realize how important it was until I left and then returned. After a couple of years of being away, I was anxious to see the Boulevard. When I came back I moved to Venice, because I really didn't want to be around the East Side. It was one thing to see the Boulevard in the daytime, but to see the Boulevard at night was entirely another.

The first day I came back to East L.A., I walked over to the corner of Whittier and Atlantic. I stared at the orange sign. I kept thinking, "This is a world famous corner." The orange sign hung in testimony that nothing had changed. Throughout the Southwest all the signs had come down, yet here, from where I was standing, where it all had begun, the orange sign prohibited cruising on weekend nights. In the summer of 1981, I couldn't believe that the Boulevard had been shut down for nearly two complete years. As I stood on the corner, I kept thinking to myself that people had taken the closure for granted. Nowhere else had the Raza given up. Sure, the Raza still cruised between Atlantic and Garfield, but it wasn't the same thing. The cruising may have been even better. The point was that nowhere else had the Raza allowed the barricades to stay up. Maybe I was just looking at symbols. To me, a barricade represents repression, a denial of rights.

The ACLU, the American Civil Liberties Union, a legal outfit that fights against the mass denial of rights, defends those denied rights whether they are women, youth, Nazis, or the elderly. They defend rights whether the group affected is radical or conservative. They don't care what the politics are of the groups affected. They would defend the rights of the KKK as easily and as readily as they would defend the rights of Blacks or Jews. The reasoning behind their philosophy is that everyone's rights must be protected, that once some rights are denied to one specific group, other rights to another group would follow. People argue that the idea is backwards because, "Why should the KKK be protected, or the Nazis?" The response is, "Who determines which groups are OK?" A board? The president of the United States? The Supreme Court? Should it be left to someone like Richard Nixon or Ronald Reagan to determine who are the good guys? Reagan supports confirmed blood thirsty butchers in El Salvador, who he claims are "democratic." Furthermore, the United States supports the most racist country in the world, South Africa, because that government is anticommunist, meaning that maybe groups like the KKK are OK as long as they are anticommunist. This means that groups like the NAACP (National Association for the Advancement of Colored People) could become the bad guys. The ACLU is correct in defending the rights of everyone because nobody is blessed with the wisdom to distinguish good from bad. I'll take my chances with the ACLU philosophy because if someone says, "Don't defend the rights of Mexicans, they're illegal subversives who are potential terrorists," it would follow that groups like the United Farm Workers or the American Indian Movement could be considered terrorist subversives. To me, it is obvious that the KKK are the bad guys, but to those in power, maybe they consider us the bad guys. In fact, I know they do. That's why they're always trying to deport us. The reason I bring up the ACLU philosophy is because it is very important. "Once some rights are taken away, others will follow." Someone may wonder, "What does that have to do with East L.A. and the Boulevard?" The thing is, when rights are taken away, if people don't fight against those who are taking away the rights, then people forget about it and say, "It's not that important." After people surrender their rights, then they dismiss it or take it for granted. A long time ago, the residents of East L.A. surrendered the right to vote and the right to representation. Years have gone by and nobody complains anymore. When the county shut down Whittier Boulevard, when the barricades went up, it was another case of denial of rights. Since the ordinance affected mainly the youth, it was seen as something minor, a nuisance at most. Actually, I don't even think it was perceived by many as a denial of rights because "it only involved cruising." That's why I mentioned the philosophy of the ACLU, because once one right is taken away, then others follow. People take the right not to vote in East L.A. for granted. People also take for granted that barrio schools are severely over crowded and that students get inferior education. People take for granted that universities are practically off limits to the Raza, except for tours. It's no surprise that "stopping the cruising" was not seen as a denial of rights. The closure of Whittier was an admission on the part of the county that it could not service the Raza.

The orange sign that hung above the intersection of Whittier and Atlantic reminded me of that realization, that we had surrendered our rights. When I stared at the sign, I wondered if it would ever come down. At that time, I don't think I had been down the Boulevard in a couple of years. I walked back to the office a couple of blocks away, got in my car and headed toward Atlantic on Whittier. Passing Atlantic, it was like stepping into a time zone, like another world. Passing the New Silver Dollar, it reminded me of when I was in the tenth grade. I kept going until I got to the corner of Whittier and McDonnell when I hung a left and parked on the corner. It was like I was doing what I had done the day I was released from the hospital. I walked in the middle of the intersection to where the puddle of blood had been. I looked at the spot. I looked at the street signs. To me, that corner was like a nightmare, a memory, a reminder. It was over two years after the incident and it all seemed unreal.

For reasons beyond my control, I didn't remain with the magazine too much longer after I returned. I had a lot I wanted to say, things I wanted to write about based on the previous three years. The first year with the magazine I had learned a lot, but during the next two, I had seen enough to last me a lifetime. When I left the magazine, I still had too much ink in my blood. I still had too much on my mind. I didn't really like any of the other Raza magazines because they weren't righteously Chicano. They were trying to escape their real roots and become "hispanics." If I hated anything, it was the "hispanicization" of the Raza.

In 1979, only a few government employees and heads of programs were trying to call us "hispanics." When I returned to L.A., it was as though we had lost the war against the government's efforts to impose an inaccurate and a derogatory label on us. With what I had seen in three years, in all the barrios of the Southwest, the Raza didn't go for that label except those who wanted government or corporate money or those who actually thought they were from Spain. The reason this was a big concern is because people were also using the word "hispanic" because it sounded more respectable. In other words, they didn't want to offend white ears. The words Chicano, Mexicano, or Raza are offensive to some people. That's really what's behind all this. People are once again ashamed to speak up. They are getting silenced by government money.

That was a big concern of mine when I returned to L.A. I was feeling that all the government bureaucrats and all the "hispanic" politicos were selling us out, that they were not really expressing the true sentiments of our Raza. It was like everything had returned to the days before the Raza started rebelling. The big push was to Americanize the Raza. Our own Raza were putting down our own Raza because many had come over from Mexico and refused to become citizens and refused to be "Anglocized."

When I came back, I realized that there are leaders who claim to represent us and who put forth views which they claim are ours. On the contrary, there are voices from the streets, voices that are rarely heard.

One thing that I am convinced of is that there is a whole generation of Raza who have yet to express themselves. When I was a kid, the Raza were rioting in the streets and walking out of school. When I got to college, we were marching and taking over buildings to protest the lack of Raza in the universities. In recent years, the Raza have rallied around a lot of things, from protesting the denial of rights to the ending of varrio warfare.

From the elementary schools to the colleges and beyond, the Raza have stopped rioting, but they have not stopped thinking and reflecting. Maybe not now, but in the near future, all those voices will come together. I hope it will begin here, from East L.A. in the Heart of Aztlán. Then, all the government stooges and politicos will say, "So that's how they really think?" And they'll probably be surprised that we even know how to write.

19 / Moving On:
Rejecting the Poison

Quitting my job at *Lowrider Magazine* was probably the hardest thing I ever had to do although the circumstances left me with no other choice. Before the incident, my role was just that of someone who could contribute something to the magazine. I had a writing background and I knew L.A. pretty well. I didn't know how to take pictures when I started out, but by the time of the incident, I had been taking pictures for a while. After the incident, my role changed 180 degrees. I was not merely a *Lowrider* photographer (which was enough), but now I became something more. I became, not by my choosing, part of the core of the magazine.

A lot happened from the time of the incident till the time I quit. The main thing was that I won my case, I filed a lawsuit, and I left the state because I actually feared for my life. Not until I left California did I realize the impact the magazine was having throughout the Southwest. I thought I was hiding out. I thought if I remained low-key, everything would be cool. I had been getting arrested like it was going out of style. I figured every cop, thanks to unwanted publicity, knew who I was. I figured that if I went to Arizona, nobody would know where I was, especially the cops. When I left, my picture appeared in the magazine for the third time. By this time, everyone knew me as "the guy with the scar on the forehead." Prior to leaving California, I had been to almost every barrio in Southern California. After leaving the state, I went to almost every barrio in the Southwest. It was a three- to four-year journey that I can't write about in a single book. I learned a lot, probably ten times more than I learned as a student at UCLA. After a four-year association with *Lowrider Magazine,* I didn't receive a degree, a diploma, or even a certificate to show for it, but I did receive an education that I will never forget. Whatever people think of the magazine, it did something that nothing or nobody else has ever done. It truly was the voice of the streets, of the varrios. When I finally quit, it was hard to do so because I felt I was a benefactor of the magazine. Thanks to the magazine, Raza from throughout the Southwest, from throughout Aztlán, were backing me up. I know that without a shadow of a doubt, because I saw it everywhere I went. I can never explain the feeling from knowing the Raza were backing me up. Sometimes I was treated like a hero, with respect and sometimes with admiration. I didn't understand it because I didn't feel I had done anything. I could be somewhere in nowheresville, and people would tell me they were supporting me. I would freak out because I would wonder how they knew about an incident on McDonnell and Whittier in East L.A., but I didn't have to ask because I knew how they had heard. In town after town, city after city, state after state, in every barrio I went to, people had heard about the case. Except in L.A., the majority of the Raza heard about the incident through the magazine. Sometimes, when I would go somewhere, and they would recognize me, they would tell me they were proud of me or something like that. I would tell whoever I was talking to that "I didn't do anything." It's not like I had done a heroic deed. I felt I hadn't saved any children from a burning fire to deserve that kind of support. I guess at the time I didn't realize the impact the case had made. The way I viewed it, "I got hit on the head, and the guys that did it should be behind bars." I wasn't out for revenge or anything. I just wanted them to drop the charges and the District Attorney to file charges against the guilty sheriffs. I didn't want to represent anything. I just didn't want to be bothered by cops, and I didn't want to go to prison. I had a lot on my mind.

After I won my case, I knew I wasn't going to prison on the charges of assault with a deadly weapon and assault and battery on a peace officer. Because I was getting hassled a lot by cops, I wanted to quit the magazine and move to Mexico. I figured I didn't need to constantly be looking in the rear view mirror. Since I had conflicts with the owner of the magazine, I figured, "I'm better off starting somewhere new again." I wanted to quit, but circumstances didn't let me. Before I knew it, I was out of the state, and that is when I began to really value the magazine.

The first stop out of state was Arizona. There I regained my confidence if not my sanity. I didn't have to worry about cops. There was a little harassment everywhere, maybe some deserved and maybe a lot undeserved. Arizona was no exception, although I felt I had nothing to do with it. I was just trying to keep my mind off of East L.A. I don't know if it was the first time I returned to L.A. or the second time, but in either case, I was told to come to L.A. to deliver magazines. At that time, the magazine was growing in leaps and bounds. I didn't want to leave Arizona, but because it was the magazine that was paying my bills, I had no choice. I flew into L.A. in the morning, by nightfall I was behind bars somewhere in the San Gabriel Valley. I thought I would have to spend the whole night there, but luckily, I got out. Of course, when I was arrested, I thought I wasn't even going to make it to the jail, because about three different units had stopped me. On top of that, not only was I in sheriffs' territory, but I also had boxes full of magazines with my picture in it, saying that I had just won my case. What a way to get greeted on my return to Los Angeles. That incident didn't do much to my so-called recuperation. More than ever, I knew I couldn't hang around L.A. I think I flew back to Phoenix the next day. A dependence grew with the magazine. Out of state, I became very comfortable, that is, compared with L.A., I became very relaxed. I began to like it a lot. Because of that incident, when I returned to L.A., I figured I had two choices: either quit the magazine and move to Mexico, or stay with the magazine but live out of state. Even though I wanted to quit, I figured that I couldn't, because my lawsuit was connected with the magazine, and it was connected with the closure of Whittier Boulevard.

As you can guess, I chose to stay on. A big reason probably was because I had already seen the reaction of the Raza in Arizona. You couldn't compare the situation in Arizona with that in L.A. It was nowhere near the same. The Raza in Phoenix, it appeared to me, saw lowriding as righteous carnalismo. They saw it as a movement of Raza getting together, of having a good time, and when need be, backing each other up. When I saw that, it was something new to me. I think that had a lot to do with my decision to stay with the magazine. I figured I could stay with the magazine, out of state, until my lawsuit rolled around. On the other hand, I thought it might not be possible because I figured the lawsuit would probably take about seven years. I guess I was right. I wish I could have stayed with the magazine, to this day, but I finally had to quit. It was hard. Sometimes, even now, I regret quitting because few people will probably ever get the chance to not only meet Raza from all over Aztlán but also to get their solid support. That support was made possible because of the magazine, but like they say, all good things must come to an end. I thought I would never quit, at least maybe not until the lawsuit was over, but in the end I had to.

As much as I hated to quit, I was left with no choice. I had conflicts with the owner from the first day I joined the magazine, but the last straw was the July 1981 editorial in *Lowrider Magazine.* The reason I said I was writing this book was because I felt I had to speak up. At first I wasn't going to write about this, but I figured, I quit for a reason, and that reason was the poison that came out of the editorial. Everyone told me about the publisher, about his ideas, etc. I didn't really pay attention because I felt that reaching the streets was not only important but also nobody else was doing it. I had conflict from the beginning, but it didn't compare with what happened at the end. It is one thing to project negative images; it's another thing to promote and incite racial violence.

You can read about it in that issue if you care. Maybe I took it personally; maybe I even misread it. The editorial, if it had appeared in any other Chicano newspaper, magazine, or journal, probably would not have had any effect, but since I had seen the impact it had on youth throughout the Southwest, I figured I couldn't associate with a magazine that was preaching ideas that could result in death. People can argue till their hair turns gray that *Lowrider* was a bad influence in the first place, but to actually incite racial violence was another matter.

Maybe nothing came of the editorial on the streets. Maybe it had no effect. The thing is, I could not wait till I heard somewhere, "you know what, a racial war broke out because of the editorial in the magazine." I

124

couldn't wait till that happened. I wouldn't be able to live with that kind of blood on my hands. Between the time the editorial came out and the time I quit, I was praying to God that we didn't get news that something had broken out because of the editorial. Even one indirect death would have been one too many. I couldn't see how someone could stoop so low. Death in the barrios of Aztlán is ugly. It is vicious. It leaves a lot of tears. It leaves feelings that no pen could ever communicate. With all the death and destruction that exists within our Raza, I couldn't see shifting to a racial conflict as a solution. If anything, the reason I had to leave was because what the owner wrote was true: there was conflict between Blacks and Chicanos. But for that reason, because the magazine was reaching the youth from both races, because of its powerful influence, it should have been concerned with resolving the conflict rather than writing about it in such a way that it could have been seen as encouragement for a racial war. Because of that, I quit. To this day, I regret quitting, not because I think I made the wrong decision but rather because the magazine did more positive than many people can imagine. A lot of criticisms of the magazine are valid, but you have to see the magazine and what it did for an entire generation throughout the Southwest. The influence the magazine once had is no longer there, but the magazine is still around. In my eyes, the magazine is not the same. In many people's eyes, in the eyes of many whom I respect, the magazine was never any good. That is their opinion, and maybe their opinion is valid. In my opinion, I saw positive effects of the magazine. I also saw negative effects. For me, in the end, the negative outweighed the positive.

For those who heard about the case through the magazine, all I can say is that I hated to quit. If I could have stayed on, I would have. When this gets published, I want the Raza to know that whatever I get from my lawsuit, it will be put to good use, for the good of our Raza, for the good of our barrios, and for the good of all people. As we grow older, the future will be with our carnalillos, our younger brothers and sisters. That is where the money will go, to invest in our young Raza. It may be too late for some of us, but the least we can do is fight and struggle and pave the way for our young Raza to grow up to be warriors so that they will take nothing from no one, so that they will grow up to struggle against anyone or anything that puts our Raza down. I have not forgotten nor will I ever forget where my support came from, from towns that nobody in L.A. ever heard of, to the barrio I grew up in, from Chimayó, Superior, and Grand Prairie, to East L.A.

Gracias!

20 / Publicity for the Lawsuit: I Don't Want to Get Killed

In the L.A. area, it seems that every six months or so, someone dies of a choke hold, or commits suicide in prison, or is accidentally shot. Many cases cause outrage and waves of protests until the next case comes along. Over the past four or five years, I have been aware of a number of these cases. Probably the biggest involved the "Shooting of Eula Love," "The Ron Settles Case," and more recently, the case of Gordon Castillo Hall. Before Gordon's case, I had been aware of other cases that were practically horror stories, from the twelve-year -old in Texas who was shot by an officer while handcuffed, to the kidnapping and killing of a Chicano youth from San Gabriel by an officer of the law. I had heard about those cases before, so I was aware of "accidents." The thing that made Gordon's case different from the others is that, luckily, he wasn't killed.

I heard about Gordon's case around September 1979 from his cousin at Cal State Northridge. I wrote a story about it for *Lowrider,* but, for whatever reasons, the story never was published. He had been convicted of murder for a crime that even the police admitted he did not commit. He was serving time when he should have been free. When I heard about this case I was still awaiting my trial, so in a way, I was trying to avoid being in the position that he was in—that is, being in prison for an unjust reason. About a year later, on one of the times I came back to L.A., I heard that there was a fund raiser for Gordon somewhere in El Sereno or Alhambra. The reason I went is because I heard that César Chávez was going to be there. He did show up, but it didn't seem the right place to ask Chávez for help, because everyone was there to support Gordon. I felt sorry for the guy, especially for his familia. I met his familia there, his lawyer Richard Cruz, and many people who I knew from before. In a way, it kind of hit me there, the significance of his case. I felt bad. I realized that his youth was being spent behind bars over a technicality. In my mind, I thought, "I could be in his shoes," but luckily I wasn't. I think the next time I heard about Gordon was a few days after I came back from Texas or San Jose. I heard on the news that his lawyer was going to hold a press conference in his office in East L.A.

At the time, I was still working for *Lowrider,* so the next day, I told one of the people I worked with, "Now that he's released, maybe now he'll put him in." I took my camera, and we drove to the lawyer's office. Every radio and TV station must have been there including all the major newspapers. When we got there, there was barely enough room to get in.

Gordon had been released on July 2, 1981, pending a final disposition of the petition for habeas corpus. It was the first time in California history that someone who had been convicted of murder had been released on his own recognizance. The court had finally realized they had the wrong person, something that even the police knew. When everyone crowded around the lawyer's office, they stood in fascination to hear the incredible story of an innocent person being in prison from age sixteen to nineteen and a half. Seated next to him on his left was his lawyer Richard Cruz, and to his right was his mother and his sister Charlene. The expressions could not be duplicated. I snapped a few pictures. It was like history in the making. An innocent person had actually been released. Amid all the flashes, the two of us went up to talk to him and his family. I told him, "Congratulations!" We talked for a while. Then I told him, "I almost ended up going to prison too." He interrupted and said, "Hey, I know who you are. I read about you in *Lowrider*." I felt bad when he said that. I responded, "Hey, sorry for not covering your case in the magazine."

It was cool, he didn't care, as long as he was free. I didn't say anything at the time, but when he said he had read in *Lowrider* about what had happened to me on Whittier, I kind of cracked up because everyone used to say that *Lowrider* was the prison bible. On that day, he was technically not free, so he was not out of the woods yet, especially financially. The familia had incurred a large legal debt. For probably another nine months or so, there were still a lot of fund raisers and victory celebrations. In my last issue of *Lowrider*, September 1981, I wrote a couple of stories, including the story of Gordon's release. After that, I didn't write about it anymore, but it was always on my mind.

At the time, I used to go down a friend's house almost every day. We used to talk about a lot. The main thing my friend would tell me is that I should start publicizing my lawsuit. I would always tell her she was crazy. I used to tell her a bunch of things about what had happened to me because of publicity. The subject would always come up. She would tell me, "Look at Gordon's case. He won because of publicity." I would always respond, "But that's different." I kept telling her every time, "If I publicize my lawsuit, I think I'll get killed. If anything, I'll get hassled like I used to." I would tell her that I didn't want to go through that again. We got to be good friends. We were always making plans to reopen the Boulevard. We would talk about getting lawyers, of how the Coalition to End Barrio Warfare would be the key. We would talk about having a gigantic concert at East L.A. College to reopen the Boulevard. Then she would ask me how my lawsuit was going. Right about then, I wouldn't want to talk anymore. She kept telling me that I should publicize the lawsuit, and she would remind me of how Gordon had won because of all the publicity. But I always responded with the same thing, "I don't want to get killed."

She, like most people I knew, felt that publicity is what protects a person. I would tell her, "Look, if they want to kill you, publicity doesn't protect anyone. All it does is ensure that more people know about it." I would tell her, "Look at Salazar. He was a well-known, well-respected journalist. They killed him didn't they? What about Malcolm X or Martin Luther King? Everyone knew them. Publicity didn't protect them." Every time I would tell her, " I don't want to become famous. I don't want to become a martyr. All I want is to win the lawsuit and split the state . . . to where people like me." In reality, I didn't even care about the lawsuit. I really didn't like the idea of waiting a whole generation for the case to come to trial. I just wanted to get it over with.

Since we were friends, we would always talk about that. In November 1982, I remember getting a phone call to tell me that Gordon had been shot in El Sereno. The phone call was almost like the one I got when someone had given me the news that my best friend had died. Gordon had been shot twice on the corner of Eastern and Lombardy. I realized later that I worked at El Sereno Junior High that day. It must have happened, at most, about a half hour after I had left the junior high. The shooting had the same effect on me as it must have had on all who had followed his case. I was in a type of trauma, a shock. The next day, I drove by the scene of the shooting and parked. The large pool of blood was still there. It was weird for me. Like flashbacks. I remembered doing that on the corner of Whittier and McDonnell, staring at the pool of blood that hadn't been completely washed away. I think I was in semishock that whole day. After work, I decided to go to the hospital where I had heard he was taken. I went to some hospital in Alhambra. As I walked in, I asked if I could go up to the intensive care. They said that only the immediate family was allowed to be there. I was going to say I was family, but out of respect, I just asked the nurse to tell the family that I had come to show my concern. He was still in critical condition so I knew that his family was going through pain on top of pain.

That weekend after work, I went to a going-away party for someone who was leaving for Mexico. At the friend's house, I think I practically went berserk, because if I had needed reassuring, after a few bottles of wine I realized what had happened to Gordon. Publicity had not protected him. It was a cold realization. Maybe it had been a coincidence, maybe it had been a hit. Whatever the circumstances, whoever had done it, to me, it wasn't important. The thing was, he was shot, and all the publicity in the world had not protected him. I don't even know how I got home that night because I had drunk about two gallons of wine.

The next morning, my friend wasn't home. I think she had gone out of town that weekend. I waited till she came home. I left the message for her; so when she called me, she was in disbelief. I went to her house to talk. It was one of those weird situations in which we knew what was on each other's mind. Gordon, up until that point, was still in critical condition. His shooting had affected me so much that my friend thought I was going to immediately leave the state. Not that I felt an immediate threat to my life, but rather it was just an example of how it could happen, accidental or otherwise. I don't think we ever talked about the need for publicity again.

Fortunately, Gordon pulled through. From what I understand, as of this writing, he's somewhere undergoing rehabilitation. They say he's paralyzed on one side. I don't really know, because I haven't run into his family. All I know is that his family must be suffering like no other family. I remember the expression his mother and sister had the day I first met them. Words can't describe grief.

21 / Incident at Belvedere: I Didn't Go to College to Keep Quiet

I always knew I would write about the incident of March 1979, but originally, I thought I would wait until after I won my lawsuit. The reason I am writing this now is because of an incident that happened to me in March 1983. It happened at Belvedere Junior High where Ruby, a young Chicana, asked me in front of many people if I had ever experienced racism or discrimination when I was a student at UCLA. In a way, I froze because I had explicit directions from my job, teaching in a college preparatory program, to be careful when talking to students about stuff like that or not to initiate that type of conversation. In my mind, there was a fine line between talking about it and initiating the conversation. I thought to myself, I better play it safe. I told her, "Actually, I experienced it more in high school where the counselors and the teachers would always tell me that I couldn't go to college." Being that I was conducting a meeting, I told her, "You know what, let me talk to you about it another time." After the meeting, after she left, I felt terrible. I felt like, "que había bajado la bandera."

Because of instructions from my job, I had backed down. It was a feeling I had never experienced before. I felt real bad. How could I undo what I had done or, rather, what I had failed to do? I thought to myself, "What's more important, my job or my conscience. Financially, no job had ever been as important, but it could not even closely compare to my conscience. When I got home, I wrote her a six-page explanation. I explained why I froze, and I explained that the letter could cost me my job. But to me, it was more important that I let her know how it really was at UCLA. I wish I could print the letter but I didn't make a copy. What I explained to her is that racism is too nice a word for what goes on at universities. I told her that when I went to UCLA, there were very few Chicanos at the campus but that today there were even fewer. I told her that a lot of us had demonstrated, taken over buildings, had protested so that our younger brothers and sisters could go to the universities. I told her that when I went, it wasn't said, but it was understood among us that no matter where we moved to, no matter what profession we got into, we would let people know what we learned through fighting against the university. It was almost an unwritten code. It was a duty that every Chicano had.

Every Chicano who ever went to a university had the responsibility to tell our younger Raza what we had learned and what we had encountered. That's why I told her that racism was too nice of a word. I told her that what happened to me on the streets was nothing compared to what happened to me in the university. On the streets, I got my head cracked, I got my life threatened, and later I got arrested more times than I can remember. At the university, I learned why there are very few Raza there. I told her everything that I could in six pages, and still there was more to tell her.

Even though at that time I only worked at Belvedere on Tuesdays, I went to Belvedere early Wednesday morning, but I pulled a typical me. I had forgotten the letter at home. I waited until the following Tuesday to give it to her. I called her in the office sometime that day and told her that I wanted her to read this letter I had written. After she read it, I told her that I felt bad that I couldn't tell her that the other day. We had a real good talk. The main thing I told her is that if you never speak out, you will never experience racism. Even then, what she wanted to know about UCLA wasn't racism. It was ten times worse. We talked for a while, and after that I felt relieved and felt that there was nothing more important than speaking out. I told her that maybe what we had talked about could cost me my job, but I told her, "I didn't go to college to keep quiet. I didn't demonstrate so that later I could keep silent about it." I told her that UCLA should be 50 percent Chicano, but it would never happen if people kept quiet because the university is not really interested in increasing the enrollment of Raza. They are just content with justifying why there is only a handful of Chicanos, in an area where Raza make up more than 50 percent of the students in the Los Angeles Unified School District.

It was that talk that snapped my mind. It's as they say, "Se me prendió el foco." I had spoken out to her, and I was determined never to keep quiet about the status of Chicanos and education. But that's when I realized that I was quiet about something else. For over three years, I had been completely silent about something that had happened to me. I had thought that I would write about it after the lawsuit. Talking to the young Chicana made me realize that, no matter how I looked at it, I had been silenced. I didn't want to jeopardize my lawsuit, but the result was that I wasn't talking about Whittier Boulevard, and I wasn't talking about what had happened to me. I had sworn that I would write about it because what had happened to me was only the tip of the iceberg.

I was probably one of hundreds, if not thousands, who had become a victim of police brutality in East L.A. I thought that my trial would have brought all that out, but my charges had been dropped nine months after the incident, so none of the evidence ever surfaced. Now, to win my lawsuit, I had to keep quiet so as not to endanger the prospects of winning the case. It's five years later, and unfortunately the Boulevard is still closed, which is a reminder that we're not talking about history. It would be history if the Boulevard had already been reopened. It would be history if violence no longer occurred, and it would be history if the Raza had the right to be represented in East L.A. Five years is a long time to wait and a long time to keep quiet. It's a lot of time to think, and I've had a lot of thinking to do. But now, the thinking time is over. It took a junior high school Chicana to make me realize that remaining silent was doing nobody any good. I was waiting for my lawsuit, yet in the meantime I was no longer fighting. I was pretending to be low-keyed. What happened to me was serious because it happens and it has happened to many of our Raza. The only difference with me is that I have the ability to write. However, by not speaking out about what happened, I was letting that talent rot by not putting it to better use. Thanks to that young Chicana, I decided to write this. The only hope I have is that our Raza benefit from this. Even if only one Chicano or Chicana benefits from what I write, it will have been worth it. I will feel that the five years was worth it, that I didn't waste them. If only one Chicano or Chicana who has been unjustly imprisoned, if one who has been beaten steps forward and files a lawsuit, it will have been worth it.

To that young Chicana, gracias.

22 / Conclusion: A Message to the Young Raza

As I close this, I have to seriously stop to think why I wrote it. While I was writing, a friend asked me, "Are you willing to go through that all over again?" I had explained to this friend about all the harassment after the incident, about how I thought I was going to be killed and how I finally had to leave the state. I responded, "I don't want it to happen again, but I feel I have to do it." And I do feel I had to write about it. I feel I owe an explanation to the Raza who supported me and helped me win. I feel I owe it to the Raza so it doesn't happen again, so that others can speak out, so that they can file complaints and file lawsuits, and so that innocent Raza never plead guilty to anything, no matter how small the charge.

Some people may be wondering if I want to start an antipolice movement. If I did, I would spice it up a bit, but that's not the intention. The intention is to make the Raza aware that we have rights, that we don't have to allow ourselves to be stepped upon, and that we don't have to accept injustice. How does that transform into every day life? Can it help the Chicano who got hit on the head five years ago, four years ago, last year, last weekend? How can this actually help? I wouldn't want someone to view this just as an autobiography. If it was an autobiography, it would be about something else. I did write a lot about myself, because the incident happened to me. Even now, as I am writing this, I have to ask, "Who gives a you know what? Can anyone benefit from this?" I had to stop and think, and what I decided is that I wouldn't want people to say, "It's a great book!" When I wrote about my case in July 1979, some people told me it was a good story. I know it would be a compliment in that maybe it was well written, but the thing is, it shouldn't matter how I write this. The message in the book is about injustice. The word "injustice" sounds hollow in that I'm not sure it's the right word to use.

I think that, if anything, what I would like people to do is ask, "Why is Whittier Boulevard closed?" And to me, even more important, "Why are there very few Raza in the universities?" To this day, I get madder when I go to UCLA and count only a handful of brown faces. It makes me madder than what happened to me on the Boulevard. Maybe a psychologist would trip on that, but I would ask, after writing about what happened to me, "Why is the university a bigger concern than the Boulevard?" It isn't a bigger concern. I am concerned equally. I get madder about certain things. I hate when the migra go on raids. I hate when our young Raza are made to feel ashamed of their own Raza. I hate it when Chicanos are ashamed to call themselves what they are, when they think they should call themselves hispanic because they've been told it is more acceptable. I could go on and on. The thing is, I think that if I can get one Chicano or one Chicana to ask those questions; if someone, after reading this, asks, "Why do we accept injustice? Why do we have to accept things as they are?"; if someone says that and does something about it, I would be satisfied. I wish I could do more. I know I have gone through hell and back, but I am young. Those older than I am have gone through worse. There are still Raza around from the Mexican Revolution. There are still a lot of Raza around from the Zoot Suit days. There are things that they could teach us if they spoke up. I speak out now in hopes that maybe somehow someone else will speak up. If not those older than I am, then those who are still in the elementary schools, those in the junior highs and high schools. For whatever reasons, the voices in the barrios have not yet been heard. Right now is just the beginning. If I can contribute to that, I will feel that I have accomplished something, if not to help the Chicano who was beaten five years ago, then to prevent that it happens five years from now.

Maybe I'm getting carried away, but that's how I am. I grew up in East Los Angeles at a time when the Raza were full of hope and full of dreamers. That's one thing for sure . . . I'll never stop dreaming . . . but more important, I will never stop fighting.

On the
Wrong Side
of the Law

Introduction

If I testify and expose the police brutality that's rampant in the United States, I may get killed.

If I remain silent, I may get killed.

If I speak out or write about the pervasiveness of police brutality, I may get killed.

In 1984, more than four years after almost being killed by police, thinking that my trial against four Los Angeles County sheriff's deputies was just around the corner, I decided to speak out. I figured that regardless of whether I spoke or not, I would probably be killed anyway. And if I was going to be killed, then people should at least know why, I reasoned.

I was paranoid in those days, about everything and everyone. Consequently, in deciding to write *Assault with a Deadly Weapon*, I believed that everything I wrote would be used against me in court. Believing that, I wrote about everything except what happened to me in 1979. I wrote about police brutality, about Whittier Boulevard and cruising, and about East Los Angeles.

This section begins by describing, in the first person and present tense, what happened that weekend. Thereafter, it picks up where *Assault with a Deadly Weapon* leaves off, examining in retrospect the never-ending wait for the trial. Finally, it recounts the trial and the aftermath.

1 / Police Brutality: In the Glare of the Boulevard

East Los Angeles, March 23, 1979—I arrive in my car at the brightly lit intersection of Whittier and Atlantic to cover the opening night of the movie *Boulevard Nights*. I marvel at the sight of thousands upon thousands of glistening cars, converging on Whittier Boulevard.

It is 10:00 P.M., and it is bumper to bumper in all directions, as far as the eye can see. There's a festive atmosphere on this Friday night, but something is not right. The omnipresent flashing red and blue lights create an uneasy tension.

I don't feel right. I have a premonition that something is going to go wrong. Maybe they're finally going to shut down the Boulevard like they've been saying for years.

Riding shotgun with me is my friend Kiki. He hasn't been going out much lately. He was riding in a car a few months back when another of our friends, Lil' Mike, was killed. His brain was blown off. A gang killing. Wrong place. Kiki hasn't been the same since. I picked him up from his house in nearby Montebello so that he can hang out on the Boulevard, so he can forget about the killing.

I want to go to the corner of Whittier and McDonnell, about 12 blocks from this corner heading westbound toward Eastern, to where I normally take pictures, I tell Kiki. I can't drive down the Boulevard tonight because at this rate, we'll get there after midnight. Instead, I'll take the side street Hubbard. We park on the corner of Whittier and McDonnell and get out. I lock the doors and grab my 35-millimeter Olympus camera.

A mile down the street in Montebello, *Boulevard Nights* is premiering at the Garmar theater. The movie is purportedly about cruising and Whittier Boulevard. There are picket signs out front. People are protesting the images presented in the movie; they say the movie is fiction, a distortion, a glorification of gangs. The picket signs are news.

On the Boulevard, the red and blue lights are visible as far as the eye can see. They are flashing incessantly. For the media, this is not news.

On the Boulevard, a person is guilty unless proven innocent. Here, the Constitution is read upside down. Worse! Every night the Constitution is discarded. Tonight, the jails will be full.

Tonight, I want to capture on film, not the picket signs at the theater, nor the gang violence that occasionally flares, but rather the cruising and the real Boulevard. I want America to see that not everyone out cruising carries a machete or a shotgun in a coat pocket.

The atmosphere here resembles a carnival, yet the tension continues to mount. The police, with guns and riot sticks drawn, are interrogating and arresting everyone they can.

On this corner, there are about 30 people, including another guy with a camera, in front of the Pueblo liquor store. And a lot of traffic is going in and out of the liquor store. Kiki knows most of them. He stays there talking with them. The guy with the camera is taking photographs of the police.

"Be careful," I tell him.

He shrugs.

East L.A. sheriffs and the Highway Patrol are out in numbers. But there are other police—a special unit of riot control officers. On the streets, I think they call them the hard hats. It is a massive show of force.

I hadn't come to take photographs of police in action. They seem intent on causing reckless abandon and spoiling the fun for 95 percent of the youngsters who have simply come here to cruise.

I'm walking down the Boulevard toward Atlantic, with camera in hand. On the left side, the north side, of the street, a couple of sheriffs are yelling at a carload of guys and girls they have pulled over.

"Get your greasy asses out of the car!"

I want to take photographs but don't because they'll get me too for interfering with a police officer. I don't know why they've been pulled over. I don't know if they've done anything wrong. What I do know is that less than ten feet in front of me, the sheriff on the passenger side has yanked a young girl by the hair through the window.

"Get the fuck away from here!" the sheriff yells, waving his riot stick at the onlookers as he continues to yank the girl by the hair. Here, nobody wants to get arrested on someone else's behalf, so everyone moves on to the next scenario. Other people step away from the scene and view it from a distance.

There are thousands of cars cruising by, bumper to bumper in both directions. There are hundreds and hundreds of people hanging out in front of stores, bus benches, on corners, parking lots, and hamburger stands. On every block, someone is being arrested. On every block, someone is being interrogated, searched, and needlessly harassed. Police are making thorough searches of cars, looking for weapons: in the front, in the back seats, in trunks, and even under the hood. Beer is being confiscated and emptied onto the street.

The sight of all the red and blue lights gives the appearance of a dragnet on the Boulevard. Despite the police action, nothing curtails the cruising because there are not enough police to arrest everyone. The majority of the people out cruising seem undaunted. They're probably used to it. Police harassment is normal on the Boulevard. People lying face down with guns drawn on them is a normal sight. People getting handcuffed on their knees is normal. Being insulted is normal. People getting checked for needle marks or tattoos is normal. Being interrogated while being made to face a wall is normal. But the youngsters on the Boulevard, they don't take it. I've seen youngsters getting clubbed rather than take an insult from a cop. Most of the sheriffs are white. Most of the youth out cruising are Mexican. However, now one frequently sees Mexican American sheriffs, but they're no different—at least that's what the youngsters say.

"You little fuckin' beaner . . . I ought to beat the shit out of you right here and right now."

That was last week's confrontation that I witnessed on this very same spot, on the corner of Arizona. A Mexican American sheriff was berating a youngster for no apparent reason.

"Take off the badge and we'll see who the beaner is," the youngster replied.

The cop nearly blew his top, but the youngster did not back off. Eye to eye, the youngster repeated the challenge. "Can't fight without your gun?"

"You're lucky I don't blow your fuckin' head off, asshole!"

The youngster did not back down or even flinch amid the threats. This was in front of about four white sheriffs. I was there right next to that youngster. I thought he was going to get shot on the spot. I thought we were both going to be shot. He wasn't even cited or arrested.

I don't know what that sheriff actually felt. Perhaps he used to cruise the Boulevard when he was younger. Perhaps he was trying to impress the other sheriffs.

I'm recalling those events as I pass the scene of that confrontation. I can still hear the echo of the words exchanged last week. "You put on a uniform, and you think that all of a sudden you have to crack the heads of your own Raza."

Right now, another carload is being interrogated at the same spot. I don't know why I'm walking. I'm passing the intersection of Whittier and Arizona. Two other police vehicles sit at this intersection. This corner is crowded. There's another liquor store on this corner whose doors don't stay closed for more than a few seconds.

On the street, there are carloads and carloads of people. Some I recognize. Some recognize me. The last few weekends, I've taken a lot of photographs. Tonight, there seems to be a lot more electricity in the air. A thousand stereos are blasting from oldies to funk. People are singing, dancing, and yelling from their cars. It is revelry. I've never been to Carnaval in Brazil or Mardi Gras in New Orleans, but I imagine it must be something like this.

I continue walking toward Atlantic. Cruising, cars, people, music, and more red and blue lights. I go a couple of blocks. As people see my camera, everyone yells to get my attention. All are waving and posing but I don't want to take pictures. Not yet. Not until I get back to McDonnell.

I see a carload of girls I met a few weekends ago. They insist that I take their pictures. With my hand, I make a circular motion, letting them know that when they come back, I'll take their picture. I don't want to take it now because if I do, it'll be total pandemonium. I won't be able to get back to McDonnell for a while. Once the flash goes off, everyone knows *Lowrider Magazine* is on the Boulevard. And everyone wants to be in *Lowrider.*

The police say everyone out here is a criminal if not a killer, but these youngsters don't look too violent to me. Most are just looking for romance. They want to see and be seen.

As they say on the streets, the cruising is "low 'n slow."

I cross the street, in between cars, and begin walking back toward McDonnell. The Boulevard is colorful tonight, like it always is, only it looks like the better cars are out this night. There are plenty of old cars, the bombs, the 1954s and under. They draw the most admiration. Respect. Pride. Cars with hydraulics are everywhere, attracting a lot of attention as they hop at every intersection. Customized vehicles turn heads. Spoked rims. Chromed steering wheels. Crushed velvet interiors. Stereo systems that emulate concert halls. Chandeliers. Candy and pearl paint jobs. Murals of Aztec warriors and Mayan princesses adorn the hoods and trunks of many of the vehicles. This is art. Art on wheels. This is East Los Angeles. This is cruising. This is the night life—an all-night outdoor party and there isn't anyplace like it in the world.

I pass by another police encounter where the occupants of another car are being made to sit on the curb, with their hands clasped behind their heads. They're probably being asked if their mothers know where they're at tonight. I move on.

Back on the corner of McDonnell, I start taking a few pictures. I talk to the other guy with the camera. I tell him of all the busts down the street. He wants to go take pictures of the sheriffs arresting people. He doesn't have to go far as a Highway Patrol officer has just pulled over a carload of girls. They were apparently drinking because the officer is making them get out while he puts their beer cans on top of their car.

I take one photograph and back away. The other guy is taking more pictures. "Keep taking pictures of cops, and you're going to end up in jail," I tell him.

He takes another picture.

I'm thirsty. I go into the liquor store to buy some gum. I know the people who work here. Tonight, they seem to have about eight assistants. Perhaps they need them because it's as crowded inside as it is outside. The owner asks me if I can bring more magazines tomorrow or Monday.

"If we have any left, I'll bring some," I tell him. "I'm not sure there are any left. In a matter of a few days, five liquor stores on the one-mile stretch of the Boulevard sell about 200 copies each. We can't print enough. It sells out fast every month, not just here but throughout the whole Southwest," I tell him.

Back outside, there are still a lot of people on the McDonnell side of the liquor store. There are more people on the other side of the liquor store and on the other three corners. I'm on the Whittier side of the liquor store, taking pictures of the cars and people going by.

A truckload of girls goes by. I met them the night before at Yoya's Upholstery Shop down the street on Olympic. They yell they'll be back because they want their picture taken.

A couple of blocks away, toward Eastern, a fight has broken out. But it's not causing much excitement. The Boulevard is violent. Every night at least one incident takes place. Nothing's ever happened to me except one time. Someone pulled a knife on me because I told two junior gangsters not to gang up on this one guy who had gotten a beer bottle thrown at his car presumably by his ex-girlfriend. When the guy who pulled the knife on me saw that I had a camera, he got all excited and wanted to know if I could take pictures of him and his homeboy for the magazine. I said, sure. As a result, the guy they had confronted got away.

I've seen a lot of fights and a lot of bottles flying but somehow, on this corner, I always feel safe. Part of it is probably because I grew up down the street. The other part is probably because most people know that I take photographs for the magazine. People can't wait to get to this corner to pose.

The sheriffs are arresting everybody except the ones who should be arrested. Those clowns fighting down the street might end up killing each other.

Where are the sheriffs when you need them?

One day, the Boulevard is going to explode. One day people are going to get tired of being pushed around and turn their anger on the police. That's what everybody says. Most of them are too young to remember the riots of East L.A. a decade ago.

On the Boulevard, time flies. I don't know the time, but I'm sure I've been out here for at least two hours. I haven't drunk anything. I haven't drunk anything alcoholic all night, on purpose. If I get stopped by a cop, I won't be "under the influence." My friend Kiki is still talking with the crowd on the corner. I told him to be cool about drinking in case we get stopped. I've been taking pictures. I don't know if he's been drinking. Normally, I might drink a beer, but tonight, something doesn't feel right.

Suddenly and out of nowhere, there's a guy in a sarape in the middle of the intersection. He's walking in the middle of the street wearing a Mexican sarape. He's walking between the cars. He's talking about God.

Someone tells me to take a picture. I look at the guy. He looks like he's crazy. Who would be in the middle of the street, in the middle of the night, talking about God? The regular Bible-carrying Christians, a group of ex-gang members, hang out up the street in a parking lot. They preach the word. It's street ministry. Sometimes they carry a big wooden cross up and down the Boulevard, but they do their preaching on the sidewalk. This guy's not part of them. He's nuts. He's in the middle of the street.

I go inside the liquor store and buy a soda. When I come back out, he's still out there. Now that I think of it, I decide it will make a good picture. He's got his arms raised like Moses. I snap a photograph. He looks like Moses parting the cars. As crowded as it already is, it looks like he's stopped all the traffic. I take another picture. I'm taking the photographs from in front of the liquor store. I get closer.

Either he's crazy or he's on drugs.

The guy in the sarape is in the middle of the west crosswalk on Whittier Boulevard with his arms raised in the air. I snap another photograph. It probably will make for a good shot, but I don't know about the guy. He's still yelling things about God.

All of a sudden, from an easterly direction, a black and white appears, red and blue lights flashing. The sheriffs park somewhere in the vicinity of the east crosswalk, and two sheriffs exit their vehicle. There are about a hundred people who are in this general area. I step back.

The sheriffs pull out their riot sticks. They are walking toward the guy with the sarape. They approach him. He appears to be oblivious of their presence.

People start telling me to take pictures. I'm not exactly thrilled with the idea.

The sheriffs say something to him. The guy yells out something about God. As they attempt to arrest him, he bolts out of their reach, running backward. He doesn't go far. He's caught by the sheriffs about the length of three stores away in the direction of Eastern Avenue. I can't tell whether the sheriffs have thrown him down or whether he's fallen, but he's on the ground. A lot of people are looking at this unfold, partially blocking my view. He is being dragged to the sidewalk. More sheriffs are arriving. The sheriffs have made the guy sit on the curb. They are talking to him or trying to talk to him. They're yelling at him. They sound impatient. He's still talking about God. They are trying to handcuff him. He is not letting them.

Suddenly, smack! They've punched him. Again. They're hitting him. Both of them. More sheriffs have arrived on the scene. People are telling me to take pictures. I want to leave the scene. More black and whites are arriving. Red and blue lights are approaching the area. Sirens are blaring. People want me to take pictures. More sheriffs are on the scene. The assault continues. He keeps yelling. A full-fledged, senseless beating is in progress. I'm ready to leave, but the guy yells out in anguish. It's a different type of yell . . . it's pain. I want to leave. People are pleading with me to take photographs. His cries are eerie. I want to leave, but his cries prevent me from leaving. The beating continues. The beating is horrific. By now, there are about eight or nine sheriffs surrounding him. Each is beating on him. Riot sticks are flying at him. Punches. Kicks. It is grotesque. I snap a picture. More kicks. "Ahhhhhhhhhhhh!!!!!" He lets out a sound, not even a yell.

I want to leave, but I can't.

His screams are chilling. More kicks. Another picture. The flash of my camera illuminates the carnage. I've never seen anything like this. The people are pleading with the police to leave him alone. The beating turns my stomach. The sheriffs are fighting among themselves for position. They are pushing each other out of the way for a chance to beat on the guy. The guy in the sarape is not crying anymore. He is not screaming. He is wailing. My flash has recharged. I snap another photograph. This flash sends a chill through all the onlookers. It has illuminated the sheriffs mercilessly beating an already limp man while one sheriff is pointing directly at me, motioning to the other sheriffs. I know the other guy with the camera is there somewhere, but the sheriff pointed at me. The sheriffs are yelling at the top of their lungs. They are commanding everyone to leave, but everyone seems to be frozen. The onlookers have become witnesses.

The beating has finally stopped. From the crowd, someone has stepped forward.

"Please let my brother go."

"Get the fuck out of here before we arrest you too!" a sheriff shouts at him.

More helmeted sheriffs have arrived on the scene, riot sticks out.

"Please, let me take my brother home. Let him go. You know he's not on drugs."

Hearing this, I am somewhat startled. Apparently, the guy in the sarape is not on drugs. There is something mentally wrong with him. They just finished beating on an innocent individual, and the sheriffs know it.

The sheriffs ignore his request and command him and everyone else to disperse.

There is nowhere to go but in one direction, back toward McDonnell. The other side is blocked by squad cars. There are probably eight to ten squad cars, maybe more, in the area. All have their red and blue lights flashing. There are helmeted police everywhere.

Many onlookers have already left.

I, too, am leaving slowly, momentarily stunned by what I have just heard.

A helmeted sheriff is on the southwest corner of McDonnell, shouting commands to the other sheriffs. The other sheriffs start heading toward the crowd. People are being herded.

"Get the guys with the cameras!" someone yells. It isn't the commander. The shout comes from the area where they are beating the guy. A cold chill has enveloped me. People are running about. I'm not. I haven't done anything wrong, yet sheriffs are coming after me. I'm walking away calmly. A sheriff with a riot stick comes up behind me as I'm walking toward the liquor store. He jabs me with the riot stick and tells me to leave. I was already walking away so I reply, "I'm leaving."

He comes up right behind me, getting even closer to me.

I keep going forward but in a diagonal because I'm not comfortable with him following me that closely. He's so close I can't even see him. I walk in that diagonal and then another diagonal, still in a forward direction. He's still right behind me, jabbing me with the riot stick, yelling at me to leave.

"I'm leaving," I tell him again.

"Get the guys with the cameras!" I hear again.

Abruptly, he jabs me again and says, "All right wise guy, you're under arrest." He pushes me toward the intersection in front of one of the police vehicles. There are other sheriffs, with riot sticks out, coming toward me. I'm still composed because I know that they don't want me. They want the camera.

Suddenly, I'm getting hit from behind. Stumbling forward, instinctively I toss the camera in an underhanded motion to a group of about six or seven people who are about ten feet in front of me and about fifteen feet in front of the liquor store. The camera is in midair. A guy in a blue Levi jacket stretches out his hands. As I recover my balance, I turn around to face the cop who struck me. But before I see him, I'm struck again by the riot stick on my back. Stumbling once again, I can see another three or four sheriffs charging at me. In a split second, I'm getting hit by riot sticks from all directions. I really don't feel pain, just incredulity. I don't know how many times I've been hit, maybe twenty, maybe thirty times? My body slouches down but I'm still up. I think I'm being held up. I look up. There's a black object coming at my forehead at an incredible speed. I don't have time to react. The force of the object drops me to the ground.

There's a ringing in my ears.

I don't know if I've lost consciousness. I am on the ground, semiconscious. I hear a pronounced, high-pitched sound inside my ears. I am oblivious to everything. I am dazed. I don't know what I am thinking. My head is spinning. I hear faint sounds. There are people around me running. Something must be going on. I hear yelling. The yelling is far away.

All of a sudden, I realize that the yelling is directed at me, and it's a sheriff who's been doing the yelling, but I can barely hear his voice. I can't make out what he's yelling. Is he mad?

He's yelling something about my arms. What does he want?

He wants me to give him my arms. He's trying to handcuff me.

That's what he wants.

He's yelling some more.

I forget. He wants my arm. My left arm.

I can't move. I can't raise my arms. Somehow, I landed on my belly with arms crossed. My body is on top of my arms.

He's yelling again.

OK, I'm going to try to lift my arm from underneath my body. But I can't move. I better hurry. He's probably going to shoot me. He probably thinks I'm disobeying his orders. I want to raise my arm, but I can't. My mind is telling my body to move. My mind is telling my arm to move, but it won't respond.

He's yelling. I think he's going to shoot. This can't be happening. But it is. He's going to shoot me. He's got his gun right above my head. He's going to blow my head off.

I don't want to die. I'm immobile. I want to move. I think I'm paralyzed. But I will my body to move.

I roll over. I rock to the side. My arm is free. I raise it.

That was close. I thought he was going to shoot me.

What is going on?

I start hearing those faint sounds again.

They come and they go.

Those sounds are far away.

People are still running.

My God! He's been yelling at me the whole time. He wants the other arm. He probably thinks I'm ignoring him. He's going to shoot. I'm not ignoring him. I can't make out what he's saying, but I know he wants the other arm. He wants to handcuff both my arms. It's probably too late. I'm going to get shot . . . just because I couldn't hear him, just because I couldn't make out his words. I didn't know he was yelling at me.

I rock to the side again and free my other arm. I raise it. He takes it and handcuffs me.

I am lying face down on the street, handcuffed. I am now aware that I am bleeding. My face is in a pool of blood. My blood.

Why am I on the ground?

The sheriff has left me there. The street is cold. I can still hear people scurrying about. The sheriffs must be chasing people.

I can't believe this is real. It is. It's not a movie. This is really happening. It's not a nightmare. I want to shake my head. It can't be happening. This stuff only happens in the movies.

"Keep your camera with you at all times. You'll never know when you need it."

Is this what they meant at *Lowrider?*

"Be careful," Barbara kept telling me.

"Why are you telling me to be careful. You're the one who's leaving."

Why did she tell me to be careful? She's the one who went to New York.

"Be careful."

Why did she say that?

Why did I take those stupid pictures?

Why didn't I leave when I sensed danger?

Ican't believe this. I'm lying on the ground in the middle of the street in a pool of blood. This can't be real!

2 / A Trail of Blood: My Final Destination

I'm losing blood. Lots of it. The pool of blood is getting bigger.

How much blood have I lost? I don't know. I've been here, face down, on the ground on Whittier Boulevard, five minutes, I think.

Did I lose consciousness? I don't remember. I think I did because I don't remember how I ended up lying on my arms. The guy was going to shoot me.

What's going on?

Why aren't they putting me in a squad car? Why aren't they taking me away?

I wonder what happened to my camera? Did the guy catch it? Did it fall to the ground and break? Did he catch it and get away with it? How am I going to get it back? The cops probably have it. I hope they didn't beat the guy who caught the camera. I shouldn't have thrown it. They probably got him too just because I threw the camera to him. I don't even know who he was although I remember seeing him earlier. I can still imagine his face clearly. I think Kiki knows him. What about the other guy with the camera? He was there. Did he take pictures of me while I was being attacked? Did he get away? Did they get his camera? I was telling him to be careful. I hope nothing happened to him.

I'm numb. I don't feel pain. I feel shock. My body feels stiff. I can't even move my head around. The pool of blood in front of me is getting larger and larger. I can't see anything. Behind me, I hear footsteps. I can hear people running. In fact, I can see people running all around me, but I can only see their shoes. I can see reflections in the pool of blood, but I can't make out the figures.

That's why they're not taking me away. They're chasing everyone else. How much longer?

Ten minutes have gone by. I'm not sure. I can't be sure. I don't know if I lost consciousness. It's cold. The pool of blood keeps getting bigger and bigger. I can see my own reflection in it.

Two sheriffs finally pick me up. They are debating where to take me. There are three squad cars in the intersection. I'm a little dizzy. I'll probably be put into the car closest to me. Apparently not. One of the sheriffs has gone over to talk with four or five officers who are huddled nearby. They seem to be arguing about where I should go or whom I should go with.

Finally, the sheriff has come back. They're walking me over to the squad car that's in the parking lane, facing the flow of traffic. They put me in the back seat of the squad car, directly behind the driver's side. The sheriff sitting beside me is irritated. I am bleeding profusely. Blood is squirting out of my forehead. It has stained the helmet of the officer in the front seat. It's not my fault, yet he's acting like I am bloodying his helmet, bloodying the car, on purpose. He wipes his helmet. Instead of driving away, both sheriffs have gone back to talk to the other sheriffs.

With each pulse beat, more blood spurts out. How much blood can I lose? Blood is everywhere now. Blood is rolling down my jacket onto my pants. My pants are soaked.

How long am I going to wait in this car? Does anyone know I'm in this car? Where are they going to take me? Somehow, I have to let the magazine know what has happened, but how am I going to do that? I can't let the sheriffs know that I work for *Lowrider*. They'll kill me. They're probably going to kill me anyway. There are sheriffs standing around. One pokes his head through the window.

He laughs, "That's a pretty good hit."

He motions for another sheriff to come and see the wound on my forehead.

"Look at his head. They done a pretty good hit on his head."

"A perfect cross. Not bad," the other sheriff says.

They both laugh.

"We better get this guy to a hospital."

A hospital? What for? I'm startled. Why are they going to take me to a hospital. I'm conscious. I'm alert. I'm bleeding, but there's nothing wrong with me. The sheriffs walk away.

A perfect cross?

The hospital?

I want to see my forehead. I want to get word to Larry or Sonny, the owners of *Lowrider,* but they're out of town. No one is at the offices of the magazine, but maybe a message could be left on the recorder. Maybe Sal, the photographer, will pick up the message. How can I let them know? I don't want to be killed.

The hospital? I'm not dying. The wound is not that serious. Why do they want to take me to the hospital? Maybe it's better that way. They'll kill me at the sheriff's station. Maybe I'll never make it to the station. I better not tell them I work for *Lowrider*. If they find out, they'll kill me. If I live, I'll expose them. I'll sue them. I'll file criminal charges against them. If they know that I'm connected with media, they won't let me live. They won't want to lose their jobs. They won't want to spend time in prison. They couldn't survive in prison.

What about George, my brother-in-law? He's a sheriff. If he finds out, he'll help. I'm going to tell the sheriffs that I know someone at the top. My brother-in-law, he's got twenty years on the force. If he finds out, he'll put those guys away. They'll lose their jobs. I better not mention his name. If I tell them his name, they'll kill me.

Just keep your mouth shut. But I have to get word out.

There's a car passing slowly right by me. Three girls.

"Ahhhhhh," one screams.

All three look at me in horror. It looks like if they've just seen a monster.

"Please call *Lowrider Magazine*," I whisper.

I can't speak loudly because there are sheriffs around the squad car.

The girls look terrified.

"Call *Lowrider.*"

They are flinching at the sight of me.

Maybe they think I'm guilty of something. No. If they can just make out my words, they'll help.

They are throwing their arms up in the air, somewhat shielding their faces. They look concerned . . . but also apprehensive. They can't make out my words.

I want to tell them to call the police . . . but how can they call the police. Law enforcement officers are the one's who have me.

The traffic is still moving slowly, but after a few minutes the girls move on. They know I need help. Will they call someone? Who will they call? The FBI? Maybe the media?

I can't believe the expressions on their faces.

I have to see myself. Am I that bad?

If I can only inch my way up so that I can see myself in the rear view mirror.

My God. I can see myself in the mirror.

That's not me. But it is.

Blood is coming out of my eyes, out of my nostrils, out of my mouth. There is a massive wound on my forehead. Blood is squirting out of my forehead. Blood is everywhere. I am bleeding from every place imaginable. My face is a mass of blood.

No wonder the girls flinched.

"They were right," another sheriff pokes his head in. "It is a perfect hit."

"Please take me to the hospital," I ask.

The sheriff laughs.

"Please take me to the hospital. I've lost a lot of blood."

"Yup . . . you sure have . . . it's a perfect hit." He laughs again and leaves.

Why are they leaving me in the car? They can't refuse to take me to a hospital.

"Please, I have to be taken to a hospital."

Two other sheriffs have poked their heads into the vehicle. "Right between the eyes," they both laugh.

How long is this game going to last?

A cold realization sets in. For the first time, it dawns on me that there is no one to call. Those who have me are the ones I'm supposed to call for protection.

Panic is setting in. They're not going to take me to a hospital.

I have to go to the hospital. That's the only protection I have. They'll fix me up, and they'll keep me away from the sheriff's station.

Finally, both doors open. The driver is mad because I have bled everywhere. The sheriff on the passenger's side, with the door still open and sitting down, pulls out his riot stick and points it at me, "You act up, and I'm going to finish the job."

The sheriffs drive away.

Why is this guy threatening me? What does he mean by "acting up"? This guy is probably used to scaring people into submission. I don't know where they're planning to take me, but I'm going to request that they rush me over to the hospital.

"I've been hurt bad. I need to go to a hospital."

After laughter and more laughter, they agree.

There's so much traffic on the Boulevard that they can't go by way of the normal route. I'm dazed. I have lost my sense of direction. I don't know where they're at or where they're going, but they're away from the Boulevard. They seem not to know where they're going. They are driving at about five miles per hour through dark streets. This is not the fastest way to the nearest hospital.

There is talk over the radio. Can't exactly make it out. Still crawling along, the driver seems to be lost. The passenger is telling him where to go although he doesn't seem to know where he's going either. I'm starting to get scared.

"Run the red light," the passenger tells the driver.

The driver hesitates. "But it's illegal."

"Go ahead, we do illegal things all the time." The sheriff on the passenger side looks at me with the riot stick in his hand.

Yes, I know what he meant by that. The guy's trying to act tough. He's telling his partner stories about all the illegal things he does.

Something comes over the car radio. The sheriff on the passenger's side responds, "We have one case already. One more case and we're through for the night. One more case and we can party."

Are they going to take me hostage? They are either really lost or pretending to be so. They're still driving five miles per hour. There's no reason to go slow. I'm still losing blood. I've been losing blood for I don't know how long. I'm drenched. The back of the seat in front of me is stained; the floor in front of me is stained.

I don't feel weak. I feel a little scared with all this talk about illegal things he and his partners do. I can't believe them. What did they mean by case? Am I a case? Do they need to capture someone else to meet their quota to call it a night, or were they referring to a case of beer? Is that why they pull over everyone on the Boulevard? To steal people's beer so that they can drink it?

The sheriff on the passenger's side turns toward me with my camera in his hand. It doesn't appear to be damaged. The guy must have caught the camera. They must have caught him. He probably didn't have time to run. I hope they didn't beat him. It wasn't his fault. He was just an innocent bystander.

I lean forward to get a glimpse of their name tags. The name tag on the driver says Taylor. The name tag on the passenger says Galbraith. I wish I could write their names. But I can't. I can't forget their names. I'm surprised they're even wearing their name tags. Maybe they've switched them. Don't forget their faces. I won't. I won't forget their faces, especially the one who has threatened me.

This sheriff presumably named Galbraith has begun to unscrew the back of the camera.

"So you had the lens cap on all the time, huh?"

The guy starts laughing sarcastically.

This guy's real funny. He's going to open the back and claim the lens cap was on the whole time. The camera doesn't even have a lens cap. And even if it did, the camera wouldn't work that way because the viewer would be blocked. This guy's not too bright if that's what he's going to claim.

"Do you always shoot with your lens cap on?" he says sarcastically, turning away as he yanks the film.

I don't say anything.

I've been attacked severely, I witnessed a brutal beating, I photographed the incident, and now the guy has exposed the roll of film. I gulp. The tension is incredible. No one is saying anything. The three of us know what has just occurred. I think it's a felony. Is that why they've been driving around slowly? To give them time to destroy the evidence? What else are they going to do? Are they now going to take me to the hospital, or are they going to kill me?

We're driving through dark streets, gang infested streets. Are they going to drop me off in front of a gang hangout and let them finish the job? Just another statistic. In the morning papers, another gang killing?

"Where are we going?"

They're ignoring me.

They probably think they're dealing with some dummy. I better talk to them so that they know I have some intelligence. Maybe that'll discourage them from killing me. They probably think I'm under the influence of PCP, under Angel Dust. If I talk to them and I sound coherent, maybe they won't kill me.

"Are there a lot of people on PCP out tonight?" I ask.

"Every night."

I'm engaged in small talk, about drugs. I'm coherent. The driver knows he's not dealing with someone under the influence. I intentionally mentioned PCP because someone under the influence of drugs wouldn't be able to deal with such a subject coherently. Galbraith seems to be irritated.

I am starting to feel weak. They're still lost or are still pretending to be lost. I don't know how much blood I can lose.

It appears that they're taking me to Santa Marta Hospital. They must be lost because it's already been twenty minutes, and it normally takes five. The streets are dark in this area but they seem even darker right now. We finally park.

I'm walking or being led down a ramp. We are going through the emergency doors. I've never been arrested, and I've never been in an emergency hospital. Do they work together? Should I tell the doctors what has happened? Will they believe me?

I am put on a table. I am still losing blood. My pants are completely drenched in blood. The doctor examines me.

"I can't treat him," the doctor says.

My face is wiped clean. The blood continues to flow.

"The wound is too massive. We're not equipped to handle this type of trauma to the head."

A large bandage is placed around my head.

The doctor walks away with one of the officers. They are discussing what to do. The other officer follows.

I want to make a phone call. But what do I say? I'm not going to stay. I don't want to lose the one phone call that I'm entitled to. What if they overhear my conversation? What if they kill me on the way to the other hospital? I don't know whether it's a good idea to call. I remember what happened to David Domínguez. I covered the trial a couple of years ago. He called his mom right before he was kidnapped and killed by a sheriff. It doesn't matter. I have to call. Maybe they'll kill me if I call, but maybe they'll kill me regardless.

I'm shaking. The two attendants ask me what happened. I look toward the sheriffs. I don't respond. I'm trembling. I've gone into shock.

"Did they do this?" the attendants ask.

I don't respond.

I look toward the sheriffs. I can't make out what they're saying. They will probably overhear me if I say anything

"Ask the sheriffs if I can make a phone call."

I'm trembling uncontrollably. If I say anything, they'll probably kill me. After we leave, they have the perfect alibi. The doctor refused to treat me because my injuries were too severe. They'll work me over. Then they'll say I died of those original injuries, and the doctor will admit that he couldn't treat me due to the seriousness of the injuries.

The attendant comes back and says that I can make the phone call.

I change my mind. I'm thinking about David Domínguez's phone call.

I want to save the phone call for after I know where I'll be. I have to save the phone call. It may save my life.

"Forget that phone call," I tell them, "I'll call from the other hospital."

They're taking me away. There's a trail of blood leading from the emergency doors all the way to the squad car. We get to the squad car and drive away. I should have called. I'm going to regret that I didn't call. If I get killed, at least my family would have heard my version of what happened. I should have called. At least I could have talked to them for the last time.

They're hesitating. Again, they are acting as though they don't know where they're going. I don't believe this. They're driving around in circles. They're driving five miles per hour again. If my injuries are too serious for this hospital, why don't they rush me over to the other hospital.

"What are we going to do when we get there?" the driver asks Galbraith.

"I don't know," he responds.

They're talking about what they're going to say on their reports, what they're going to say at the hospital. Galbraith pulls out his riot stick, "Maybe we can convince him of what happened."

Pointing the riot stick at me, he says, "What are you going to say happened?"

I hesitate. I'm under duress. I can say anything.

"I'm going to tell them that I slipped and fell."

"Are you sure,?" Galbraith says rapping the riot stick on his hand.

"Yeah. I slipped and fell as I was being handcuffed."

We're on the freeway now. There are no other cars on the road. Even on the freeway we're going slowly. We're on the Long Beach Freeway. We're on the San Bernardino Freeway.

I feel weak. Only the thought that they might kill me prevents me from dozing off—from passing out. I know I've lost a lot of blood. I don't know how much blood a person can lose before passing out. At least it's stopped gushing out.

I can see General Hospital from the freeway. We get off the freeway.

"How do we get there?" the driver asks his partner.

I don't believe this. What a time to act stupid. The hospital's to the left. I've been by this hospital so many times it's not funny.

"Make a left right here and then make a right on Marengo," I tell them.

"I don't think so," the sheriff on the passenger's side says. He laughs.

I don't believe this. The building's so big, it's bigger than City Hall.

"Let's see," Galbraith says, "I think we can get to it by going this way," he points to the right with the riot stick.

The guy starts turning to the right.

"What are you guys doing? The hospital's to the left."

"There's a short cut this way," Galbraith laughs.

"Turn around. The entrance is on Marengo!" I tell them.

Galbraith's laughing with the riot stick in his hand. I don't believe this. To the right is the Ramona Gardens housing projects. I almost got killed there the other day. It's deadly in there. Further down, toward Huntington Drive, there are hills, and it's isolated.

My head is spinning. "Why are you guys going this way?" I ask.

They are silent. My God! This is it! They're actually going to finish the job. My God! Why? It's going to happen. I'm really going to die. This is it! God help me! Why? I can't die. Why? No! They can't. Calm down. Die like a man. My parents. My family. What will people say? They won't believe it. Are they going to let me run and shoot me in the back? Are they going to work me over and then shoot me? How will the end come?

God, if I must go, then let me go in peace. I always knew I was never going to reach my twenty-fifth birthday. How many times have I said that? I had a premonition. Over the years, I must have told my girlfriend a thousand times that I was not going to live to see my twenty-fifth birthday. Why? Why did I have to be right?

This drive is slower. Why are they going slower? No one is on the road. I could have done many things. It's too late. We die unexpectedly. There's no more time. What will my relatives think in Mexico? At least, I got to meet them. At least, I got to meet my grandmother and my godmother before they died. I should be thankful I've lived this long. Will people really believe I tried to escape? Will people really believe I died of my injuries?

No matter what happens, no matter what they ask, refuse. Don't run. Die like a Mexican. Die like Zapata: "It is better to die on one's feet than to live on one's knees." Don't run. Let them shoot you in the front. Don't plead for your life. Let them know that this Mexican did not bow down to them. No matter what you do, don't plead for your life. Don't get on your knees. Die like a man. Let them kill you, but don't give them the satisfaction of seeing a Mexican on his knees. Let them know that they killed a warrior. No one will know how the end came except for me, them, and God. They can tell a million stories. They can brag about it to their friends. They can keep it to themselves. But God will know and they will know that when they killed this Mexican, he didn't plead, he didn't beg, he didn't run.

God, forgive me for all my sins. God, forgive me for having denied you. I am ready.

Wake up! Snap out of it! This is real. This isn't a movie. You can't die. You won't die.

Galbraith is having the time of his life. He can see the tension in my eyes. The other guy looks scared. He's probably never killed anyone before. No one is saying anything. But the tension has left me. I am ready.

There's a sign on the side of the road. I think it said "L.A. County Facilities Service Road." What? We've gone a half mile. We're making a left turn. There really is a service road. There's a back entrance.

Galbraith and the other guy are slapping each other's hands. They're laughing their heads off.

This death ride. It was all staged. They knew where they were going all along. They're having the time of their lives.

They don't realize what they have just done. I can forget everything, but this I will never forget. They prepared me. I prepared for my last moments. They don't realize what they've done. They're laughing. This I will never forget.

We park. Galbraith again points the riot stick at me. "What are you going to tell them?"

"I already told you. I'm going to tell them what happened. I'm going to tell them that I fell down as I was being handcuffed. I'm going to tell them that I slipped."

"Are you sure?" Galbraith looks at me with his menacing riot stick.

"Yeah. I'm sure."

As they lead me toward the hospital, I look back. I am leaving a trail of blood. The blood is dripping from my pants. The bandage wrapped around my head has stopped the flow. The trail is from the pants. They're soaked. The trail leads from the squad car to the thirteenth floor.

"What happened?" the doctor asks.

We're up in the jail ward of the L.A. County Hospital.

The doctor removes the blood-soaked bandage. He is examining my head-wound while I am seated and handcuffed to a bench. One of the sheriffs is standing right next to me while the other one is filling out some forms. Galbraith is filling out the forms. This one is making sure I tell the story straight.

"I slipped and fell."

This guy's probably a fake doctor. He probably works for the sheriff's department.

"Seriously, tell me what really happened."

I look up to the sheriff and tell the doctor, "I slipped while they were trying to handcuff me."

The doctor puts the bandage back on and walks away in disgust. Either he doesn't believe me, or he knows what really happened.

The doctor is conferring with another doctor. I can overhear their conversation. "The guy's got tracks all over his forehead but he says he fell."

The doctor comes back and leads me away, away from the sheriff who was standing next to me.

"We're in a hospital. I'm a doctor. You can tell me what happened. Trust me. Tell me what happened."

If this is a real hospital, then why do they have bars, and why am I handcuffed? How do I know this guy is a real doctor? He's probably a cop doctor. Even if he's a real doctor, they're probably in on it together.

"I slipped and fell as they tried to handcuff me."

No matter what anyone says, I'm not changing this story until I get out. I'm not saying anything until I get out. If I ever get to court, I know they'll use my words against me, but I know the law. I'm under duress. I'm being held against my will. But I'm not worried about the law right now. I want to stay alive. The whole place is probably bugged. Don't trust anyone. No one. When you make your call, don't talk about what happened. Just have them get you out.

The doctor is conferring with the sheriffs. I think the sheriffs want to take me away. I'm not sure. I think I'm staying.

I'm taken to another room with a nurse. This nurse has an attitude. There is someone else who's in worse shape than I am. I wonder if it's the guy with the sarape? Can't tell, but whoever this guy is, he's in bad shape.

"You assholes deserve this," the nurse directs her contempt at me.

The other guy is in a daze and seems to be unable to comprehend and unable to determine where he is.

"I don't think you know what you're talking about," I tell her.

I can't believe her. She's wearing a nurse's uniform, yet she's acting like the cops. She hasn't asked me what happened, and she's indicting me already. Just calm down. She's probably baiting you, just to get you to talk. Don't say anything. It's just like I thought. She's in with them just like the doctors are in with the cops.

She continues her insults. I ignore her.

I am on the operating table now. The bandages are off of my head. The doctor's nervous hands work quickly to stop the new flow of blood that is gushing out of my forehead. With each pulse beat, blood is squirting onto the white gown that has been placed over my blood-drenched clothes. The gown is now completely blood red. My eyes are shut, yet I am completely aware of what is going on. The doctor is unable to stitch the massive wound. I want to open my eyes, but I fear the pouring blood will seep into my eyes. The doctor is working frantically. I am conscious that I have lost a lot of blood. The stitching has broken. He must start again. Though I am numb in the area of the forehead, I can sense his trembling hands. I open my eyes. My vision is blurred, but I can see that the doctor is wiping his face. The heat from the bright lights are making things worse. My eyes are shut again. Blood has seeped into my eyes. The doctor wipes my eyes. It is hot. It is unbearable. He begins stitching again.

"It's almost over," the doctor says.

I don't know what he means by that. I am lying on an operating table in the jail ward of the Los Angeles County Hospital. His voice is shaking. It is near four in the morning. He has been attempting to close the wound for more than fifteen minutes. Up till now, his efforts have been futile. I am starting to feel delirious. I open my eyes. My vision is still blurry.

"Close your eyes," he says. "There's nothing to worry about. You're in no immediate danger."

His trembling hands and his lack of composure betray his reassurances. I don't know how much blood a patient can lose, but I am feeling weaker. I close my eyes. The gushing continues. I am beginning to lose hope. My life is in his hands.

3 / False Arrest and False Imprisonment: Guilty until Proven Innocent

The bleeding has finally stopped. The doctor has finished suturing me up. I feel weak but relatively at ease. With my eyes still closed, I ask him, "When can I leave?"

"You can't leave. You need to rest. Besides, you're in custody."

"Have I been arrested?"

"Yes."

"What have I been charged with?"

"I don't know."

"Can you find out?"

"I'll ask. In the meantime, you need some rest."

"I need to get out of here. Can I make a phone call?"

"Let me find out," he says.

My head's spinning. No, it's not spinning. I'm feeling the effects of losing all the blood. Can't believe I'm actually under arrest? For what? Being a witness?

The doctor's back. It didn't take him too long.

"You've been charged with 242 and 243."

"What's that?

"I don't know?

"Who knows?

"I'm not sure?"

"Can you find out?"

"I'll probably have to wait until the morning."

"What about my phone call?"

"You'll be called as soon as a phone is available. Right now, you'll be assigned your bed. Wait there until you are X-rayed."

The X-ray machine looks old, probably emits excessive radiation.

While waiting to be assigned a bed, the doctor returns.

"I found out what the charges are. They're felonies: assault with a deadly weapon and assault and battery on a peace officer. Two counts of each."

I'm at a loss for words. I can't believe this. It's true. It's just like in the movies. Fake charges. A frame-up. They actually made up a story. I attacked them. Incredible.

"What happened out there?"

I don't trust the doctor. He works here. He'll probably go tell the cops as soon as I tell him the truth.

"The marks on your forehead are not from falling down. Tell me what really happened. Trust me. I'm a doctor."

I don't trust anyone.

I can't believe this. They almost kill me, and I'm charged with trying to kill them. A weapon? What weapon do they claim I had? This can't be real. The only thing I had on me was a camera. What did they plant on me? I never believed that police actually plant things on people, but they apparently have. A gun maybe? A knife? A crow bar? A bumper jack? They've really planted something on me.

"Do you know what weapon I'm supposed to have assaulted them with?" I ask the doctor.

"No. It doesn't say here."

Assault with a deadly weapon and assault and battery on a peace officer. Two felonies. Two counts each. What a joke. But the joke's on me. It's not a joke. It's real. But it can't be. Things like this don't happen in this country.

I finally get my bed. It's now five in the morning, and I'm being allowed to make a phone call. It's been an incredibly long night. I can't believe what has happened. I don't want to call my parents, but no one from the magazine is in town. What will I tell my parents? I should wait until I get out to tell my parents. They'll probably be alarmed. They'll probably get worried. I don't want them to worry. I'm twenty-four years old. I don't live at home, and I've never been in trouble, but who am I supposed to call? I'll have to call them, who else would bail me out, especially at this hour?

At least, I remember their phone number. It's my youngest brother.

"They already know," he says, "Kiki called."

I didn't even know Kiki had my parents' number. Apparently he followed the police car and then called my folks.

"Everybody's out looking for you. They've been going to all the jails."

"If they call, tell them I'm in the jail ward of the L.A. County Hospital. I'm on the thirteenth floor. It's the General Hospital in Lincoln Heights. Tell them I'm OK, but I've been arrested. I'm not sure what they're claiming I did, but have George find out. Tell him to get me out."

"He knows already. He's going to get you out in the morning."

"Make sure he knows. He has to get me out of here quick."

I'm back in my bed. If all goes well, I'll be out in no time. I'm not that close with my brother-in-law, George. I don't talk to him much, but he is my brother-in-law. I have probably put him in a difficult position. He's in the same department as these guys. But I'm not exactly calling him by choice. I hope he comes through.

If all goes well, I'll probably be out by eight. I'd probably be out by seven, but with red tape, they'll probably keep me in for another hour.

There's no clock in here, but I know that a couple of hours have already gone by. I need to go to the bathroom.

I'm stiff already. Stiffer. I'm aching over every inch of my body.

My God. Who is this person in front of the mirror? It isn't me. It can't be. My eyes are swollen shut. I can barely open my eyes. My vision is blurred. The face in the mirror bears no resemblance whatsoever to my face. The face in the mirror is bloodied. It is black and blue. It is purple. It looks worse than when I saw it in the back seat of the car, when the girls flinched. My face is not just swollen. It's distorted. It's disfigured. This can't be real. My forehead is protruding. My God. My forehead looks twice as big as it normally is. My black hair is mixed with blood. The stitching is right between my nose in a cross. The cross protrudes to the forehead. That can't be me.

I'm tired. Weak. I can barely walk back to the bed. I'm stiff. One step at a time. Slowly. I'm walking like Frankenstein. I look worse than he did.

I'm in bed not believing what has occurred, what is occurring. Stay awake. Don't fall asleep. Just wait. You'll be out soon. You'll be out in no time. No matter what you do, don't fall asleep. They'll probably kill you while you're sleeping.

Some time has passed. My eyes are flinching. I can see the black riot stick coming at my head. Again and again.

More time has passed. I wonder what's happened?

"There's someone here to visit you."

Finally.

Apparently, I had lost track of time because I find out it's three P.M.

"Where am I going?" I ask the guard.

"To the visiting area."

I reach a booth with glass separating the visitors. My parents, two brothers, and my sister are in the lobby. They look at me with a mixed expression of horror and concern. The overriding expression is that of concern. My dad and my sister come to the booth.

We converse in Spanish.

My dad says, "We raised the bail money, but now they say you have two warrants."

"They're making it up. I don't have any warrants."

"They won't let you out until we pay the bail money for the warrants."

"Where's George?" I ask my sister.

"He's working."

"Can't he get me out?"

"He's trying?"

"Tell him the warrants are fake."

"What happened?" my sister asks.

"I'll tell you when I get out."

"We'll be back after we raise the money for the warrants. We have to raise it before five or else they say we have to come back tomorrow."

"Tell George I don't have any warrants. Tell him they're not mine."

As they leave, I see my mom give me a reassuring look. She doesn't say it, but she motions for me to be strong. I'm amazed. I thought she'd be crying or something. I guess you don't know people, even your own family, until a crisis comes up. I didn't want my family to know. I didn't want them to see me in a jail, especially like this. I think they're the last people in the world I would have wanted to know about this. I probably would have called them after my face looked OK, but . . .

It is now five o'clock.

It's six o'clock.

I'm staying another night.

I'm even stiffer now than I was earlier.

Everyone in the room has a story to tell. Everyone is in worse shape than I am. I want to tell them what happened to me, but I don't trust anyone. I'm not saying anything until I get out. For all I know, there are rats or hidden microphones in here. Don't say anything. Don't trust anyone.

The hours are dragging. There's nothing to do but think.

I can still see the guy in the sarape being viciously beaten. I can clearly see the camera in midair. The witnesses. There were a lot of witnesses. I can still see their faces. I talked to a lot of them. Right before it all happened. I'm going to need to track them down.

As soon as I'm out, first thing I need to do is get a lawyer. I wonder what happened after they arrested me? I wonder what's going to happen tonight?

Nine o'clock.

Ten.

Eleven.

Twelve.

One A.M.

There's nothing to do but think. They're holding me on false warrants. As soon as I get out, I'm going to sue them for false arrest and false imprisonment. I've never had a warrant in my life. I didn't do anything but I know they can keep me for three days, not counting weekends. If they don't kill me in here, they'll probably let me out on Wednesday. They don't want anyone to see me in this condition. I have to get out of here.

Three in the morning.

Tonight is extremely busy. The room I'm in was already full, but they're bringing in more people.

"Where is everyone coming from?" I ask one of the custodians.

"From the Boulevard."

"You serious?"

"From what I heard, they're arresting everyone."

I wonder what's happening?

"Is that where they got you?"

"Yeah."

This guy probably works for them. Don't say anymore.

At three in the morning, it seems like it's daytime by the amount of activity.

Time is crawling.

Everybody's talking about the Boulevard. The other room is filled with people who were brought over from the Boulevard. Everybody's been charged with assaulting police officers. I'm sure they assaulted sheriffs just like me.

The sheriffs on the Boulevard must have finally gone berserk. They were always threatening to close the Boulevard. If they really wanted to close it, I'm sure they could have barricaded it, but it appears they've chosen to close it with riot sticks.

Six in the morning.

I wonder what time they open on Sunday. I still haven't slept. I don't want to sleep. I just want to get out of here.

Seven in the morning.

We're given the option of showering. I'm stiff from head to toe. I'm not showering until I get out. As soon as I get out, I'm going to get photographed, then I'm going to shower. I want people to see exactly how they left me.

Everybody's talking about what happened to them, about how they were arrested. I feel sorry for them. Most of them are in worse shape than I am. They're the ones who were assaulted, but they're the ones who are going to end up doing time. And nothing will happen to the cops. They'll be free to terrorize; they'll be free to brutalize because they know nothing will ever happen to them. Everybody's going to do time except me. They went after the wrong guy. I'm going to fight them, and I'm going to win. And they're going to pay. All I have to do is keep my mouth shut until I get out, and I'll be OK.

Time continues to crawl.

"Rodríguez," a guard says, "get ready."

Get ready? I've been ready since the doctor finished suturing me.

"As soon as we're ready to process you, we'll call you."

I'm getting out. They're probably fuming.

I have to plan things. What am I going to do? Did they tow my car away? Who knows about this? I wonder if the media knows what's happened on the Boulevard? What has happened on the Boulevard? I don't know. I'm going to have to fight a frame-up.

I don't know what's taking so long. I wonder if they've forgotten about me? I wonder if they've changed their mind?

164

Maybe they found out that I work for *Lowrider*. Maybe they've found out that George is my brother-in-law. Maybe now they realize that they're going to be in trouble and have decided to keep me in until they decide what to do with me. They're probably trying to figure out how to cover their tracks.

Get ready. What did they think I needed, hours to get out of the hospital bed?

Hours later, the doors finally open.

"Let's go," the guard tells me.

We're walking down the corridor.

"I don't know how you know George Blair, but he's getting you out."

Of course you don't know. He's my brother-in-law. Don't say anything. Not a word.

"Before you get released, you have to sign some papers and get fingerprinted."

You're almost out. Don't blow it. Don't say anything, and don't get smart.

The guy doing the fingerprinting, a marshal, is talking to me in a sarcastic way. He's baiting me. "So you think you're a big man going around attacking police?" he says.

"You think you're tough, don't you?" he asks.

The guy's jamming my fingers instead of pressing them against the ink.

This is the first time I've ever been fingerprinted in my life.

"Why aren't you tough in here?"

I can't believe this guy. He could pass for a fat little pig, whom I could probably flatten with one punch, but in here, he's rough and tough.

"You want to try something with me? Let's see how tough you are? You go around beating on cops and then getting out. We'll see if you get away with this."

Don't say nothing.

"Aahhh!" The guy has just jammed my left ring finger. It's still swollen from Friday night.

"You ain't nothing. I'll be seeing you behind bars."

"I doubt it," I tell him. "I'm innocent."

"Is that right. Then why are you in here, asshole?"

"I'm not saying anything until I get out."

The marshal is giving me a sinister look. He turns me over to another guard.

Why did I say that? Why did I even open up my mouth. Shit! There's only so much abuse a person can take. But why now? Why didn't I wait until I got out?

A guard is leading me away.

I turn around and face the marshal, "Don't I get photographed?"

I don't know why I asked. I didn't mean to be sarcastic. It's just that in the movies, they always photograph criminals.

"Get the fuck out of here, wise guy, before I change my mind and keep you here."

I didn't really expect them to photograph me. They'd be handing me a victory in court.

The guard directs me to a booth.

"Wait here," he says.

He comes back a short time later and gives me a bag.

"Change," he says.

I take the bag.

Everything seems to be in here.

I take off my blue jail ward shirt and put on my regular shirt. I take off the blue pants and . . . My pants are not in this bag. Is this a joke or what? Maybe they have them in another bag.

"Excuse me," I call the guard, "my pants are not in this bag?"

"What pants?

"What do you mean, what pants? The pants I was wearing?"

"If they're not in the bag, it means we don't have them."

"How could you not have them? Everything else is in here."

"Maybe you came here not wearing any pants."

"Why don't we quit playing games? If you're not going to look for my pants, I want to talk to your supervisor."

"I am the supervisor."

"Then look for my pants. I need them to leave here."

"I'll be back."

I don't believe these guys. I'll sue them for destruction of evidence. I don't blame them for destroying the pants. They were drenched in blood. If the jury sees the pants, I'll win hands down. I can't believe this is happening.

The guard is back.

"It says here that you came here from Santa Marta Hospital. You probably changed clothes when they treated you there."

"The refused to treat me at Santa Marta's. They sent me here."

"I don't know what happened there, but you came here without pants."

"That's a lie."

I'm silent for a moment. They've already destroyed the pants. They probably got rid of them Friday night. If this guy wanted to give back my pants, he probably couldn't.

"What am I supposed to do now. What am I going to go home in? My underwear?"

"Take those," he points to the blue jail ward pants that I'm wearing.

The guard walks away.

I can't believe this. They've destroyed my pants, and they're going to let me walk out with evidence, evidence that they destroyed my pants. I better hurry up before they change their minds. Maybe the marshal who fingerprinted me told this guy that as soon as I was out, I was going to talk. I shouldn't have said anything.

I'm ready to leave.

My ring that was on my left ring finger doesn't fit anymore. But it doesn't matter. It was a special ring, and they took it off. I'm not going to put it back on until I beat them. I'm not going to put it back until this is all over with. I don't care how long it takes.

My wallet's here. My money's even in it. My camera's missing. They probably brought it in separately. It was in the car when they brought me here. The guy even opened up the camera in front of me.

I call the guard over.

"I'm ready to leave except I want to take my camera with me."

"What camera?"

Again. I can't believe these guys.

"The camera I had with me."

The guard leaves and comes back.

"We're holding your camera as evidence."

"Evidence! What evidence?!"

"It says that you used it in the commission of 242 and 243."

"What!"

"You can go now, but you can't take the camera."

This can't be real. My camera was the deadly weapon?

Incredible.

4 / Seven Years:
The Longest Wait

As might be expected, after getting out of the hospital, my primary thoughts were consumed with revenge. During those first few days after I was released, I had to contend with, if not balance, my irrational thoughts with my rational thoughts. My rational thoughts were in the legal world. My irrational thoughts were in the underworld of violence and retribution.

Before the week was out, I was approached by three different street gangs who offered to carry out the retribution for me. They wanted to take out any sheriff's deputy or any police officer. Despite my total rage, I did not want anything done at random. If there was to be revenge, it could not be random. But in my irrational state of mind, I mulled over the offers. At the time, there was a lot of rage in East Los Angeles and in most other barrios. I wasn't the first person to be victimized by police brutality. Everybody who lived the streets of Los Angeles had had his or her share of run-ins with law enforcement officers, and it seemed that things were just about to explode. It seemed that people had had enough. That many people were willing to go to war, an all out war, just seemed to be the logical conclusion of living and being treated as less than human. The brutality had to end, and it was not going to end voluntarily. To me, the gang members were like Moslem holy warriors who were not only willing to kill for their cause but were willing to die for it.

That three separate gangs offered to carry out hits for me convinced me that I was indeed living in a dangerous world. Night after night after agonizing night, I contemplated my options. I wasn't sure what I would do, but I was certain that I would not be content allowing myself to be stepped on. Many of my thoughts were not of killing but fear of being killed. I had unwittingly become part of a world in which respect for human life meant little.

Fortunately, I didn't trust anybody. I was suspicious of anyone offering to carry out a hit for me, fearing entrapment. Not trusting anyone didn't stop me from creating numerous plots. I thought about staging a coordinated attack by the different gangs against the Third Street sheriff's station in East Los Angeles. I was sure many lives would be lost in the process, including my own, but I was convinced I was going to be killed anyway. Street lore had it that something like that had occurred in the past, somewhere in the San Gabriel Valley.

For a while, I checked out the logistics of a bomb or grenade assault on the station via the Pomona Freeway. I even thought about becoming a suicide bomber—crashing my vehicle, packed with explosives into the Third Street station. For a while, I conceived every plot imaginable. The only good thing about all this is that I kept those irrational thoughts to myself, always fearful of entrapment, never trusting anything or anyone.

At a certain point, I ceased plotting and determined to follow through with a legal course. That's not to say that the rage faded. Instead, it was simply channelled into the legal arena. The quasi-rational mind won out over the irrational mind. From that point began a seven-year wait.

Counting the Days

Seven years seems to be a difficult concept to explain. For me, for my case, it's not sufficient to say that seven years was 1979 through 1986. It was much more than that. Seven years equals 2,555 days. If I count from March 23, 1979, to July 31, 1986, when my case was legally disposed of, then it was actually 2, 686 days. If I count to when the last legal maneuver was made regarding my case, then it was 3,091 days. And I could go on and on because something will always surface, whether it's legal, medical, emotional, or psychological. But in terms of actual wait, it was a seven-year wait to get to trial.

In 1979, I was 24 years old. In 1986, when I had my civil rights trial, I was 31. But grasping the concept of time alone cannot adequately give a person an idea what it is to wait seven years.

In my mind, I still believe that if justice had proceeded as it should have, that is, if the officers had been criminally convicted, I would have healed from the trauma that I am still recovering from, perhaps within a year or two after the incident. As a result, instead of prompt recovery, due to endless wait and uncertainty, my mind went through seven years' worth of cataclysmic changes.

Lacking training in medicine or psychology, I am incapable of conducting a psychological analysis of what happened to me as a result of this trauma. Nonetheless, I still feel I can convey, in lay terms, what happened to my mind.

During those seven years, I experienced every negative emotion possible: fear, anxiety, paranoia, hatred, loss of confidence, loss of self-respect, loss of self-esteem, loss of dignity, insecurity, and, most of all, loneliness.

For me, as a Mexican, it was important for me to win to set a precedent. But for me the individual, it was more important to regain my self-respect, my dignity, and my confidence.

More than anything, the seven-year wait was an emotional journey. It was a journey that took me to a bottomless pit. I emerged from that pit, from a world filled with violence, and moved on to a professional world; from the streets to halls of power; from a world where rights do not exist to a world that was unaware of what took place after dark; from a world of lowriding, khakis, and bandanas to a world of suits, ties and $500-aplate dinners; from a world of funerals, jails, and police brutality to inaugurations, speeches, and political promises to cure all evil.

Despite the change of clothes, throughout the seven years there was one constant: the preparation. I was always waiting. And perhaps it was for the best that the wait took so long because at certain points, many times in fact, I would not have been in the proper state of mind to face my opponents. During the seven years, I was in virtual physical pain for almost three years straight. During six of the years, I lived in fear. Up until the time of the civil trial, I was possessed by a rabid hatred of anyone white and anyone who wore a badge. And throughout, I was driven to drinking excessively. Perhaps the greatest casualty was my mind, scattered at best, and, at worst, beset with insecurities that did not enable me to think or function properly. The psychological strain was tremendous. Because I was determined to win on the merits of my case as opposed to my psychological or medical condition, I refused, up until the time of the civil trial, to see doctors or psychologists to treat my trauma.

Unscrambling the Scattered Mind

Five years into the wait, I wrote *Assault with a Deadly Weapon.* Although I wrote it because I thought I was going to be killed, writing it, I believe, is what triggered the recovery of my battered mind. Until then, I hadn't written anything that required analysis since I was in college. Of course, I wasn't killed, but I was still living in fear. Writing released all that had been eating away at me for five years or so and allowed my mind to start thinking clearly again.

At about that time, I began reading and studying in Spanish with a circle of friends. I had to read a lot of material, but more than read, I had to explain my thoughts. Week after week, I felt my mind getting sharper. By then, I began writing weekly opinion columns. All the studying and the writing enabled me to walk into court with a fairly analytical mind, a far cry from the first few years after the incident.

To be truthful, I never thought anything had happened to my mind. At times, I heard people who were close to me describe a person with whom I was not familiar. The person I knew lived in almost constant pain for three years and in total fear for six years. But living in pain or living in fear had little to do with intelligence. The only negative effect the blows to my head created was the inability to recall things and constantly losing track of what I was saying. Aside from losing my train of thought, I thought I was OK. But the person who friends described bore no resemblance to me. Of course, I recognized and still realize that I was in no position to analyze myself, especially while I was fighting my case, but it just didn't seem that they were talking about me.

Prior to any of this happening, I used to like to write fiction. Throughout the seven years, I continued writing fiction. A psychologist friend of mine once analyzed my writing and came to the conclusion that writing fiction, for me, was an escape, especially when I wrote science fiction. She said that I wrote the most fiction, the most science fiction, when I wanted to escape the most, and when I began writing analysis anew, that represented the beginning of my return to normalcy. Although she's probably right, I could not accept it as true, because to my mind, I simply wrote fiction because it was fun and I had nothing else to do. I was, in a sense, muzzled while waiting the seven years because I couldn't write about my case. Neither did I keep a diary or a journal, and that was intentional because, mentally, I could not do that. I felt that keeping notes and keeping diaries and journals meant that the person was intentionally preparing to write a book, as opposed to concentrating on winning. I couldn't do that because, in my mind, I was living an actual life-and-death situation. It wasn't fun, it wasn't exciting, and I didn't enjoy the excruciating pain that had been thrust upon me. And legally, nothing was happening, year after year after year. Turning to fiction, for me, was like a hobby. That's why I never thought anything had gone wrong with me. But despite my penchant for writing fiction, I knew that writing fiction required a different skill than having an analytical mind. In fiction, I created things. I invented worlds no one had ever been to, dimensions that no one had ever thought of. As time drew near my trial, I knew that I would need a sharper mind, a mind that would be able to recall, that would be able to respond immediately and instinctively. For most of those seven years, I did not possess the mind that would be locked in a mortal and intellectual combat.

5 / Conquering the Fear: "The Song of the Quetzal"

As a result of the incident, death threats, and the never-ending harassment, I didn't simply develop a fear of police, rather I lived in fear. The difference between having fear and living in fear is the difference between being hungry and starving, between being cold and freezing, and between being broke and being poor.

At certain points, the fear I lived with caused me to want to purchase a number of weapons—including a machine gun—for purposes of self-defense. The inordinate fear I lived with had caused me to want to protect myself at all times and to fortify my house. I figured, if I was going to be killed by police, perhaps I could take out a few of them in the process. Having seen enough police violence out on the streets and knowing I wasn't on law enforcement's ten most popular list, I feared that if I was stopped and if I was ever killed by a police officer, the weapons in my car, whether under the seat or in the trunk, would be used as evidence that the police killed me in self-defense. I decided against carrying weapons, on my person or in my car, for the sole reason that it would be more dangerous to carry a weapon than not to have one in case I ever needed one to protect myself.

Despite having left the state for a few years, despite quitting *Lowrider* and leaving the streets, five years later, I still feared for my life. I wasn't being pulled over every time I got behind the wheel of my car anymore, yet despite wearing suits, I still feared driving at night. That fear had more to do with my past, but was also exacerbated by the color of my skin. People with black or brown skin, regardless of educational or social level, know what that feeling is.

Five years after the incident, I was editor of a national magazine, yet I still loved to play basketball in the East L.A. neighborhoods where I had grown up. The combination of gang and drug wars placed me in the police line of fire and occasionally exposed me to the dangers of getting caught in the cross-fire.

I was no longer part of that world, but because I determined that police couldn't chase me away to a yuppie health club, I was still able to see how police treated people who didn't wear suits. On the basketball courts, no one wears suits.

I could have left the barrios of Los Angeles, but that was the point. Police harassment wasn't about me. It was about anyone with black or brown skin. I could have left for the safety of the suburbs, and perhaps my fear would have subsided, but harassment of Mexicans and Blacks

172

would not end. That's why I was fighting. That was the purpose of the lawsuit, to put an end to the harassment and brutality once and for all.

Of course, my thoughts were Quixotic, even naive, in believing that I could help end police brutality by exposing it in court, but that's how I thought. The harassment and the fear was simply the price I had to pay.

Sometime in the spring of 1984, while I was still writing and rewriting *Assault with a Deadly Weapon,* the attorney representing me in the civil suit informed me that by the fall of that year we would be in court. After five long years, there seemed to be light at the end of the tunnel. He assured me that by October or November, we would have a decision. In other words, the end of my case. After years of living a tortuous and nightmarish existence, I could not fathom a conclusion to my case.

My feelings of anxiety and fear were heightened by the thought that I would not be permitted to testify. In my mind, I created the scenario that the police would stop at nothing to prevent me from taking the stand, from exposing the brutality of the sheriff's department. All of a sudden, finishing the book and getting it published became a race against time. I figured, if I was going to be killed, at least I was going to let people know why. And that meant finishing the book and getting it published in a matter of months.

When I resolved to write the book, I already knew that Gordon Castillo Hall had been shot, despite publicity, but that did not deter me perhaps because I thought no one would know that I was writing the book. But when the attorney assured me that my trial was set, I assumed that obviously the sheriff's department knew, and somehow I would not be allowed to make it to trial.

Of course it's possible that nothing was planned for me, but it shows what had happened to my mind. I had allowed myself to be overcome with fear; so the race to publish the book became very real. I wanted to have it come out at least three months before going to trial. In my mind, my life depended on it.

The next few months, in the spring, summer, and fall of 1984, became the most tense months of the entire ordeal. Many tense things happened during this period not the least of which was that the printing was delayed for a variety of reasons. I truly believed that the longer the delay the bigger the chances of something happening. Of course, considering my state of mind, I had concocted the theory that the printers had sent the book to the sheriff's department, if not the FBI.

With the assistance of the Presbyterian Synod of Southern California, the book came out sometime in October 1984. And of course, I did not end up in court that fall. The wait was to continue for another couple of years. Though the book projected a scattered mind, nonetheless, it expressed pure and raw emotion, fueled by a desire to express the truth. I was still in fear for my life, but the one thing I was not afraid of was contradicting myself in court. In five years, my mind had regressed severely, but at the same time, I was very conscious that the book could be introduced into evidence. Therefore, everything I wrote was calculated. Perhaps calculated is not the right word; rather, I was not afraid to say anything because I didn't have to invent anything. The incident was engraved in my mind; therefore, when I would get to court, I would be able to recall, in detail, everything that had occurred that weekend without fear of contradicting anything I had written or stated earlier.

At about the time I began writing the book, I met Noemí, a young Guatemalan woman, to whom I owe my sanity today. That individual allowed me to conquer the fear of police.

Of all places, I met her in Venice, California, at a theater in which three movies were premiering. One of the movies was a powerful documentary titled *When the Mountains Tremble*, about an indigenous woman, Rigoberta Menchú, from Guatemala.

At the time, perhaps I was as well aware of the political situation in Guatemala, as was most everyone who was attuned to world affairs. Guatemala had the dubious distinction of having the worst human rights record in the Western Hemisphere. That particular movie showed one of the worst examples of man's inhumanity toward man; it showed actual footage of government troops in 1981, setting the Spanish Embassy ablaze in Guatemala as the trapped Mayan Indians inside were burned alive.

After that showing, everyone in the audience emptied out their wallets and donated generously. I didn't have any money on me, but I had been affected just the same. Outside in the lobby, I began speaking to Noemí. I told her that I didn't have any money but that I would like to donate a fiction story, "The Song of the Quetzal," that I had written recently.

The Quetzal is the national bird of Guatemala. As I told her of the story, she of course was familiar with the legend of the Quetzal, that it can not live in captivity. I told her that I had woven the legend with a story about a little boy who goes looking for the mythical bird which was thought to have become extinct after the arrival of the Spaniards. The truth, so goes the story, was that, in actuality, the Quetzal had gone into hiding in the jungle to avoid being slaughtered by the Spaniards and that now, after five hundred years, it was once again emerging.

After I finished telling her about the story, she liked it, and I agreed to give it to her and the group that had shown the movie. The only thing, I told her, was that it was in English and I had to translate it before I could give it to her.

From that moment I met her, I knew that there was a special quality about her. For about a year, I spoke to her about three or four times, over the phone, telling her that for one reason or another, I had not finished translating the story. For that year, I didn't really know what it was about her that made her special until one day, I saw her at a function. Shortly thereafter, I ended up going to see her at her office with the copy of the story which was still in English. She radiated an aura that made me want to be around her. I thought her political views were those of an astute intellectual. Her thoughts were sharp and clear. More than anything, she spoke with a burning desire to one day see her people free in Guatemala. Soon, I began to go to their group just so I could have the chance to talk to her. It was about that time that I learned she had been a political prisoner in Guatemala and that she and her brother and sister had been brutally tortured by the military of her country. In all the time I had known her, even though our conversations had been brief, I had not once mentioned to her what had occurred to me. All of a sudden, I had a desire to know about her, but I did not know how to go about asking her about being tortured.

In 1976, as a journalist, I had interviewed Olga Talamantez, a Mexican American who had been jailed and tortured in Argentina for 18 months. When I interviewed her, it had been a most uncomfortable feeling, especially since she had been back in the United States for less than a week.

Because of that previous uncomfortable experience, I didn't know how to bring up the subject of torture to my new friend from Guatemala. Besides, I didn't want to interview Noemí; I just wanted to know about her. The reason I wanted to know more about her is because she projected love in her eyes, a love for her people and a fierce determination. Her eyes projected strength, yet they could not hide a hurt, a hurt that seemed to fuel her desire for freedom. I had never seen that strength and determination so strongly in anyone else. I was puzzled, or perhaps, I must have thought that she should have been broken and unable to function. In any case, another few months went by when she called me to tell me that I should go see this movie titled *El Norte* about a Guatemalan brother and sister who escape the repression in Guatemala and come north to Los Angeles. I didn't see that movie for a few months, but after I saw it, I was now more determined to talk to her about it because I had been told that her torture and flight to freedom had actually been more gruesome and more dramatic than the movie depicted.

Because my mental health wasn't improving and because I was still running around in fear, I finally got enough courage to ask her about her torture. I figured that, no matter what had happened to her, it had not weakened her and it had not deterred her desire to see her people free.

As I listened to her, I was spellbound and humbled. She told me that what had happened to her was not unique, that it was happening to an entire people. It was then that I understood the difference between individual suffering and the suffering of an entire people. Individual pain, individual tragedy was part of a larger tragedy in which death, disappearance, torture, genocide, and massacres of entire villages were ingrained as part of the national psyche. It was commonplace for students to witness the kidnapping of their fellow students, the murder of their teachers in class, and the torture of their parents in their own houses. In

Noemí's case, she and her brother and sister along with 19 other students had been kidnapped and abducted off the street by government security forces for protesting for educational reforms. For fifteen days, they were continuously tortured, witnessing the group of kidnapped students, reduced from 22 to 16, with some of them executed in front of their very eyes. The torture was physical, and it was psychological.

When she finished telling me about her trauma, she relayed to me that she had a deep faith in God because, according to her, "there are no political prisoners in Guatemala." The genocide taking place in Guatemala, she said, precluded the need for jails. She stated that she didn't know why they and the other students were released, speculating that perhaps it was because they were only fourteen, fifteen, and sixteen years of age and only for propaganda purposes. She stated that when she was being interrogated and tortured, she was well aware of the fact that no one in her country had ever survived a torture session, that no one had ever lived to tell about it. When they were miraculously released, she stated, who else could she thank but God?

I felt embarrassed at the thought that I had been running around like a scared chicken merely because I had been clubbed on the head and because I had been harassed. When I saw her body, I saw a Guatemalan Indian. When I saw her mind, I saw a warrior who had not let torture get in the way of her desire for freedom, freedom not just for her but for an entire people who had known nothing but continuous dictatorships at the cost of over 100,000 lives and close to 40,000 "disappearances."

She was living testimony, one of only a handful from her country to have survived torture and to have lived to tell about it. Her faith was incredible. Incredible for many reasons.

As a result of listening to her recount the tragedy she and her family had personally undergone, I developed a close affinity toward her. I knew that if anyone could understand my state of mind, if anyone could help me conquer my fear, she could. For the next few months, I learned more from her than I had ever learned from any book. Through being around her, through debating with her, through political discussion, eventually, without thinking about it, one day I realized that the whole concept of fear no longer existed within me. Through her, I had come to understand the meaning of life. Through her, I learned that when you struggle for justice, when you struggle for freedom, when you fight for your people, your enemy can't take your life because you are willingly giving it.

For six years I had been living in fear of law enforcement officers as if I had been a criminal. It was as if I had been living in some kind of draconian society in which everyone's moves are watched, every conversation listened to, and where death and violence are the order of the day. But from that point on, I conquered fear. It left me completely. And to underscore the meaning of conquering fear, I would compare it with having a blind person see once again. But it was more that, because my spirit had been destroyed, my will to live, my will to fight had been at its lowest. So to have conquered that fear at that particular time was what enabled me to prepare for my trial. After six years of walking around in fear of every law enforcement officer anywhere, conquering fear enabled me to confront my accusers. It enabled me to march forward as a soldier in battle, to know that, win or lose, the outcome was secondary, for I would walk into the courtroom and face them with strength and without one ounce of fear.

6 / Racial Poison: Rejecting the Venom

Without question, one of the resultant traumas of the incident was to instill in me an extreme hatred of whites and members of law enforcement. It was a hatred so bitter, so deep that it rotted my very essence. But just as I conquered the fear of police, I also conquered that hatred within me. It took a little longer, but I conquered it just the same.

I had so much racial hatred that if it had been water, it would have been enough to overflow the Amazon, and if it could have been measured in height, it would have dwarfed Mount Everest.

I had so much racial hatred that there wasn't a white person alive whom I didn't distrust. But in my own distorted mind, I didn't think of myself as having hatred; rather, I thought of myself as not only a victim of hatred but as an individual who was responding to hatred. And I didn't think of it as wrong. I thought I had a legitimate right to hate. In fact, I saw my views as not only a normal response but a healthy response.

Racism, it has been said, is a disease. Those who perpetuate racial ideas are diagnosed as sick individuals. What is not normally acknowledged is that the victims of those racial ideas are, if not also sick, at minimum, infected. Generally, when an individual is hated, the natural response is to hate back. It's a different kind of hatred, but it's a hatred nonetheless. Perhaps not every victim of racial hatred responds with hatred, but everyone is affected in some form or another. It is not normal to hate or be hated so that when one lives under an environment full of hatred, it almost renders an individual incapable of producing clear and normal thoughts regarding race and racial matters or anything for that matter.

For years I was filled with hate. It wasn't that I enjoyed hating. It's just that I couldn't recognize it, and I couldn't recognize what it was doing to me. Perhaps even worse, I didn't know how to stop hating. But fortunately, the extreme feelings of hatred I had toward police and white people began to break down a couple of years before my trial.

About two years before my trial, I was asked by a 15-year-old student, Consuelo Preciado, from Fremont High School in Los Angeles, if I hated white people. I had met Consuelo sometime around the end of 1982, when I was working at UCLA. Because she lacked transportation, I had given her a ride to a gallery so she could write a review of a "Day of the Dead" art show for *La Gente,* the student newspaper at UCLA. She was extremely bright, yet her question startled me. At the time, it seemed to be such a ridiculous if not a naive question. I shook my head in disbelief.

"Of course I hate white people," I told her.

Implied in my response was, "How would you feel if you got your head cracked?"

She looked at me as though I had fallen from grace. I responded, "You don't understand. When you grow up—when you learn what they've done to us—you'll understand why I hate them."

I shook my head in disbelief at the idea of how despite her intelligence, the educational system had deprived her of her history and of knowledge. This student was a genius, yet she couldn't figure out why I hated white people.

Perhaps it was from that conversation that I finally got a glimpse of how I, as a victim of racial hatred, had had my normal thought processes damaged. Here was a young, brilliant fifteen-year-old student, proud of herself, proud of her culture, yet not one ounce of hatred resided within her. And I thought something was wrong with her. In the opposite corner, I stood, supposedly full of knowledge, full of pride, yet full of venomous racial hatred.

I remember specifically, at that moment, after speaking to her, realizing that I indeed had been damaged in an extreme way. When I tried to explain to her the reasons why I carried this extreme hatred in me, I realized that the main argument I was using was her purported ignorance. In other words, I was telling her that my knowledge of history, my knowledge about how the world functions, gave me the license to hate. I was telling her that knowledge produced hatred and that as soon as she knew as much as I, she would also hate as much as I.

The thought was abhorrent and it was sobering. I realized at that time that what I was saying could not be right. It wasn't right because if this student who had a pure heart and not one ounce of hatred was taught by me to hate, rather than passing on knowledge, instead, I would be passing on poison.

At that point, I realized that I, the victim of hatred, was as sick as the perpetrators of that hatred. It was one thing to recognize the hatred, but it was another thing to conquer it.

Since speaking to that student, I was consciously no longer attempting to fuel myself with the same ideas that had fueled me in earlier years. I no longer wanted to win because I hated white people or law enforcement. I wanted to win because what I was pursuing was right. At that time, even though I recognized the hatred in me, I knew it was wrong to teach hatred, but I still didn't think it was wrong for me to harbor those feelings. However, little by little, I tried to get rid of my racial ideas. The problem was that the nature of my struggle was very racial. To win in court would have meant upsetting history. So as long as my trial was in front of me, no matter how hard I tried, my fight for justice was equated with racial justice.

The year before my trial, after I had conquered the fear of police, my normal thought processes began to return to me. On a conscious level, through a number of friends of mine, I was made to understand that my way of thinking had become distorted long before I had been clubbed on the head. At the time, many of my friends were from Central America, including Noemí. They knew a lot about their own countries, I thought, but they knew very little about the United States. I viewed them as being oblivious to the racial realities of the United States. I perceived a polarization. They did not. They mixed with whites freely. I despised whites. They saw whites as potential friends, friends who could help them raise awareness about the tragic conditions of the wars in their countries. I saw whites as my mortal enemies, who looked down on nonwhites with contempt. I saw the good ones at best as missionaries, as paternalistic, always trying to lead, always assuming that Mexicans and Central Americans did not have the capacity to lead.

I couldn't figure out my friends from Central America. I viewed whites not only with suspicion but with extreme hatred. To me, my friends were consorting with the enemy, my sworn, bitter, and mortal enemies.

But the hatred I had did finally start to melt down. The year before my trial, I learned that to fight for something or that to fight against something did not require hatred. Up to that point, I had the view that to fight against injustice meant fighting against whites.

More specifically, in my case, the fact that I was confronting law enforcement didn't mean I had to hate law enforcement. I was fighting against four sheriff's deputies. But even more than that, it wasn't a battle against four police officers as much as it would be a battle of truth versus untruth. All my energies had to go into winning the hearts and minds of the jury. There was no time for hatred. It had become a useless emotion.

Throughout most of the seven years, when I was ready to give up, I had been driven solely by racial considerations, and it was destroying me. It was then that one of those friends explained to me the whole notion of hatred as a useless emotion, as useless energy. That friend explained that to hate requires and expends an enormous amount of energy. Essentially, this friend reaffirmed the idea that you can fight for what you believe in without having to hate. Not only that, but not hating gives you more energy, allowing you to use extra energy in a constructive way. This made me understand that hating was a waste of time.

On an intellectual level, I already understood all that. I already subscribed to the theories that white people or law enforcement were not my enemies, but it was a far cry from a theory to the reality that I knew. Nonetheless, as time went on, I came to believe. I struggled, albeit slowly, to cleanse myself of useless emotions.

Conquering the fear of police had taken me six years. Overcoming the hatred of police took a little longer. However, the two were inexorably intertwined because as the fear subsided, so did my hatred. During that final year before the trial, I began to refocus my energies, from hating to a pure desire to win. Although, initially, I had reason to hate police, by the time of the trial, I had not been harassed by law enforcement in a couple of years. As the trial finally approached, this business of hating police wasn't even part of my conscious mind anymore. If it existed, it was buried deep within my subconscious. I not only no longer had a fear of them, but more important, the hatred had simply been part of my initial reaction seven years earlier.

Seven years before, when I looked at myself in the mirror, in the jail ward of the hospital, my thoughts were not whether I was going to get revenge, but rather when. But as the years went by, the bitter feelings of anger had to be repressed because the battle had shifted to the legal arena. And repressing that anger took its toll on me. The endless waiting without a minimal sense of satisfaction caused anguish and sleepless nights.

But the idea of hating police was conquered nonetheless. And I conquered it in the same manner as I had conquered the notion of hating whites. Essentially, I realized that I was emulating behavior that I abhorred. I was emulating the behavior that I was fighting against. Because the police cracked my skull, I hated all police. Because the police were white, I hated all whites. Obviously, I ended up realizing the ridiculousness of my ideas. If I objected to people generalizing, then what I was doing was equally wrong.

My enemy was not law enforcement nor was it the white race. My opponents were four police officers. Their race was irrelevant. They violated their oaths as peace officers, and they violated the sacred public trust. If they were in the wrong, it was they who would be found guilty, not every member of law enforcement or every member of the white race. If the jury could perceive that, then the judicial system would work as it was meant to work.

7 / 1985: After Six Years, Back in the Courtroom

After the dismissal of the criminal charges against me in 1979, I didn't step back into a courtroom for six long years. Interestingly enough, in between court appearances, I never again saw the sheriff's deputies I sued until 1985.

In 1985, after years of complete legal inactivity, I participated in three separate court-related matters. The first was the taking of my deposition. Officially, twice I had related what had happened the weekend of March 23–25. I had done so on March 26, 1979, at the Center for Law and Justice, and I did it again when I retained the services of a lawyer for the purposes of a lawsuit. But the deposition was much different. The deposition I gave in 1985 was for the opposition. I made my deposition to Gordon Trask, the Los Angeles County attorney who was representing the sheriff's deputies. The purpose of the deposition was for preparing the opposition's legal defense. The idea of a deposition, which is taken under oath, is so that the opposition can study the statements for inconsistencies, discrepancies, and contradictions. This deposition in 1985 was taken about six years after the incident, meaning that my memory should have been somewhat impaired. And about many matters, my memory was not only impaired, it was severely damaged. But not about the incident. That was crystal clear. My memory had always been crystal clear regarding the incident and the trip to the hospital. In fact, the whole weekend was crystal clear. I could still remember minute details that took place that weekend.

When I gave my deposition, I could recall every detail effortlessly. When I spoke, when I was questioned, I was not afraid to reply, to repeat things. Neither did I have qualms about elaborating. I know that Miguel García, the attorney who was representing me cringed every time I volunteered or expounded upon a point, but what did I care? I was telling the truth, and nothing I could say would trip me up in court. From my point of view, the taking of the deposition amounted to preparation for my cross-examination when I would take the stand during my upcoming trial.

In between giving of the deposition and the next court proceeding, the attorney asked me to give him a figure that I would be willing to settle for. Of course, the idea of settling out of court after six years of waiting didn't appeal to me. At the time, I was being told by the attorney and other attorneys that my case was worth $5,000, maybe $10,000. It was beyond my comprehension how the figure could be that low, considering other cases in which plaintiffs received sums of millions for less damage. After six years, I had made a habit of keeping abreast of lawsuits. If handled properly, I figured my case would also be worth millions. The idea of settling for a paltry sum or any sum at all turned my stomach. Nonetheless, amid pressure from the attorney, he went to a mandatory settlement conference willing to accept the sum of $25,000.

Not only was I not enthusiastic about the figure, but I was prepared to reject the offer even if it was accepted. The idea of rejecting a settlement had more to do with pride and with a sense that a settlement would absolve the sheriff's deputies from having to account for their actions. Furthermore, it would preclude the Los Angeles County Sheriff's Department from having to answer about its pervasive patterns of police brutality and its failure to prosecute and or to institute corrective measures.

By then, after having waited those long years, I was more concerned with the fulfillment of justice than collecting a few thousand dollars.

At the mandatory settlement conference, the attorney representing the four deputies offered a sum of $1,000 to settle out of court. Needless to say, the offer was not only insulting but it was rejected out of hand. Of course, offering $1,000 was a way of ensuring we would reject the offer, indicating they felt they had an open and shut case. The next step before the trial was the arbitration hearing.

The arbitration hearing was essentially a trial without a jury. Despite the tension of not having faced the officers since the incident, the proceeding took place uneventfully. Had the arbitration hearing been held in a normal manner, the case could have been disposed of within two days. Instead, because of delays and scheduling problems, the proceeding was broken into four night sessions over a span of five months. The proceeding began in February and ended in May. The decision was rendered in July.

At work one day, I received the crushing news from my attorney's office that I had lost the decision. It was devastating news. I was more devastated than I should have been because the significance of an arbitration hearing had not been fully explained to me. When I was given the news of the decision, I thought that was the end of the case. But when I was told that not only had I lost but that I should start looking for another attorney, I was confused. It was explained at that time that, though it was mandatory for both sides to participate in the proceeding, the decision was not binding.

Devastated by the loss nonetheless, I went into a deep depression, and I doubted everything surrounding the case. Though I had not been satisfied with the legal representation on my behalf, I didn't think that the faulty representation would have been reason enough for the loss.

Despite the flaws of the representation, I had thought the weight of the facts would have been enough to convince the judge. In the back of my mind, when we had finished our presentation, I indeed felt the judge had believed our side of the story but that we had not proved our case. Perhaps that was the problem. We just needed to prove the case. Perhaps another lawyer would be able to do a better job, or perhaps the decision had nothing to do with the representation.

Suddenly, at that particular moment, the cold realization set in that, had we been in a criminal court, I would have lost. I would have been convicted, and I would have been writing this from prison. I remembered that I used to think there was no way I could lose, yet I knew that, despite the overwhelming evidence, it was possible. The decision rendered by the judge in the arbitration hearing had confirmed that an innocent person could indeed be framed.

Though I knew the battle was not over, I no longer had the complete confidence that a victory was certain. Now, I knew I could win, but I knew I could also lose.

To win, I wondered, what we could do differently or, rather, since I no longer was going to have the same attorney, what I could do differently? It seemed hopeless. Hopeless only because the illusion I had held onto for over six years was shattered. I really had believed that given a fair trial, I could win. All the jury had to do was listen to the facts, and perhaps that was the problem. This court proceeding had not been in front of a jury. Perhaps with a jury, there was hope.

I could not accept the reality that we had lost. After all the years of waiting, a feeling of hopelessness set in.

8 / Fire from Within: Never Give Up

Even though I did not know the specific date for my trial, I knew that it was around the corner, because after losing the decision at the arbitration hearing, I learned that the next step was the trial itself. Losing that decision was not only sobering, but it placed me in a different frame of mind. First off, my lawyer was no longer willing to represent me. After six and a half years, I had to make a decision of whether to go forward or to give up. Obviously, there was no decision to make. That decision had been made the night I was struck by the riot sticks. It was made the night I lay drenched in my own blood on Whittier Boulevard in East Los Angeles. It was made the night my life was threatened, the night I prepared to face my maker. And it was made the night I lay in the hospital bed with a disfigured face and a completely numb body.

Before the arbitration hearing, I had been guided by a commitment to never give up, but after the hearing, I felt like giving up. Whatever energy I had left was practically depleted. My will to go on dropped to its lowest. The loss had been a crushing and devastating blow. The loss brought on the realization that if I lost this decision, then it was conceivable that I could lose the upcoming lawsuit.

At about this time, I read a book titled *Fire from the Mountain* by Ómar Cabezas, which had a significant effect on my thoughts. Essentially, it helped me regain my energies. It helped me to recoup my mental strength and my physical strength as well. It prepared me for my trial, and it created a consciousness within me of being morally and physically indestructible.

Fire from the Mountain is an inspiring book about Nicaragua. It is an account of the way the guerrillas were able to overthrow the Somoza regime in 1979. The account of the uprising delved into the psyche of a people and dealt with Cabezas's personal transformation, from student to guerrilla, from romantic notions of revolution to the realities of survival in the mountains. More than anything, the book was an account of "the building of the new man," the building of a new society. The book's power stemmed from a description of the process by which he and his band of guerrillas became powerful. At a certain given point, the guerrillas came to believe that they were indestructible because their ideas were indestructible. That belief enabled them to weather the elements, to conquer any and all obstacles they encountered, and it enabled them to survive against all odds. More important, it guided them to eventual triumph.

How they arrived at the mental state of invincibility was due not to ideological beliefs but to what they encountered in the mountains. In essence, what they encountered was themselves. They discovered their strengths and their weaknesses, their many weaknesses. The moment they made the decision to go to the mountains is the day their transformation began. And the mountains were symbolic. When they took their first step, they were ideologically strong, yet they were morally weak. Stated differently, their minds were in the right place, but at the time they did not possess the moral strength to overcome all odds. They did not have the moral strength because they had not yet been tested, had not been pushed to their limits. Up in the mountains, their biggest enemy was not the Somoza National Guard but rather loneliness.

When Cabezas wrote about combatting his loneliness up in the mountains, it struck a chord with me. At the time, the most difficult aspect of my fight had not been the battle against the sheriff's department nor the fear involved but rather the loneliness. Writing about loneliness is somewhat cultural. You don't admit to loneliness even if it tears you apart. And at different times throughout my longest wait, it tore me to shreds. So to read that a triumphant guerrilla, a triumphant people, encountered loneliness in the mountains made my situation somewhat bearable for me, bearable because I believed that, in the end, the rewards would be worth it.

Of all the emotions I experienced in those seven years, none was more difficult to grapple with and cope with than the loneliness. Fighting against enemies is difficult, of course, especially when they have not only a propensity for violence but also a propensity to use deadly force. When I decided to take on the sheriff's department, I knew that I was encountering a formidable and powerful enemy. But at least, the enemy was identifiable and only too visible. It was extremely difficult dealing with the constant threats, the intimidation, and the harassment I received at the hands of law enforcement, but dealing with loneliness was more difficult than any of that.

The principal reason for this is that loneliness is not tangible. You can't see it, you can't touch it. Thus, you can't fight against it the way you fight against an enemy. With loneliness, the enemy is yourself. Loneliness is an internal enemy.

Living away from someone you love is difficult, more so if the separation is forced. It's difficult to describe how I lived for seven years. It wasn't so much that I was forced to live away from a loved one. It was more than that—in my mind, someone was taken from me.

Not to mislead anyone, at the same time I was experiencing these difficult times, it was like Dickens' famous line, "It was the best of times, it was the worst of times." I was partying all over the country, and I was being paid to party. And it was fun! But having fun cannot compare or compete with the feeling of loneliness.

Love, it is said, can be described in a thousand ways. Loneliness, perhaps, can also be described in a thousand different ways, except that loneliness hurts more. Loneliness is perhaps the result of the denial of love. Even though loneliness has a multitude of descriptions, I find it nearly impossible to put into words. All I remember is that I was feeling overwhelmed. Night or day, I felt totally dominated by loneliness. I felt as though my other half was missing, that I was an incomplete individual. Nothing in the world could replace that other half. Partying was fun, romancing was fun, but when all was said and done, I felt a void. That's what hurt: the empty feeling, the illusions, the knowledge that one day the case would end but even then perhaps that void would never be permanently filled once again.

Reading about the way in which Cabezas conquered loneliness, in which the guerrillas conquered the elements, conquered all obstacles, and became invincible was inspiring to say the least. The account of their moral indestructibility is a chapter in human history that would give anyone courage, strength, and determination to overcome any obstacle.

Up in the mountains, according to Cabezas's account, as they marched, the ragtag guerrillas would be driven hard by their leader. They marched uphill. They marched onward. They marched, and they rested. They marched, and they rested. They marched against the elements. They marched with swollen feet. They marched through rain and mud, through insect-infested jungles. They marched when their bodies would no longer allow them to march. At a certain point, the heavily armed guerrillas rebelled against their leader and refused to march onward. The encounter was dramatic, for this was where they finally realized what it was they were fighting for, and this was where they found their strength.

When the guerrillas refused to go any further, Cabezas related, the leader went off by himself and cried. He cried incredulously at their lack of will, at their lack of determination. When he came back, he gave them an inspiring speech that instilled in them the moral strength to once again go forward. Paraphrasing, the leader explained, or reiterated, the cause of their revolution: "the creation of a new society," a society of equality, of dignity. Their society would be one in which the new man would be valued, where men and women would shape society for the benefit of the entire country as opposed to the Somoza regime which benefitted only a few.

He explained that to create that new society, it would require the creation of the new man, and that the new man would have to be stronger, would have to be morally superior, to be able to defeat his enemy. And to defeat their enemy, he stated, they had to build a nucleus of men and women, an invincible army, who were morally superior and morally indestructible, who would have strength when others grew weak, whose minds would allow their bodies to go forward when their bodies would no longer allow them to go forward, who would never give up when confronting a superiorly armed enemy. What was the strength that would allow them to defeat their enemy? Their belief in the new man.

"And where is that new man?" the leader asked, and Cabezas related, "He's over there," the leader pointed. "He's on top of that mountain."

Cabezas related that, though tired, the guerrillas got up and went up the mountain. They climbed the mountain, oblivious to the pain, to the insects, to the elements and went five times further than they had ever gone until they reached the top of the mountain. And when they reached the top, they knew they had become new men. They knew at that point they could not be defeated, they were that invincible army that would defeat the dictatorship. They would defeat their enemy because they had become morally and physically indestructible. They had become invincible.

As I prepared for my trial, that passage of Cabezas's book was engraved in my mind. At times, when I wanted to give up, when fleeting thoughts of hopelessness began to overcome me, when doubts crept in, I recalled that passage. I remembered that to defeat my enemy, I would have to be morally and physically superior.

Thus, I understood that to prevail in court, to triumph, to triumph against my enemy, I would have to be in the best mental and physical shape of my life. I would have to feel strong. I would have to be strong. I would have to walk into the trial not only without one ounce of fear but also with the knowledge that I was morally superior, that I was morally indestructible. And in relation to the trial, I was. I was superior because truth was on my side. There was nothing in the world that my enemies could do that could alter the fact that they could be broken, that their lies could be detected, and that we would triumph.

Shortly after losing the arbitration hearing in July, I woke up one morning feeling a little down and decided to run. When I started running, I didn't know how far I was going to run. All I knew was that, at the time, I hadn't run in a while. After going down the hill a ways, I was going to stop, but I said no. I remembered the passage in which reaching the top of the mountain meant conquering their enemy. As I wanted to quit, I remembered their determination and their will, and even though I knew my legs would kill me in the morning, I kept on and on until reaching the top of the hill. After reaching the top, I nearly collapsed, but I had accomplished my objective. I conquered the hill. I defeated my enemy.

In the morning, I woke with my legs stiff, not wanting to get up, unable to get up. I decided not to run and to sleep a little longer. I was too out of shape to be running up and down hills, conquering mountains and invisible enemies. I laughed to myself at the thought and got myself up and ran like the day before, except a little further.

After I began running, after feeling good and feeling strong, I convinced myself that nothing could prevent me from achieving my objective: getting into shape, into the best shape of my life.

Paradoxically, the last time I had been in superior shape was right before the incident in 1979. At that time, I was doing 300 push-ups and 300 sit-ups. I was running, playing basketball, and a little bit of handball and racquetball. I remember that some time after the incident, after being examined by one of the doctors, he exclaimed that it was perhaps due to my superior conditioning that I had survived the riot-stick attack.

Six and a half years later, as I prepared for my civil trial, I had determined that I would get in the best mental and physical shape of my life. By the time my trial came around, I was not only running but I was working out like I had never worked out in my life. The workouts were exhausting, but the actual physical and mental challenge came when I ran, when I struggled to reach the top of the hills, the top of the mountain.

At times, the ascent seemed insurmountable, but each day I would conquer the hills. Every day, as I conquered the hills, I would feel that I had conquered my enemy. Every day, as I ran, when I reached the point at which I wanted to give up, I would say to myself: "Never give up. Have to reach the top, farther, faster. Never give up." No matter how exhausted I was, I would not allow my body to quit. I would not allow my body to dictate my mind. My body and mind became stronger as I would not allow myself to stop or take shortcuts by running less on any given day. When I began, I was running about half a mile up in the hills of Mount Washington. By the time I received notice of my trial, I was running daily perhaps six to seven miles up the hills of Mount Washington, Cypress Park, and Highland Park. Every day, as I ran farther and faster, I began to feel indestructible. I began to feel invincible.

At a certain point, reaching the top of the hills was no longer enough. I was driven by the idea that I had to reach the top because that's where "the new man" was. That's where the new society was. But each day, as I ran farther and farther away, as I returned to the top of the hills, I was overcome by a new idea. "What if instead of the new man being on top of the hill, what if my enemies are there waiting for me? What if I reach the top and collapse? What if I have no strength to fight them off?"

That thought allowed me not only to reach that top but also to continue. That thought allowed me to persevere. I had to continue running once reaching the top because I had no choice. If I encountered my enemy at the top, then I would need more strength. I would need more strength to either outrun them or to confront them. And so after reaching the top, I continued faster, farther, faster farther.

"Where are you going?" I would ask myself. "To the top."

"And what if they're waiting for me at the top?" I continued.

"Then I'll keep going, faster, farther."

And at that, I would run faster and farther. I ran another block, another two blocks, another mile. I ran on raw energy, fueled by pure desire, on fierce determination and on an inextinguishable will. I could defeat my enemies anywhere: on plain ground, on my run down, on my climb up, or on top of the hill. I was ready for them. Anywhere. Anyplace. Anytime.

When I was set to go to trial, I was five months into my superior conditioning. My mind was strong. My mind was focused. And my body was sound. Whereas in the previous seven years my conditioning had fluctuated, by the time of my trial, I had never been in better shape. At that point, I was mentally and physically strong. I had made myself strong by willing myself to be strong. I convinced myself that victory was within my grasp, that victory was possible if I wanted it bad enough. And I wanted it bad enough. More than anyone in the world. But more than a victory, I wanted a confrontation. Every day, as I ran up the hills, I had a showdown, and each day I triumphed. Not once did I give up. Not once did I allow the hills to conquer me because despite the climb, despite the gruelling wear and tear, I was engaged in a daily struggle for survival, a struggle between life and death. My battle in the hills was not simply a battle of endurance. Instead, I converted the physical battle into one of ideas.

The idea I was fighting against was the belief that I was the bad guy and that they were the good guys. I knew I was in the right, yet law enforcement and the judicial system were attempting to turn justice on its head. I had done nothing wrong. I had never disrespected the law, yet for seven years, I had been forced to prove that it was I who had respect for the law, that it was they who had broken the law, and that it was they who should have to pay for their crimes.

Theoretically, I knew there was a chance I could lose my case, but as I prepared, I did not let thoughts of possible defeat enter my mind. The only thoughts on my mind as I ran up the hills were that it would be a clash of titans. And despite the astronomical odds in their favor, I did not feel like the underdog. Yes, they were strong, but I would be stronger. History was on their side, but what did that matter to me? That's why I was battling them, to put a stop to history. Time was on their side. I had waited long enough. Society? I was there to prove society wrong. Legal precedents were on their side; I was to be the example, the exception. Race was on their side; I was going to prove that justice had nothing to do with the color of one's skin.

No possibility, no scenario had escaped me. I had lived a clean life. I had nothing to hide, no regrets, and nothing to be ashamed of. And yes, they had messed with the wrong person. They had nearly killed me, and they had nearly destroyed me, but they had failed to break my spirit. I would win because I had convinced myself I would win.

When I did in fact walk into that courtroom, I felt morally and physically indestructible. And, in fact, I was invincible, and I was indestructible.

Nothing or no one could defeat me. Not a thousand armies. Not a thousand lies.

9 / Dropping the Bombshell: Two Days till Trial

It was 7:00 P.M. on a Tuesday night, January 15, 1986, when the phone rang. It was one of my brothers.

"Your lawyer called the house. He says that you're set to go to trial in two days. He said he hopes you have another attorney because he's not going to trial for you."

It was a devastating call. It is difficult to convey what I felt as I hung up the phone.

Seven years after the incident, after the longest wait, I was two days away from trial, and I had no attorney. How could it be? How, after all this time, could I be facing this latest blow? It wasn't possible. It wasn't supposed to be this way. It was supposed to be a showdown. It was to have been a classic trial. Countless thoughts raced through my mind, not the least of which was convincing myself that it was real. Reality had arrived. The long-awaited trial was finally here. All the time, all the lonely nights, all the fear, all the wait; and all of a sudden, all the sacrifice was in danger of being for nothing. All of a sudden, seven tortuous years of waiting were going to be for naught. The devastating feeling had a similar impact to the head strike of seven years earlier. A billion thoughts were crammed into a split second. Every possible thought, every possible scenario, every possible ramification, and every possible outcome flashed before me in a matter of moments. I never knew it was possible to have so many thoughts at one time. After momentary shock, a feeling overcame me which was none I had ever experienced. It was a sensation of going into war, of going to battle. Reality had indeed arrived. There was no time for fear. There was no time to panic. No time to be confused. No time for contemplating. Only action.

Prior to that phone call, for about five months, after losing the arbitration hearing, I already knew Miguel García no longer wanted to represent me; however, he was still the attorney of record. In fact, for the last couple of years, he had indicated that I should retain the services of another attorney, but his insistence was never an ultimatum. It was on-again, off-again. Because of that uncertainty, I had been unable to secure the services of another attorney.

After losing that arbitration hearing, Dolores Huerta, the vice president of the United Farm Workers Union, offered her help or rather, suggested an attorney who might be able to take the case. With a strong recommendation from the labor leader, I felt confident the lawyer she was recommending would take my case. Shortly thereafter, I went to see the attorney. To state that the meeting was humiliating would be an understatement. The lawyer let me know, in no uncertain terms, that a lawyer would have to be crazy to take a case like mine, especially when I was but months or possibly weeks away from trial.

I told the attorney that I had no choice in the matter, but beyond the time element, he stated that my case was worth between $5,000 and $10,000. He went on to tell me his opinion of police abuse cases. He stated, as attorney Miguel García had told me, that cases like mine were hard to win, and that if we were lucky and did win, the most we would get would be $15,000. He went on to tell me that he had recently won a $50,000 settlement for a case in which a woman had slipped and fell in front of Beverly Hills High School. I asked him if I'd be better off slipping in front of a school. He said yes. He further stated or rather reiterated his belief that any lawyer who would take my case would have to be out of his or her mind.

"The only reason I'm talking to you is because of Dolores Huerta," he said.

"You mean," I responded, "that if it weren't for Dolores, you wouldn't give me the time of day."

"That's right," he said.

I got up, thanked him for his time, and left.

After that episode, I tried to get a couple of other attorneys to take the case, but the closest I got was one of them saying that he'd consider it only after I brought him my file. He said it was somewhat ludicrous to switch lawyers after six and a half years and right before a trial.

I told him that I had no choice.

When I talked to Miguel García, he communicated that he would not release my file until I obtained the services of another attorney. Obviously, this put me in a Catch-22 situation. Even though the attorney acknowledged this, he did not relent.

How was I supposed to find an attorney who would consider my case if he or she couldn't look at my file? After the arbitration hearing, I also asked Antonio Rodríguez, the attorney who had represented me during the criminal proceedings, whether he could take this case. He said that he was not available because he was in another trial and he was campaigning for City Council for the City of Los Angeles. Regardless, he told me to find the date of my trial and that perhaps at that time he might be available.

Again, I went back to Miguel and reported the situation. Actually, by this time and in fact in the last couple of years, I had little contact with him. The primary contact I had was with his secretaries and with one of his assistants. So when I went in to see him, I was told by his assistant that I would be given a notice of when the trial would be. I told them that

I possibly had a lawyer but it was dependant upon the date of the trial. I was assured that I would be told as soon as they knew. That's what I had been told after the arbitration hearing and that's what I was told again.

For the next five months, I called about every two or three weeks to see whether I had a trial date. Always it was negative. But around December, I received a call from the attorney's assistant telling me that I finally had a trial date but that he wasn't sure when. A few anxious days went by, and the days turned to weeks. I was still not given a trial date. After repeated calls, I was told that he believed it was sometime in January but that he couldn't be sure.

During the funeral of a good friend, Carlitos Vásquez, I ran into Antonio, the first attorney. He asked me if I had a trial date. I told him that apparently I had one but that I wasn't being told the exact date. He restated his offer that if he was available, he'd consider representing me.

Finally, on that Tuesday in January, I received the devastating news. Of course, I was angry. I was fuming. I was angry that the attorney hadn't had the decency to call me personally. I was angry that even his assistant hadn't had the professional courtesy to call me directly. Instead, the call was placed in the evening by the assistant to my parents' house two days before my court appearance.

When I hung up the phone, I had no time for anger. All of a sudden, seven years of preparation had to be compressed into two days. Despite not having an attorney, I convinced myself that somehow things would turn out OK, that somehow, even if I had to represent myself, I would do it.

Instinctively, before doing anything, I called Consuelo, who by then was seventeen and had become a most special friend. She represented the most special person in my life, and, incredibly, by then she had become my best friend. Call it fate, destiny, or anything else, but instead of calling a lawyer or my girlfriend or anyone else, in this moment of crisis, I called her.

At the time, my entire life revolved around waiting for my trial. It was a painstaking wait, never understanding why it was taking so long. To kill time, I spent my free time writing.

Consuelo was also a writer. She enjoyed writing and loved to read. She probably read everything I wrote, including drafts of the earlier book. She had an insatiable thirst for reading, and at the time, I had an insatiable thirst for escaping.

In my tempestuous world, she brought solace to my life. She had a spiritual quality about her that was missing in my life. Ironically, just about everyone I was close to was spiritual. They were always praying for me. I figured, with friends and family praying for me, I didn't need to pray for myself. I not only didn't have the time, I was what one might call, antireligious. For intellectual reasons, for racial reasons, for cultural reasons, and for any other reason I could think of I had turned away from religion. To me, religion was what held Mexicans back. Thus, my simple deduction led me to equate religion with oppression. To have friends who were very religious didn't bother me unless they tried to impose their ideas or beliefs upon me. And perhaps, that's why I allowed Consuelo near me. In time, I shared with her all my fears, my doubts, and my ideas. She rarely spoke to me in religious terms. It wasn't that. It was her innocence and her spiritual nature that attracted me to her. At a time when I trusted few people, I turned to her for spiritual comfort and reassurance, and perhaps that's why I was turning to her now.

On the Tuesday on which I was informed of my trial date, I came face to face with my very essence. On that night and for the duration of the trial, I would come to know what I was made of. Either I would buckle under the tremendous pressure or I would walk into the courtroom fortified with nerves of steel. Seven years had done something to me, and I was about to see what it was. Would I walk in like a warrior, or would I throw my arms up in despair?

When I called Consuelo, I didn't know what to tell her except to let her know the news: after seven tortuous years, I was to face my accusers. She told me to have faith, but at the time I didn't understand the meaning of faith. I didn't know what it meant to have faith. The word was hollow. Here I was facing the crisis of my life, and some naive kid was telling me to have faith. Faith in whom? Faith in what? I had been betrayed. I had been thrown out to sea in the middle of a storm without a life-jacket. Faith? What a repulsive thought. Who was looking out for me? Who had caused me all this pain for seven years? Who had caused the loneliness? The hurt? The suffering? Who had caused me to go insane? Who had caused me to lose everything I had and everyone I was close to? Who was it that she wanted me to have faith in? God? Where was this God when my skull was cracked? Where was he when I lay drenched in a pool of my own blood? Where was he when I was forced to live in terror? Where was he when I was torn away from the one I loved? Where was he now?

I was infuriated at the thought. All the hatred became focused. I was to go on trial and I had no lawyer. Why had I been abandoned? Why? Why in the times of my most critical need did God always abandon me? What had I done? Had I done something wrong when I was a kid? Who had I harmed? Why couldn't I have been spared from the seven years of waiting and from the crisis I was now facing? Why, now when I was at the moment of truth, had I been abandoned? This wasn't a movie. How could seven tortuous years of my life suddenly come to a screeching halt, without that confrontation, without that long-awaited showdown? Is this what justice was all about? As I spoke with Consuelo, my situation seemed without precedent. I knew I could look for a lawyer, and perhaps I could even find one. But that would only bring me to the ring. Speaking to her, I nearly went insane. Taking on law enforcement was difficult, extremely difficult, but I was prepared for that fight. Why was this latest monkey wrench thrown into an already complicated situation? It's as if someone had messed with the brakes on the eve of a big race. Sabotage? Perhaps. But that was the least of my problems.

Again, as I was about to get off the phone with Consuelo, she told me to have faith, to place my life in God's hands. I must have replied sarcastically, but just as I was about to hang up, she stated, "When you go to trial, just remember that I love you."

I was putting the phone down when I heard that. I put it back to my ear and said, "What did you say?"

"I love you."

I froze. For a moment, I didn't know what to say. Of course, I knew she loved me as I loved her because we were the closest of friends, but hearing her say those words shocked me. I responded, "I love you too."

Suddenly I was overcome with a new strength. The panic was over, that is, there was no time to panic. The mental paralysis was over.

After getting off the phone with her, I recollected my thoughts and calmly called Antonio, hoping that perhaps his calendar was clear. Luckily, he was home. I explained the situation. Common sense would tell anyone the reaction to expect from any attorney being asked to take on a lawsuit against law enforcement on a two-day notice. He knew the impossibility, and so did I, but there was no time to quarrel. His calendar was clear, and he was willing to take the case. There was no time for anything but preparation. In terms of crisis and urgency, whatever he felt, I felt it tenfold. Incredible pressure was thrust upon him.

How does someone prepare for a trial on a two-day notice? There were legal theories to deal with. Evidence. Witnesses. Documentation. The list was endless. I cannot begin to relate the level of intensity this crisis produced. From the moment of that initial phone call, I was focused on one thing and one thing only.

Mentally, I was up to it. Physically, I was in the best condition of my life. We were in a crisis, and there was extreme tension, but the tension was directed at one goal: defeating my mortal enemies. Witnesses were hard to find. Some had tantrums. We had little time to prepare. All of that produced an incredible amount of tension, but it was all directed, all focused, on winning. There were a number of major decisions that needed to be made, and during these moments of decision, some tense moments arose, including thoughts we had regarding the attorney who dumped the case, but we had no time to vent out our anger or even think about the guy. Everything else became secondary, a blur. Only the trial mattered, and the trial had to be won.

10 / The Trial: Thirty-Six Days of Irreality

After Antonio agreed to take the case, we immediately went over the record. Because he had handled my criminal defense, he was somewhat familiar with the issues involved in the lawsuit, though seven years had lapsed since the incident and more than six years had passed since we had been in court battling the criminal charges. In going over the case, he had to be refreshed about what had happened on the March 23, and he also needed to know what had happened in the intervening seven years. We went over the case, once, twice, as many times as time allowed. During those frantic days, more than preparation, what we needed was to track down those witnesses.

I would like to say that we devised a brilliant strategy, but we can't make that claim because, with only two days, we were at the mercy of fate and circumstance. To win, from the moment we walked into the courtroom until the last day in court, everything had to go our way.

The first thing that didn't go our way was that we found out that the statute of limitations was due to expire just two days after I had received the phone call. That, of course, meant that we were not entitled to a delay, not even another day.

With that squared away, prior to the commencement of the trial, we had to decide whether we wanted a jury trial. There were two factors to consider. The first factor had to do with money. To have a jury trial meant that we would have to pay the jury costs. Specifically, I would have to raise that money. Of course, I had no knowledge that that was the way justice worked. Jury costs were estimated to be several thousand dollars. Because of the suddenness of the notification of the trial, I was penniless in terms of cash reserves. All along, I had assumed that, because I had signed an agreement with the previous attorney that stated I wouldn't have to pay a penny unless and until I won, court costs would be picked up by my attorney or the courts. Whatever the arrangement had been with the earlier attorney, he was no longer representing me. Thus, if I wanted a jury trial, I would have to pick up the costs. If need be, I had been prepared to raise money for a trial, but in a matter of two days, it didn't seem humanly possible.

The other factor to be considered, which should have been the only consideration, was whether we would get a fair trial, that is, could we get a fairer trial through a judge or a jury trial? On this matter, I received conflicting advice. If there had been no consideration of money, I would have automatically opted for a jury trial. But money was a factor. I wanted a jury trial only because I had thought all trials were conducted with a jury. My arbitration hearing had been held in the presence of a judge only, and we had lost. Though I could end up with a biased jury, I was willing to take my chances.

Many attorneys advised me to go with a judge, but they also advised that it should be my attorney's decision. So, on the day the decision had to be made, I told Antonio that I was willing to go with his choice.

"No," he replied, "this is your decision."

Having only minutes to make the decision, I felt a surge of adrenaline flowing to my brain. One of the most important decisions of my life had to be made, and I alone had to make it. I already knew what I wanted, but the possibility of raising the money instantly seemed out of my reach. Nonetheless, I stated, "Let's go with a jury trial."

From that point on, the adrenaline did not cease. The incredible tension did not subside until the verdict was read.

Surprisingly, after we got back to the office later that day, Antonio informed me that I didn't have to pay for the jury costs after all because the lawyers for the sheriff's deputies had insisted on a jury trial, meaning that not only did they pick up the costs, but I had gone through needless financial worries.

After the decision to go with a jury trial was made, the opposition lawyer made a series of motions to disqualify my evidence, including the color photographs taken of me hours after I had been released in 1979. The photographs were graphic. They were gruesome. Not only had I gone to great lengths to ensure their safety, but I was also careful and insistent that they never be published anywhere for fear that they would be ruled inadmissible during the trial. As it was, their attorney proposed the idea that the photographs would be prejudicial if the jury were to see them. Fortunately, the judge ruled in our favor. With the pretrial motions out of the way, it was now time for the trial.

Prejudicial?

As an aside, after returning to Los Angeles from living out of state, I feared that my assassination was imminent. As a precaution, I gave copies of my well-guarded color photographs to a good friend, a well-trusted friend. It must have been my fortune to find out later that he was employed by a law enforcement agency. I never asked whether he turned in the photographs. I didn't need to. It was just another factor that made me suspicious of almost anyone.

The Charges and the Defendants

The civil trial took place in Superior Court in the City of Los Angeles. The object of the lawsuit were four Los Angeles County sheriff's deputies. The officers were Patrick W. Soll, Gheral Taylor, Paul Rapisarda, and John Galbraith. The charges filed against them were: assault and battery, false arrest, false imprisonment, intentional infliction of emotional distress, and violation of civil rights (a federal statute).

At the time of the incident in 1979, the identities of the officers were not positively known. Their identities were revealed in the arrest report.

On the drive to the hospital, in fear for my life, I had learned the identity of the officers who drove me to the hospital by casually leaning forward to get a glimpse of the names on the badges of the two deputies. The driver was named Taylor. The passenger, the one who had issued the threats, was named Galbraith. I believed this to be their identities for six years.

Six years after that drive to the hospital, during the arbitration hearing, it was revealed that the driver's name had been Rapisarda, not Taylor. It was a startling revelation.

There was no confusion about who the sheriff's deputies were. What was in question was their names. For six years, I had believed the driver's name to be Taylor and the passenger to be Galbraith. Either deputy Rapisarda had switched badges with Taylor, or I had genuinely forgotten Rapisarda's name.

Essentially, if not for the arrest report, I would not have known who to sue. I would have known the identities of only one of the officers, Galbraith. If not for the arrest report, I would have had to go through photographs to be able to make positive identification of the driver, Rapisarda. Perhaps, due to the trauma and the fact that I was dazed, I did indeed forget Rapisarda's name. But his face, both faces of the sheriff's deputies who drove me to the hospital, I have never forgotten.

Besides Rapisarda and Galbraith, I wasn't able to identify any of the other deputies who assaulted me or attacked the guy in the sarape because it was dark and the majority of them were wearing helmets. If only two names would have appeared on the arrest report, I would only have been able to sue two of the officers. Had ten names appeared, I would have sued ten officers. Perhaps they never expected a lawsuit because, inadvertently, in an effort to frame me, they volunteered their identities and ended up indicting themselves by signing their names to the arrest report.

With the names of the defendants known and the charges filed, after the pretrial motions were out of the way, it was time to get on with the trial.

11 / Born in East L.A.:
Selecting the Jury

A Jury of One's Peers

The precept of being tried by a jury of one's peers has always been omnipresent in my mind. Never, however, did I ever expect to be in a courtroom to experience the consequence of this idea.

In 1979, as I faced criminal charges, I thought that either the jury would laugh at the ridiculousness of the charges or the judge would simply throw out my case before it reached trial. The latter happened. Not lost on me was the realization that we could have gone on to trial and that I could have been judged by a not-so-fair jury. Luckily, at that point, my life was not placed in uncertain hands.

In the intervening seven years, I occasionally thought about the composition of my would-be jury, but that reality did not dawn on me until we saw the fifty or so potential jurors file through the courtroom doors. As each potential jurist walked single-file into the courtroom, not one brown face could be seen. Perhaps for cultural reasons, without saying a word, Antonio and I looked at each other, keenly aware of the racial composition of the potential jurists. It was going to be a tension-filled, racial trial. In my mind, there would be no one in the jury box who would be able to comprehend my psyche.

Being that we had but two days to prepare for the trial and due to our crisis state of mind, when we realized the racial composition of the potential jurists, we had no time to strategize.

What would be the implication of not having one Mexican or other Latino on the jury? Would it hurt? Would it help? Did we have a say in the matter?

The concept of being tried by a jury of one's peers applies to a defendant in a criminal trial. In 1986, I was no longer facing a criminal trial. I was the plaintiff. The sheriff's deputies were the defendants in a civil trial. If anything, they would be the ones who would be able to insist on a jury of their peers. The potential jurists who walked through the courtroom doors of the Los Angeles Superior court definitely satisfied that requirement.

But realistically, it was I who was on trial. I had dared take on law enforcement, and in this country, Mexicans don't prevail against white police officers. In fact, no one triumphs against law enforcement in the courtroom. Legally, I had no option. I could not demand a jury of my peers; thus, I was already up against incredible odds. To not see a brown face was disheartening. Before the trial had begun, I had constantly thought about the idea or concept of a fair trial. A fair trial included having an honest judge and an unbiased jury.

Perhaps I had already assumed that the judge would be white, and he was, but I was not prepared for race to be a factor with the jury. The possibility of the judge being nonwhite had not entered into my realm of thinking. The jury however, was another matter. With a heavily charged racial trial, pitting a Mexican against white police officers seemed absolutely biased without even one Latino jurist? Could a jury of non-Latinos be fair and unbiased toward a Mexican?

The trial had not even started, and I questioned whether I could get a fair trial. It was the realization of my worst nightmares. I was going to be lynched if not overwhelmed. All my hopes, all my faith, would be placed onto the hands of twelve total strangers, people with whom I had nothing in common.

Having earlier made the decision to go with a jury trial, we now expected to be tried by a fair jury. Needless to say, seeing the potential jurists walk through the double doors, I began to think that my decision had perhaps backfired on me.

I peered over from where I was sitting and looked at each potential jurist. They looked nervous to me. They were mostly white, yet there were a number of Blacks and a few Asians. I looked and looked. Perhaps one of them was Mexican; perhaps one of them was a light-skinned Latino. But I looked to no avail.

I tried to put myself in the shoes of the opposition. What was the opposition lawyer thinking? Were they on easy street? Was there anything he could do that could work against them? I came to the conclusion that the only thing he could do wrong was show an appearance of racial bias.

As we began the process of selecting the jury, I learned that both sides could each reject nine potential jurists without a reason. After nine potential jurists were rejected, one could attempt to disqualify a potential jurist, but at that point, the reason did matter. A valid reason would exist if it could be determined that the jurist would be predisposed toward one side or the other.

Because the selection process takes place in open court, in front of all the potential jurists, I was conscious that their lawyer, Paul Paquette, could not exercise his option to dismiss the Black or Asian potential jurists. The dismissal of the Blacks or Asians would be interpreted as racial bias by those individuals who would eventually comprise the jury. From that perspective, we had nothing to lose. This could only work in our favor. Because there were no potential Latino jurists, we were not in the same predicament. In a sense, we did not have that same racial pressure on us. In terms of the jury selection process, we were not in a position to be judged as having racial biases, but we did have biases. The more Blacks, the more Asians, the better for us. At least we thought so. So when a Black or Asian potential jurist was called, we crossed our fingers, knowing that their lawyer couldn't reject them.

In the end, eight whites, three Blacks, and one Asian became the jury. The two alternates were white.

But the drama of selecting the jury was multifaceted. There were two other factors independent of race that were critical in the selection process. Whereas the race factor was on our side, we had another pressure that could have potentially worked against us. Just as their side could not appear to be racially biased, we could not afford to appear to be prejudiced against law enforcement.

We faced two situations in which we could have rejected the prospective jurists because of their law enforcement affiliations. The first situation was a security guard. Of course, we thought that he would be predisposed to support law enforcement, but he was Black. With all the white candidates, we took our chances with him. Deep down, I figured that he could be against us, but at the same time, I thought that, given the facts, he would vote his conscience. So we went with him.

The second situation was purely diplomatic. By the time we reached this potential jurist, we had already selected the jury. We were selecting the last alternate. As he was questioned by Antonio, he revealed that he worked closely with law enforcement in a volunteer capacity and, also, that he was or had been an Eagle Scout. We discussed the idea of rejecting him, but I told Antonio that, since he would only be an alternate, we should take the chance. If he remained an alternate, he couldn't hurt us, but more important, if we rejected him, it would send the wrong message to the already selected jury. We couldn't afford that. Besides, I thought to myself, in court, I would later reveal that I had been a cub scout, creating a camaraderie of sorts. We chose to keep him.

As far as the selection process went, we did nothing wrong. In fact, where their side faltered, we shone.

One factor we hadn't considered, but of which their side made us aware, was the gender makeup of the jury. There were nine women and three men. This was not a factor, until their lawyer appeared to treat the women in a condescending manner.

Besides the racial and sexual composition of the jury and besides the law enforcement factor, there was another aspect that dominated the jury selection process and the trial itself. That factor was fear.

As was revealed during the jury selection process, only one of the jurists had ever been to East Los Angeles. One of the women had worked at a job which brought her into East L.A. once a week. Other than her, the jurists had never even visited East L.A. It was an incredible situation, an incredible revelation, that, despite all the talk about equality and progress, for the most part we still live in a segregated society in which the races apparently don't mix, don't even cross the river to see how the other half lives. Their lawyer decided to exploit that.

From the very beginning, a picture of East L.A. was painted as one being dominated by wall-to-wall, cutthroat hoodlums. Gangs, gang violence, and gang murders permeated the courtroom air. For those who had never been to East L.A., the opposition lawyer painted a frightening picture of gun-toting and knife-carrying Mexicans who had little respect for the law or law enforcement. The tension was thick, and the tension was pervasive. How could we counter the picture being painted of East Los Angeles?

Near the end of the jury selection process, Antonio leaned over and asked me if there was anything I wanted asked of any of the potential jurists. Aware of the incredible tension, I told him, "Ask the last jurist if they've seen Cheech Marín's video *Born in East L.A.*"

Antonio looked at me with a puzzled look and asked, "What?"

"All these jurists think that everyone from East L.A. is a hoodlum. If you tell them about Cheech's video, we'll not only break the tension, but they will hear another version of East L.A.," I said.

After questioning the last jurist, as Antonio was about to sit down, he said, "I'm sorry, I do have another question."

He addressed the jurist. "Have you seen Cheech's video *Born in East L.A.*?"

She smiled, and everyone in the courtroom laughed, the other jurists, the sheriff's deputies, their lawyer, and even the judge. "Yes," she responded.

"The reason I ask you is because today you've heard a lot about East L.A. You probably believe that East L.A. is violent and that everybody who lives there is a gang member, ready to shoot and stab each other. If you've seen the video, that's how I want you to think about East L.A. Those of us who have grown up there, who work there, are decent people. Our community is composed of hard-working people. And yes, we love East L.A."

Born in East L.A. was a humorous adaptation of Bruce Springteen's hit, "Born in the USA," depicting the life and the people of East L.A. It was not about gang members but, rather, the everyday people who call East L.A. home. Smiling, cheerful people full of pride. Its plot was about the Immigration and Naturalization Service deporting a Mexican American by mistake and his successful effort to return to East L.A. More than anything, it was light, it was funny, and, most of all, it gave the country a glimpse of East Los Angeles.

Though we took a chance, the strategy worked. Introducing the video into the trial not only broke the incredible tension, but it also accomplished another point. With it, we subtly accused their lawyer of attempting to foist racial myths about Mexicans and East L.A. With the jury relaxed, an advantage went to us.

202

Essentially, there were two views of the jury. Our view and the opposition's view. From our point of view, we would have wanted a racially balanced jury, but once we knew that such would not be the case, we had to proceed with what we had.

That's not to say that we weren't shocked. We were. Perhaps if we were living in eastern Idaho, we could have expected no Mexicans or Latinos on the jury, but in Los Angeles? And it wasn't just that we didn't have Latinos on the jury. What was more bothersome was that there were no Latinos in the entire pool of potential jurists. It appeared to border on the intentional. The jury pool was drawn from voter registration lists; thus, either no Latinos were voting in 1986 or having no Latinos in the pool was simply coincidental.

Faced with this circumstance, there was nothing we could do. We couldn't dwell on the matter. Instead, we made an assessment. Our assessment was that all human beings are essentially the same. There were no tricks up our sleeves. If we lived in a society in which truth conquered over lies, then the composition of the jury would be inconsequential. When something is right, it's right. When it's wrong, it's wrong. What had happened to me was a blatant disregard for my human rights.

If our view of society was that people are basically bad, then we would have felt we had no chance. But we operated on the opposite premise, on the opposite thesis that regardless of race, people are basically good. This is when we realized that the jury itself was on trial. Because only one of the jurists had ever been to East L.A., anything the other jurors thought they knew about that side of town most likely had been shaped by the media. If that was their point of reference, we were in trouble, deep trouble. The opposition's lawyer didn't help as he fanned the flames of their fears. But we decided that, as individuals, regardless of their social/political views, once they stepped into the jury box, their consciences would compel them to shed their biases and listen to the facts. And being unbiased meant fighting against societal views.

As each jurist was selected, as each one took his or her seat in the jury box, in the back of their minds, they were undergoing the litmus test. It wasn't the government that was going to decree guilt or innocence. Instead, they as individuals and they as a group, regardless of whether they had previously espoused biased views, as they took the oath to mete out justice, upon their shoulders lay the awesome responsibility of determining guilt or innocence.

We believed they took their oath seriously. We believed that if they were exposed to the facts, they would have no choice but to rule in our favor.

We treated the jury with respect, with intelligence, and without bias.

On the other side of the table, it appeared as though the opposition treated the jury in a condescending manner and also attempted to exploit their biases and their fears.

12 / The Criminal: Indian in a Three-Piece Suit

As the jurists filled the jury box and as they awaited instructions from the judge, a nervous tension prevailed. Even though the trial had not begun and even though they were not aware of the charges, by the nature of the attorneys' questions, the jury and the two alternates could already sense what was to come in the emotion-charged courtroom.

On the right side, in front of the jury, were four sheriff's deputies and their attorney. Antonio and I sat on the left side.

Now that they had been selected, it was the jury's turn to judge. As the instructions were being read to them by the judge, their eyes focused on me. I imagined their thoughts as they looked at me, an Indian in a three-piece suit. For the duration of the trial, this jury would not only probe my mind and my character, but figuratively speaking, also strip me down to my essence.

As the judge continued the directions to the jury, I became keenly aware that all that I had ever done, the person who I had become since my birth in Aguascalientes, Mexico, in 1954, since crossing the border in 1960, was now on trial. I would have to account for every day of my life, for every move and for every thought. My mind drifted.

Indian in a Three-Piece Suit

I did not visit my place of birth until I was 22 years old. The stars under the sky in Mexico seem to be more numerous than in the United States, the earth richer, the air cleaner, the sky bluer. For the first four years of my life, I inherited something that was to remain with me until I was 22 years old. When I was four years old, my family made the trek north to the land of milk and honey, settling in an alley on Whittier Boulevard in East Los Angeles. Along the way north, we paused in the border town of Tijuana for approximately two years. That is where I received my Mexican education. My only thoughts, my only recollections, and my only relationship to things Mexican up until I was 22 years old were etched in Tijuana. All else was an illusion.

From the time I was five and half years old, a whole mythical world had been created in my mind. At 22, armed with a college education, I believed Mexico was the land of Aztecs and Mayans, of temples and pyramids and of Indians fighting off Spaniards. The images of Mexico were things I had read and things I had imagined as opposed to experienced.

Like most people, most experiences in life are forgotten, yet certain images persist. My first trip back to Mexico is still etched clearly in my mind. On that first trip, I went straight to the world I had created. To the pyramids. Symbol of ancient Mexico. A world that predated European intrusion. Lost roots. Preserved for time immemorial. Ready and waiting for every and all transplanted Mexicans in search of their culture. And that was me.

Growing up in an environment in which things Mexican were despised, the illusion of pyramids was sanctuary. There are few sensations I remember as vividly as my ascension of the pyramid of the Sun in Teotihuacán, just south of Mexico City. Each step up the pyramid took me one step closer to that illusion, that illusion of a past grandeur. When I reached the top, I reached not an illusion but rather a reality previously unknown to me. The feeling was awesome. Overwhelming. It was more than cosmic. For a transplanted Mexican, it was vindication. Every putdown, every insult, every denigration I had ever received or witnessed since crossing the border was now erased.

While one of my uncles waited for me at the base of the pyramid, he probably thought I was going through the motions of a tourist, but he could not comprehend the significance of the pyramid to a displaced Mexican who lived in a state of perpetual conflict. On a cultural and psychological level, I must have been hurting so bad inside that I didn't go to Mexico to simply visit my relatives but to connect with my lost roots, to receive a reassurance that there was nothing wrong with my culture and that there indeed was pride in my blood, in my history, and in the color of my skin.

So on top of the pyramid, I received spiritual fuel and revindication. As fate would have it, upon descending the pyramid, as if summoned by a beacon, I walked over to an undeveloped area and almost immediately found an arrowhead. For a battling warrior, there was nothing like bringing back to Los Angeles an ancient arrowhead to be used in my struggle against those who had made me their enemy. Because the arrowhead became my most valuable possession, I gave it to Barbara, my girlfriend at the time, as a symbol not solely of our shared love but also of our shared determination to hold up the Mexican flag in the face of cultural onslaught. The arrowhead represented a special connection with my indigenous past.

When I walked into the courtroom in 1986, Barbara was waiting for me in the hallway with that same arrowhead. She gave it back to me and told me to carry it with me "into battle." Barbara had been in and out of my life for over ten years, yet there she was, giving back what had at one time been my most special possession. Why did she give it to me? I don't know. Perhaps I would need to grasp for every ounce of strength, and the arrowhead, a symbol, would provide that strength. It would allow me to withstand anything that came my way, would allow me to draw upon all the inner strength that resided in me.

I didn't think much about it, but I put the arrowhead in my inside coat pocket and brought it with me to trial every day. What else did I bring with me? A lot of bitter memories. From the moment I crossed the border, I was constantly reminded by a hostile society that I was Mexican, and being Mexican was supposed to be less than being American.

When I was sworn in as a citizen at the age of 15, I was asked to pledge allegiance to this country against all enemies, foreign and domestic. When this ceremony took place, the Vietnam War was in full swing. I got the distinct impression that I was welcomed in this country as a citizen so that I could promptly fill the ranks of the armed forces and join the multitude of soldiers who were being sent to fight a war in another part of the world. The other and perhaps more lasting impression was that pledging allegiance to this country against domestic enemies meant warring against myself. And truthfully, I was the first casualty of that war. At the ceremony, I was encouraged to change my name. My name Roberto was to be changed to Robert. At that time, I had no option. Not only was it a symbolic rite of passage into this country, but it was also something almost inevitable.

From the day I changed my name, I regretted the action. Of course, I changed it right back.

What other memories did I hold? Still fresh in my mind in those days was the silencing of the journalist Rubén Salazar. Seventeen years after having to change my name and sixteen years after the death of Salazar, I was still preoccupied with racial matters, but I had long ceased to see the need to prove my ethnicity.

But who was I now? Yes, I was an Indian by appearance, but what else? While the jury was listening to the opening remarks, they were subconsciously judging me before I had the chance to utter a single word. As they looked at me, I felt they were not about to make a judgment about an incident in 1979, nor the individual in front of them in 1986, but they were going to judge the character of someone who was 31 years old, dressed in a three-piece suit, who had been in this country for a little over 26 years.

Here was an individual who should never have been in front of them. Everything was the opposite of what it should have been. I was not the hardened criminal projected in their minds. I had been a Cub Scout, a newspaper boy, an excellent student, a UCLA graduate, former teacher, former counselor, and seven years later, at the time of the trial, I had the fortune to have been the editor of a national magazine. It also did not hurt that two days out of the week, I was an intern with the *Los Angeles Times* writing staff. If my attorney had wanted a better client, he couldn't have been found. Nowhere to be found was the East L.A. hoodlum, cut-throat gang-member that Paquette, the opposition attorney, would try to project.

Their side had to take on me and my attorney on an equal footing.

They had to deal with intelligence versus intelligence. They would choose to depict me as a hoodlum, and it would rest with the jury to determine the credence of such depictions.

What if I had indeed been a hoodlum or a gang member, or what if I had been unemployed? What if the same incident had occurred to another individual with a criminal past? Would the odds have been different because the person did not have a university education and a respectable job? As I was conscious of the jury's presence, I was keenly aware that we would be engaged in a psychological war. On the surface, all the odds favored the sheriff's deputies. They had the superior weaponry of societal attitudes. We were combatting not strictly four sheriff's deputies but law enforcement itself. And in actuality, we were combatting society's preconceived notions of Mexicans and law enforcement. Who can say if society or juries will ever be able to judge guilt or innocence based on the evidence rather than on preconceptions of character and or appearance.

As the judge closed his opening instructions, I stood before the jury. This is the individual the prosecution had to contend with. This is the person the jury had to judge. There were no video cameras present at the incident; thus, the jury would be making a determination on guilt or innocence based on the evidence, and they would determine the credibility of that evidence based on who was telling the truth. Essentially, it would be my character and the character of the sheriff's deputies that would be on trial.

13 / Star Witness: Miracle on Ditman Street

The opening arguments went true to form. Their side presented a picture of four officers in distress, attempting to make an arrest, besieged by a Mexican mob, on a highly volatile crime- and gang-infested Whittier Boulevard. The plaintiff, a gang leader, not only urged the mob to attack the deputies but himself ended up attacking the sheriff's deputies with a deadly weapon.

Our side presented an altogether different scenario. Eight or nine deputies attacked an innocent individual. The plaintiff witnessed and photographed the attack. In turn, and as more officers arrived, he was viciously attacked by club-welding riot officers. There were many arrests.

Two versions, diametrically opposed to each other. Who is the jury supposed to believe?

The reason it is difficult to win cases involving law enforcement is not simply because of the attitudes of society but also because witnesses disappear. That is how my trial began.

When people witness violence, they disappear almost instantly. When people witness violence involving law enforcement, witnesses become nonwitnesses. By nature, people would rather not be involved. Ingrained in their minds is the notion of danger associated with being a witness. Normally, the danger is supposed to come from the bad guys. Scenes from gangster movies are ingrained in people's minds where witnesses are shot by Mafia hit men. In cases involving police brutality, fear and intimidation are magnified tenfold. Witnesses who come forward and testify against the police are in the awkward position of testifying against the guardians of peace and justice. Police are supposed to be the good guys. The victims of police brutality are normally perceived to be criminals who deserved the brutality. A witness who testifies against a police officer goes against the grain. The witness stands in the way of the perception that the police officer is the upholder of truth and justice. If the witness convinces the jury, it could cost the officer his job. The witness knows this. To a witness, the use of force by police officers is not a theory. The use of or the threat of retaliatory violence by police officers to maintain their innocence is not a concoction but, rather, in the eyes of a potential witness, a very real possibility. If the person has witnessed police exercise unlawful violence, what is to prevent the officer from using more violence to retain his job, to avoid prison? This fear factor is exaggerated tremendously because the intimidation is supposed to come

208

from the bad guys, and in this instance, it is coming from those to whom we are normally supposed to turn for help.

If by chance a person is willing to come forward in a case involving police brutality, as time goes on, on top of the fear factor, time becomes the principal enemy. Years can drag on, and the perfectly credible (and scared) witness can be discredited due to memory loss and inconsistencies in the testimony that normally occur after a lapse of time.

In my case, I was up against the disappeared witnesses, fear, intimidation, memory loss, and a seven-year lapse between the incident and the trial. What happened in my case was right out of a movie.

Of 75 to 100 witnesses, by the time of the civil trial I was down to about five witnesses, and none was able to testify that he or she had actually seen me get struck by blows by the riot sticks to my forehead. Though I was struck indiscriminately by four or five club-welding deputies, the main damage done to me was a head strike to the forehead that knocked me senseless if not unconscious. Despite the disfigurement of my face and the spillage of a massive amount of blood, without a single witness, in a court of law, it's as if the brutality had not occurred.

During the arbitration hearing, my witnesses testified about what they saw. Though they saw me getting clubbed, none of them was able to testify with certainty that he or she saw me get hit by a riot stick to my forehead. We lost that decision, perhaps for that reason, and when I went into trial in January 1986, in terms of witnesses, I was in worse shape than I had been at the arbitration hearing.

Although we were able to reach five witnesses, we elected to call on four: Kiki, Dina, Rick, and Reyes. It wasn't that we planned it that way or that it was part of a master legal plan. Instead, we went with the four perhaps because we were in a state of panic, looking for other witnesses, looking for the best available witnesses. Of the four witnesses we chose, none would be able to corroborate the head strike to my forehead. Each one saw the events leading up to the attack, but by then, they too were fleeing for their lives. None had functioned as a stationary video camera. None remained in a fixed position to be able to testify that he or she saw everything, blow by blow.

As perhaps could be expected, one can imagine my frustration over the inability of my witnesses to testify about what I had seen. By the time of my trial, frustration was no longer the feeling. In my eyes, perhaps 100 people witnessed what occurred that night. Etched in my mind, I can still see the people in front of me as I was attacked. When I threw the camera so that the witnesses would take the camera and the evidence with them, I remember seeing the camera in midair. I still remember their expressions as they rushed into the liquor store. I even know who they were. One can imagine how it was when I was released from jail to learn that my witnesses had disappeared. To this day, I can still remember witnesses I was never able to track down. There were about eight employees of the liquor store who all supposedly had gone back to Mexico. I remember two girls from Artesia; one of them limped. And I remember their friend, someone from the 18th Street neighborhood of Los Angeles. I remember speaking to him, a year after the incident. He was willing to testify, but as fate would have it, he was subsequently killed in a gang slaying about two years later. I even went to the houses of other witnesses. They had seen everything, and they were willing and prepared to testify. Some witnesses early on had told me of other witnesses. I remember meeting the mother of a witness. I remember some witnesses telling me that they couldn't testify because of their criminal backgrounds or because they in fact were outlaws. Imagine seven years later. Now when I needed those witnesses, when it was now or never, they were nowhere to be found. Ultimately, I had to rely on only four witnesses who would not be able to complete the puzzle. But what a puzzle. The four witnesses corroborated the violence, the omnipresence of the police, the abuse, the degradation, and the attacks. The only thing they could not do is testify that they had actually seen the blows that crushed my skull. They could not attest to the fact that they saw a riot stick make contact with my forehead. Despite that, we were (we had no choice) prepared to take our case to the jury. They would see the photographs of a bright, 24-year-old college-educated individual whose face had been disfigured, face sutured, eyes swollen shut, nose busted, and forehead protruding. They would see gruesome photographs, in full color, of a victim who had supposedly attacked four heavily armed members of the Special Enforcement Bureau of the sheriff's department with a deadly camera. What more did we need? We had truth on our side. Gruesome photographs. A credible plaintiff. But if the arbitration hearing was any indication, what we had would not be good enough. When up against law enforcement, the truth is not good enough. Only a miracle could save us.

On the Saturday night before going into the second week of the trial, I was buzzing with nervous energy. My girlfriend and I were going to go to the Los Angeles Theater Center, and I was late. I came home to my apartment in a hurry to pick up something when the phone rang as I was locking the door behind me. I was going to keep going out, but since I didn't have a recorder on my phone, I decided to pick it up.

The conversation just about gave me twin heart attacks.

It was Dina, one of the witnesses. She was animated. She stated that she had received my book that I had left at her mother's house earlier that morning. She stated, "You're not going to believe this," she paused, "but I took your book down a friend's house, and after seeing your picture, she said she was there. She said she saw you get hit on the head. She saw everything."

I was stunned. I didn't say anything. Could this be real? A witness who had actually seen the whole thing? It couldn't be possible. Things like this didn't happen in real life.

She continued, "She said she saw the cops grab you by the hair, pull your head back, and then they struck you in the head with the riot stick."

She paused again, "There's only one problem. She's crazy." Then she laughed, "I'm just kidding."

At that point, I nearly had the second heart attack. Of all the cruel jokes that could be pulled on me, especially at that time, none could be crueler than to pull that stunt on me. She knew how bad I needed a witness. She knew that none of the other witnesses had been able to say that they saw me get hit on the head. Yet here, she had pulled a juvenile prank, telling me that she had found a witness, only to tell me that she was kidding.

I shook my head. "You know I need a witness. How can you make a joke like that?"

She started laughing again.

"I was kidding that she's crazy," she said, "but I'm not kidding that she was there."

"Don't play with my head," I told her.

"I'm not. It's true. She was there."

Somehow, knowing her, I couldn't get myself to believe her. After nearly all my witnesses had disappeared and after those who had testified had been unable to corroborate the head strikes, all of a sudden, as if heaven-sent, a witness had surfaced. It was something right out of the movies. Right out of *Perry Mason*. A secret witness. A mysterious witness. The idea of a secret witness surfacing after seven years boggled the imagination. It couldn't be real.

"Are you serious?" I asked her.

"Yes, I'm serious," she replied.

"Is she willing to testify?"

"She doesn't believe I know you. She doesn't believe that I testified at your trial."

"Why?"

"I don't know. You're going to have to come down and talk to her yourself."

"I'll do it. When can I meet her?"

"Come by tomorrow, to her house."

"Will she be there?"

"Yeah, she'll be there."

"What about you?"

"I'll be there too."

"Are you sure?"

"I'm staying there at her house tonight."

"She won't mind if I bring Antonio?"

"She won't mind. Come by about noon."

At the Los Angeles Theater Center, Antonio was talking to City Councilwoman Gloria Molina about the trial. I told Antonio the news, and for the tenth time, I pleaded with Gloria to help me in case I lost. She was someone I looked up to highly and the only politician to whom I didn't have to keep reintroducing myself. In a world in which politicians scurried for cover at the mention of police brutality, she was at least willing to listen.

The next day, Antonio and I showed up at the house Dina had directed us to on Ditman Street, in East Los Angeles, right behind Rubén Salazar Park. In the barrio, where she lived, her street would be considered a dead-end. In a suburb, it would be called a cul-de-sac. We approached the house at noon. We knocked on the door and met Dina. She let us in. The witness with whom we came to speak was named Josie. She wasn't in the living room at the time although a couple of other people were, including Josie's mother. Josie's husband came out first. Being that it wasn't Dina's house, the situation was somewhat awkward if not tense. Dina apparently had not told Josie or her husband that we were coming over. Dressed in suits, we looked a little out of place, making the situation even more awkward.

When Josie stepped into the living room. She didn't acknowledge us. Instead, she stared at Dina. In fact, she flipped her off and tried to stare her down.

"Why did you bring these pigs here?" Josie said.

Dina responded, "They're not pigs. This is the guy who's on trial. And that's his lawyer," she pointed at Antonio.

The situation seemed to be somewhat volatile. Josie continued flipping Dina off and began anew to accuse her of bringing the police into her house. Josie seemed more resentful than irritated. We were not exactly welcome. After some yelling and more accusations, I got the nerve to speak up. I knew we were not welcome, but I had no choice. I went to her and practically got on my knees.

"I'm sorry for intruding, but I need your help," I told her. "I'm on trial right now, and, from what Dina tells me, you were there. I know I have no right to ask you, but I'll tell you this much, if you testify, we win. You see, we don't have any witnesses who saw what you saw."

If I was ever sincere about a request, about anything, this was the time. And this request was to a homegirl, a total stranger who probably couldn't care less one way or another, about the outcome of a trial that didn't affect her.

"Look," I continued, "I know I don't know you, and I know you don't have to testify, but please help me win. I've waited seven years, and now it's come down to the end."

I know everyone in the room was looking at us, but I was oblivious of everyone but Josie. It was an incredible surreal, feeling. My fate was

212

going to be determined by someone I didn't know, by someone who 12 hours before I had never even known existed. At that point, only she and I existed in the room. My eyes were transfixed on hers. Our visual contact was direct. Again, I don't know if I had ever had to plea to anyone before, but here and then, I was making the plea of my life. And it was the ultimate plea.

"Please, help me," I said. I was going to say no more. It didn't matter what else I said. She had already stared into my soul. Whatever she was going to do was already decided. No more pleading was necessary. There was a long silence. Only our eyes spoke.

After a few more seconds, with our eyes still fixed on each others', she nodded her head, "I'll do it."

I breathed a sigh of relief, perhaps an indication that someone upstairs was with me.

Josie began to recount the events of the night in question. Her recall was clear. Her memory sharp. It was as though the incident had taken place the night before.

As she described the attack, for the first time ever, I heard a description, by someone other than myself, of what had occurred to me, in chilling detail. I hadn't realized the gruesome nature of the attack. Her description put me into a trance. It made me aware that what had occurred to me must have looked brutal to an onlooker. Her description slowed everything. She described everything vividly, in slow motion. Being struck repeatedly by the deputies. My head being yanked, being yanked by my hair. The blows of the riot stick landing on my head, not once but twice, the second one landing on my forehead, cracking my skull. The repeated strikes after I was down.

As the jury listened to Josie's account of the attack, everyone in the courtroom was stunned, particularly the sheriff's deputies and their attorney.

Corroboration.

Something we didn't have at the arbitration hearing.

As she finished relating her testimony, I was in a trance. I found it near incredible that we had actually found someone who was there, who had witnessed the most critical moments of the attack, and who had actually been willing to testify.

When we met her, I hadn't been sure she was going to make it to court. Nothing had happened to this witness overnight, and she had not backed down. In my eyes, her testimony practically assured us of a victory.

It was hard to believe, but during the eleventh hour, a star witness had surfaced. A miracle on Ditman Street. A miracle in East Los Angeles.

14 / Another Bombshell:
A Second Surprise Witness

Still incredulous over Josie's testimony in court, Antonio and I went back to his office to plot the next day's strategy. We were certain that Josie's testimony had rattled the opposition and thrown their whole defense plans into complete disarray. After savoring that major coup, inevitably, we got to a subject I would rather have avoided.

"You think he'd be willing to testify?" Antonio asked.

"I don't know," I responded.

I froze.

"Why don't you call him and see if he's willing to testify?" Antonio asked.

I stood silent.

I knew he would testify. That wasn't it. I didn't want him to testify.

Josie had been the ultimate surprise witness. She was heaven-sent and every lawyer's dream. Her testimony was the element that had been missing at the arbitration hearing, corroboration.

Before her unexpected and miraculous appearance, I had a trump card, a secret witness, so to speak, who without question would make an impact on the judge and jury, equal to that of Josie's explosive and damaging testimony. It would also rattle the opposition.

This other witness would not offer corroboration, but just as valuable, his testimony would counter the thesis being presented by the defense attorney.

"Why don't you call him?" Antonio again asked.

"I can't," I responded.

"What do you mean you can't?"

"Now that Josie's testified, we don't need him to testify."

"It's not a matter of needing him to testify. If he testifies, they won't know what hit them. They won't know how to react, and there's nothing they'll be able to do about it."

"But I don't want him to testify."

"Why not?"

"I've waited seven years. No one wants to win this more than I do, but I don't want to win that bad."

"I don't understand."

"I can't have him testify against the police."

"Why not? Kiki and Rick did. Dina and even Josie testified, and she lives in the heart of East L.A., in sheriff's department territory."

"You don't understand."

"Even Larry [from *Lowrider Magazine*] and Barbara [my ex-girlfriend] testified."

"It's not the same."

"You think he'll get into trouble behind it?"

"No, it's not that. It just seems his testimony is no longer necessary."

Again I stood silent.

I walked toward the window of Antonio's office to think.

That I was on edge would be an understatement.

I was tense.

Antonio was tense.

We had literally been operating round the clock. We were chasing and finding witnesses during breaks, had been tracking witnesses as best we could, and we had even been going to people's houses at all hours of the day and night to get them to testify. Yet with this witness, there was no question he'd testify, and there was no question about his value. It's just that I was dead-set against him testifying.

After a long silence, I walked back.

"Look, I'm going to trust you on this. If you think he should testify, if you think his testimony is vital, then I'll call him."

"It's not only vital. It's critical," Antonio responded. "His impact on the jury would be immeasurable," he added.

I picked up the phone and slowly dialed the number.

The next day, my surprise witness was seated in the audience until he was called to the witness stand.

"Raise your right hand and place your left hand on the Bible."

The witness complied.

"Do you promise to tell the truth, the whole truth and nothing but the truth, so help you God?"

"I do."

"Be seated."

The judge looked at Antonio. "You may proceed."

As on all the previous days, the environment in the courtroom was tense, though the officers were laid-back as usual.

Antonio stood up and addressed the witness.

After asking the witness his name, he asked, "Will you tell the jury your occupation?"

"I'm a police officer."

The officers, though still laid back, changed their demeanor. They looked at each other and they looked at their attorney.

A police officer testifying on behalf of the plaintiff?

There was a noticeable increase in the amount of tension in the court-room.

The drama was inescapable. A police officer was on the stand, and it was our side who had called him to testify.

Only seconds would tick before the next question would be asked, yet the incredible drama that was unfolding in the courtroom was pronounced. The sheriff's deputies had a puzzled look in their eyes. They looked at the police officer on the witness stand and they looked at me.

"Do you know the plaintiff," Antonio glanced at me.

"Yes I do."

"In what capacity do you know him,?" Antonio asked.

The police officer looked at me. There was a momentary silence.

"He's my brother."

It was as though a thermonuclear explosion had been set off in the courtroom.

My brother was light-skinned, husky, and close to six feet tall. I was 5'6", thin, brown eyes, and dark-skinned. When he had first taken the stand, no one would have imagined there was any relationship. And most of all, no one had a clue he was a police officer. We didn't physically resemble each other, but even more important, their attorney had painted a picture of me as a hoodlum and a gang leader. Now, before the eyes of the jury, before the judge, before the prosecution, and before the four sheriff's deputies was the antithesis of that notion.

The symbolism did not and could not escape the jury.

My brother testified about my demeanor and my character. Independent of what he was saying, his mere presence was sending shockwaves throughout the courtroom.

Under cross-examination, Paquette seemed disoriented and off balance. The psychological advantage must have escaped him, because after my brother finished his testimony, Paquette aimlessly tried to impugn the testimony, but to no avail.

The jury wasn't interested in the attempt to discredit my brother's testimony. The attorney clumsily had missed the point, had missed the whole point of him testifying. The more questions he asked, the more he showed he was incapable of comprehending the damage he was causing his clients. The best thing he could do was accept the bombshell and sit down, which he finally did.

Family Feud

Adding insult to injury, my mother followed my brother to the stand, dropping another bombshell of her own.

The purpose of my mother taking the stand was simply to testify regarding my character and the character of my family.

The trial began to resemble the game show *Family Feud*.

Speaking in broken but comprehensible English, she stated, "We have raised a good family. None have ever been in trouble with the law. I have three sons who are police officers."

216

Even I raised my bowed head. I hadn't even known that. Something had been lost in the translation. As far as I knew, I had one brother who was an officer.

What my mom had meant was that, in addition to my brother, my sister had studied to be a police officer and in fact worked in some capacity in law enforcement, and her husband, the one who had gotten me out of jail ward of the county hospital, had been a Los Angeles deputy sheriff for over 20 years. Technically, my mom was incorrect, but we weren't about to correct her.

As can be expected, my mother's testimony sent more shock waves throughout the courtroom. It was a nightmare for Paquette and the four sheriff's deputies. Their side had begun the trial by trying to paint me as a hoodlum, but slowly, the jury was beginning to get another picture. It was a picture of complete irony.

Remaining silent for all those years was finally beginning to pay off. They hadn't known about my brother, and neither did they know about my sister and her husband. There was more they didn't or couldn't have known about but were about to find out.

15 / Taking the Stand: Reliving the Trauma

It was now my turn to take the stand.

A week into my trial, before Josie had miraculously appeared, as I was tracking down my witnesses in the streets of East Los Angeles, I ran into Ana, a friend of mine I hadn't seen in about ten years. When she asked me what I had been up to, I told her I was in the middle of my civil trial.

"You need to see a psychologist," she said.

I shook my head. "No I don't. What I need is a miracle."

I told her how the trial was proceeding, explaining the tension and the inability of my witnesses to corroborate the most critical moment, the head strikes.

"It's going to take a miracle perhaps, but you're going to need some help regardless," she insisted. "When you go up on the stand, you're going to relive everything." She paused. "If you like, I can recommend someone for you to see. He underwent torture in a Cuban prison."

I looked at her with a puzzled expression.

"Torture is torture no matter where it takes place," she said.

I shook my head. "You don't understand. I lived in fear for six years. I'm not scared anymore. I don't need a psychologist. I don't need medical help."

"You are the one who doesn't understand. It has nothing to do with being scared. You're going to relive everything."

Just then, my friend Jessie pulled up in his Volkswagen.

"This is the guy I was looking for. He knows how to track down one of the witnesses I've been looking for. Catch you later."

As I headed for the car, I turned around and told Ana, "Don't worry about me. I'm OK, and I'll be OK. I'm as strong as I've ever been. I don't need psychologists. What I need are witnesses."

We sped off, with her words echoing in my mind.

Because of the suddenness and shock of having to track down witnesses and having to plan an overall strategy for the trial, I did not think about what I was going to say. In one respect, I had already thought about everything, year after year after year. Everything that had happened that weekend was ingrained in my mind. I had no mental block about the incident. About other things, my mind was scattered, but about that weekend, I had a perfect, photographic memory. Aside from having a photographic memory, I also had my book, *Assault with a Deadly Weapon,* and my deposition to contend with.

I wasn't sure the book would be used against me in court. Nonetheless, I was prepared to defend every word. And in regard to the deposition, I had no fear of contradicting myself. The reason I had no fear of the book or the deposition was for two reasons: (1) I never lied about anything; and (2) I intentionally withheld information in both instances, knowing that if I revealed everything, I would be tipping my hand. The last thing I wanted to do was prepare my opposition for the trial. In everyday life, when you intentionally withhold information, it is wrong. It is tantamount to lying, but when you're in litigation, the withholding of information is not lying. Instead, it is outsmarting the opposition.

I withheld information when I was giving my deposition, but I also did that when I wrote the book. I was conscious of not revealing damaging evidence that would allow the sheriff's deputies and their attorneys to better prepare for the trial. I assumed that, based on what I wrote in the book, they perhaps would try to rule something inadmissible. Perhaps they would even ask for the case to be dismissed. Whatever happened, I was positive that there was nothing in the book of which I was unsure. Besides, the book was more my thoughts about what had happened to me as opposed to an examination of the circumstances behind the incident in question. Nowhere else did I provide details of that weekend. As a result, I wasn't afraid of being tripped up, of being caught in a contradiction.

And in regard to the deposition, it wasn't so much that I withheld information but that I had learned never to answer anything that was not asked. Never volunteer information. The more yes and no answers, the better. The less words, the better. At first, I don't think I did very well in terms of applying that strategy because when I was asked a question, I would immediately go into an elaborate explanation. Only after a while did I catch on that the elaboration was not only unsolicited but also helpful to the opposition. In other words, the less they know, the better.

From a legal point of view, as I prepared to take the stand, I was conscious of both the book and the deposition. Conscious, I was. Worried, I wasn't.

As I prepared for the trial, I was aware of the jury, the judge, and my opposition. In my mind, everyone was on trial. The trial was one of bias. It was racial, and it was cultural. Who would be fair? Who would be biased? All had to be asking themselves if they had any biases. At this trial, everyone's soul would be questioned. Most of all, I knew that at a certain point in the trial, I would come face to face with my very essence.

When this happened, would I stand defiantly and proclaim the blood that flowed through my veins? I knew that at a certain point, I would have to make that choice. In my everyday life, I was pure Mexican, defiant; and I proclaimed it so in everything I did, in everything I said, and in everything I wrote. But I had never been on trial before. Would I be defiant or would I humble myself and pass off as the assimilated Mexican

I wasn't. Or perhaps I was assimilated and the outward appearance, the outward defiance, was but an overcompensation. Perhaps, but I had never been put to that test.

I knew that when I came face to face with the very soul of the matter, it would be in response to a question asked of me. The decision and the answer would be instantaneous. I would freeze up. My mind would freeze, but, in an instant and instinctively, I would find out what I was made of.

When I went on the stand, all my witnesses had already testified on my behalf, including Josie and my brother. I couldn't count on any more help. Now, it was just me.

In a blue, three-piece, pinstripe suit, I took the oath. The moment I had waited for seven years was finally to be. I sat down, looked around the courtroom, not cocky but not submissive. From the stand, the courtroom looked different. The sheriff's deputies, in casual clothes, appeared to be taking the proceedings in a nonchalant manner. They looked disinterested, almost aloof. From where Antonio and I had been sitting, the judge was the imposing figure. From the stand, the jury—not the judge, not my lawyer, not the sheriff's deputies nor their lawyer—was omnipresent. It was the jury who would decide. It was the jury who would determine my fate.

Upon taking the stand, I was prepared for that moment in which I would question my essence, but I wasn't prepared to deal with it on the very first question.

"State your name please," Antonio asked.

With everything on the line, I chose to assert and affirm my Mexicanness by answering and pronouncing my name with a Spanish inflection as opposed to English: "Roberto Rodríguez García."

My refusal to Anglicize the pronunciation of my name and the addition of my mother's name—as is customary in Mexican/Latino culture—set the tone of my testimony and the rest of my trial. By asserting my Mexicanness, I knew it could cost me the trial, but I determined that, even after all these years, I'd rather lose than sell my soul. Since it was an instantaneous and reflexive decision, I didn't think about it much. But when I was asked, my stomach turned, and at that point, I knew there was no turning back. My wait was over.

Being up on the stand was a surreal experience. It was the trial within the trial. Who would win? I was confident, but once that first question had been asked, it was as though I continued on automatic pilot. As my lawyer began to ask me questions, as I began to testify, slowly, I was in a trance. But worse than a trance, I was aware of what was about to happen but was incapable of stopping it.

At the beginning, the questions simply dealt with my background. The opposition lawyer objected to all my answers. I could say nothing without him objecting. My answers bothered Paquette and the protestations of my attorney raised the ire of the judge and also caused him to admonish both Antonio and me. It didn't look good, but eventually, we made it to the night of March 23, 1979. Slowly, my mind began to take me back. I began to recall everything. The sights. The sounds. The cars. The people. The sensation of the Boulevard. The red and blue lights.

Next thing you know, I was back on the Boulevard. But I could see everyone in court: the judge, the jury, my lawyer, the sheriff's deputies, their lawyer. And I could see the audience. But I could sense the Boulevard. The tension. All of a sudden, all was quiet in the courtroom. But I was no longer in the courtroom.

I'm in the middle of the street taking photographs. People are cruising. There are red and blue lights everywhere. Something's going to happen. My body is trembling. I'm going back into time. I'm there again, except I already know what's going to happen. I want to stop. I don't want to be there, but the lawyer is beckoning me, asking me to explain, to paint a picture for the jury. They're chasing the guy in the sarape. They're beating him. I want to leave, but his screams, his chilling cries for help are preventing me from leaving. I'm taking photographs. They're beating him senseless. The deputies are fighting with each other. Another photograph. They've spotted me. They're coming after me. I'm leaving. I want to leave. I'm hit from behind. Four or five sheriff's deputies are attacking me. A black object is coming toward my head. Stop. I don't want to continue. I'm in court. Why am I going through this again. I have to stop.

"Would you like some water?" the judge asked.

I nodded my head.

I was trembling, and I had been trembling throughout. My testimony was coming out of me as if in slow motion. When I could no longer continue, when the judge asked me if I wanted a glass of water, I felt that there were bright lights and television cameras intensely focused on me, and I wanted them turned off. I could see my mom and my brother looking at me. I was aware that they were uncomfortable. I could see my friends. I wanted to stop. I felt weak. I almost wanted to cry out. When the woman in the courtroom brought me the water, my hand was trembling so uncontrollably that I had trouble getting it from her and when I got a hold of the glass, I spilled the water on her. I was totally on the verge of mental and physical collapse. Incredibly, I remembered being in a similar situation a few months before when I had testified at the arbitration hearing. This time, when I thought I could go no further, I drew upon extra, inner strength. As I closed my eyes, the images of three special friends came to me. Each one had given me a special message of strength, of hope, and of courage, in the event I were to break down while testifying. As I closed my eyes, I pictured my friend Reyna. The words she had given me would not allow me to quit. Through my book, I had inspired her to write, and now I could not let her down. My friend Arminda unexpectedly was one of the images. A pillar of support, she was there for me as I had been there for her. And finally, my friend Consuelo. She was faith. She was hope. I regained my composure. I opened my eyes, and I had to continue.

No matter the trauma, no matter the difficulty, I was going to proceed. And I did. As I began answering the questions anew, I was once again in a trance. Step by step I relayed the events of that night. Each step, each explanation created a picture. Slowly, I took the jury through the assault, the fear, lying in my own pool of blood. The degradation, the threats, the imminent danger. The girls looking at me in horror. I took them on that slow drive through darkened, isolated streets. Blood gushing out. Trembling throughout. I took them through the first hospital where I had regretted not making that phone call. Remembering how David Domínguez had been killed by a deputy right after he made his phone call. I took them on the last ride to my final destination where I prepared to face my maker. I could barely continue. I took them through the corridors of the second hospital where my pants left a trail of blood. The collusion. The operation. The wait. The charges. The incredulity. My release.

I could barely maintain my composure. Three hours later, by the time I had finished my testimony, I was no longer outwardly trembling, but I was totally and completely drained. I was trembling inside. Something had happened to me while testifying which had produced a hurt in me, a resentment. I felt catatonic. When I stepped down from the stand, I went over to Antonio and told him, "You know what? Because of what they just saw, I know we have just won the trial, but believe me, it wasn't worth it."

And I meant it. He responded, "I was crying, *carnal*."

"Tomorrow," I said, "you're going to have to help me, you're going to have to coach me because when their lawyer cross-examines me, I am not going to allow him to question my integrity. No way in the world will I allow him to question my integrity."

I walked back to my seat and sat motionless for a time. I could not snap out of the trance. I resented what I had been put through, coming close to breaking down on the stand and being seen in public. I had returned to a place, the last place I would ever choose to return to. I squirmed, I shook, I trembled, I did everything but cry. And perhaps I wanted to cry. But I couldn't. Why couldn't I cry? Because I was strong. Because I could not be broken. I couldn't cry probably because I didn't know how to cry. I couldn't cry because a Mexican isn't supposed to cry. It wasn't fair. Seven years before, my treatment had been inhuman. Seven years later, in court, it was worse than cruel. It was unnecessary. No one deserved to be put through something like that for any reason. And I resented it. And I would always resent it.

What more did they want? More humiliation? No, not for one second was it worth taking the stand. After coming down from the stand, I knew that no reason was strong enough to convince me that the public degradation, the public torture had been worth it. All the years of haphazard healing had been undone. The hurt was tremendous, but tomorrow, tomorrow would be another story. I had fire in my eyes, and I had the sensation of fire burning through every inch of my body, especially in the gut. I was breathing fire. I was determined. All the hatred I had purged myself of had returned, and now it was all focused on their lawyer. Tomorrow, I would tear him apart. I would not give him the opportunity to humiliate me. I would humiliate him. I would tear him apart, and I would tear the deputies apart. My heart had been ripped apart, and I was not going to let anyone question me. How dare the guy even think of cross-examining me, of questioning me? Fire in my eyes, fire in my heart.

I sat there thinking about what my friend Ana had told me. Indeed, I hadn't been able to comprehend her because I had never relived anything before. I had thought that to relive something meant to recall, to remember. I now knew different.

The Cross-Examination

The next day, as their lawyer took me through cross-examination, I snapped at everything he said. As he tried to punch holes into my testimony, I not only repelled his futile attacks, but attempted to play with his mind. My mind, I felt, was superior to his. He was working from concocted stories. I was speaking from memory.

During the break, everyone, including Antonio, rushed to me and told me to calm down. "You're yelling at the lawyer," they said.

"Calm down," Antonio said, "just answer the questions."

"I told you I needed some help. I don't like the idea of him questioning me. Does he think what I did yesterday was for my health?"

"Just calm down and answer without snapping at him," Antonio said.

I was still fuming. Still tense. Still resentful of yesterday. Somehow, I managed to gain relative calm, and to my surprise, I was able to continue to repel his attacks in a more subdued manner.

As a result, he was getting nowhere. Not one opening. No contradictions, no slipups, no discrepancies. He was scoring zero points with the jury. It was a shutout. Nothing he said was going anywhere. Everything I had said was a model of consistency. Nothing from the book or the deposition or my earlier testimony aided him in his cross-examination.

Finally, there was an opening, and I took it. He made a slipup. The slipup was slight, but only I was aware of it. I hadn't snapped at him since the morning so I felt I had to seize the opportunity.

"Mr. Rodríguez, you stated yesterday that you were threatened by the deputies on the way to the hospital."

"Excuse me sir. I did not say that."

His eyes lit up. Everybody in the courtroom raised their eyebrows, including the judge and the jury.

It was a perfect setup.

My answer seemed to have knocked Paquette off balance as he apparently was preparing to drive home a different point. He appeared to be somewhat happy about the matter but also rattled.

"Wait a minute," he said, "yesterday you testified that you were threatened by the deputies, and today you're saying that you weren't threatened on the way to the hospital?"

"That's correct sir."

"You're contradicting yourself," he said.

"No, I'm not."

The judge and the jury were looking at me as though I had finally slipped. They flipped through their notes of my earlier testimony.

Paquette went through his notes and the deposition. He flipped through the pages until he found what he was looking for.

He read out loud from his notes and he read from the deposition where I talked about the threats.

"Do you agree with what I just read?"

"Yes. I said that."

I continued, "Sir, the problem is not with what I said; the problem is with your question. I did in fact say I was threatened, but I was threatened not on the way to the hospital. I was threatened before we even went to the hospital. I testified that as soon as deputy Galbraith opened the door, with the door open, he threatened me. The engine wasn't even running at the time."

I added emphasis to my last statement because I had intentionally outwitted him. I took whatever argument he was going to use and turned it against him in the process, and I did it with a satisfaction.

The whole ride to the hospital had been under duress and under threat—implicitly and explicitly—but literally, only one threat was verbalized. The other threats had been implied; thus, my answer to their attorney technically had been a correct response. If their attorney wanted to prove me wrong, he would have had to acknowledge that his clients continued actions and their other statements had also constituted threats. He preferred not to swim in those waters because doing so would have clearly aided our case.

I could sense the jury knew what I had done, and I sensed that they did not object. In fact, I sensed that they had also enjoyed that episode.

Disconcerted, he appeared unable to return to his original point.

Up on the stand, I had one more opportunity to turn another of his arguments against him. I was enjoying the exchange, not out of mean-spiritedness but rather as a form of revenge, as a form of healing. There was no other way to release my pent-up rage, to express my resentment from the day before.

Throughout his cross-examination, not once had he even come close to tripping me up. The jury had not even once come close to hearing anything spectacular in their defense. No holes. No nothing. Zero.

At a certain point, since he couldn't catch me in a contradiction, he resorted to another strategy.

"Mr. Rodríguez," he stated, "you supposedly were injured, but if that's the case, why is it that when you were examined by the psychologists at UCLA last year, the results don't bear this out. Let me give you an example." He took out a report. "It says here that you scored a 99 of a possible 100 points in the English portion of the exams. If you were injured so badly, how could you have scored so high?"

At this point, he turned to the jury and addressed them. Sarcastically, he stated, "to score a 99 borders on genius. As a matter of fact, I believe that rather than being damaged, it appears that the blow to the head actually improved his intellectual capacity."

Already smarting from some stinging racial remark he had made previously, I was fuming when he implied that the blow to my head had somehow been good for me.

"Sir," I responded, "I did not score 99 points."

He looked at me as though I had fouled up. He flipped through the pages of the psychological report.

Attempting to look authoritative, he faced the jury while addressing me, "It says here that on the vocabulary portion of the tests, you scored . . ."

Before he had a chance to complete his statement, I interjected, "Sir, if you read it correctly, it will show that I scored 99.9 percent."

It appeared that my strategy had worked. His only potential artillery had been taken out from under him. Of course, I looked at him with a straight face, yet inside, I was laughing and he was fuming. Again, I had taken his thunder from him. The jury, again, responded favorably.

He threw his documents on the table and stated, "No further questions."

When I walked off the stand, I wasn't cocky, yet I knew he had gotten nowhere. Had I overdone it? Perhaps, but if I was to get any justice, part of it had to do with regaining my dignity. And prior to that, there had been no other way.

I had almost been destroyed the day before. I had almost broken down. Whereas the day before I had relied on every last ounce of strength, this day, on my cross-examination, it was a complete intellectual duel. And the duel had to be tempered by the knowledge that I couldn't afford to go overboard. Wherever the pendulum had swung the day before, it had swung to the opposite extreme on this day.

Soon, it would be their turn to testify. There would be a thousand ways to destroy their lies. In this case, a thousand lies.

16 / The Trial Takes a Bizarre Twist: The Defense Is Snowed In

After we finished putting on our witnesses, it was their turn to present their concocted case. And after our surprise witnesses had taken the stand, they would be hard-pressed to convince the jury of what they had been alleging all these years.

A Case of Selective Amnesia

During the arbitration hearing, deputy Galbraith, the main deputy involved in this incident, claimed that he had not even been on the scene, that he had not even seen me until he saw me bleeding inside the police vehicle. Other than that, out of about a hundred questions asked of him, he claimed a total loss of memory. Either on his own volition he decided that he didn't remember anything or he was instructed by his attorneys to make that claim. Essentially, he took the Fifth Amendment. His total lack of recall apparently had no negative impact on the judge.

At the actual civil trial, we had a new judge, I had a new attorney, and their side also had a new attorney. This time, we also had a jury.

During the little time that we had to strategize for the trial, Antonio wanted to know about deputy Galbraith, about his demeanor, and about his responses. That's when I explained to him that he claimed zero memory. As the trial progressed, as we continued to strategize, the key seemed to revolve around what deputy Galbraith would do or say on the stand. Perhaps at the arbitration hearing, he could afford to conveniently forget everything, but could he afford to do the same in front of a jury? Facing damning evidence, corroboration, and unfavorable testimony, could he afford to remain silent, or would he suddenly recover from his amnesia and remember the incidents of the night in question?

Perhaps part of his posture at the arbitration hearing assumed that there would be no actual civil trial. Most likely, he was instructed by his attorneys not to open his mouth. But he did open his mouth. He stated that he did not see the incident in question, thus rendering him a useless witness in the civil trial. He would not be able to corroborate anything because he had already stated that he had not been in the area in question.

Based on the scenario painted by my witnesses, he was going to need to remember something or else he'd leave the impression that he had conveniently lost his memory. On record, one of the other defendants, deputy Taylor, had claimed that this particular incident had made an indelible imprint on his memory, that it perhaps had been the most memorable incident in his career. Contrast this with deputy Galbraith who remembered nothing, and a picture of cover-up and contradiction emerged.

The problem for them is that to present a credible case, they were going to need the testimony of deputy Galbraith. That he claimed zero memory didn't mean that he couldn't suddenly and miraculously recover his memory. If he were to remember, it would be permissible. Besides, through a legal maneuver, their attorney could have ensured that the jury did not know that at the arbitration hearing he had a total lapse of memory. In fact, I believed that their lawyer, through a motion, could have ensured that the jury would never know there had been an arbitration hearing. Regardless, to the judge or the jury, the sudden recovery of his memory would not present a problem. His problem would be cross-examination. Based on what I had seen at the arbitration hearing, if indeed he were able to remember anything, it appeared that he would be unable to fend off Antonio's cross-examination. The lies that were alleged on their part would have to be compounded by more lies.

As bad as it looked for them, we determined that deputy Galbraith would hurt them more if he spoke. We determined that he would stick to his story of not remembering anything. Testifying would unravel their carefully contrived scenario. Under cross-examination, the whole scenario would come apart. Thus, we determined that, despite needing Galbraith's testimony, they would rely on the word of three law enforcement officers instead of all four. In most circumstances, the word of three law enforcement officers would be enough to convince any jury, and perhaps with the knowledge of having won the arbitration hearing, employing the same strategy, they would take their chances with deputy Galbraith's silence.

Throughout the first two weeks of the trial, we mulled over the thought of whether Galbraith would testify. Over and over. On Friday of the second week, a most bizarre request was made by their attorney. The attorney requested a motion to postpone the trial to allow deputy Galbraith to take his scheduled vacation to Montana. As the judge listened, he told the attorney that it was a highly unusual request. He denied his motion. The judge told him that this being a civil trial, deputy Galbraith was under no legal obligation to be present, and thus, he did not need permission to go on his vacation. The judge, however, admonished Paquette, telling him that if his client felt like leaving, he should go, but that he would not postpone the trial for him. At this, the trial adjourned until Monday.

Over the weekend, we began to prepare for our response to their strategy. We went over what they would be claiming. We went over the picture they had created at the arbitration hearing.

On Monday, we arrived at the courtroom wondering whether deputy Galbraith had gone on his vacation anyway. When the trial resumed, he was not in the courtroom. He could have been caught in a traffic jam. A few minutes went by. Still no deputy Galbraith. An eerie feeling settled over the courtroom because his absence was very pronounced. The first break came, then lunch, and still no Galbraith. Unbelievably, an incredible scenario was unfolding. It appeared that deputy Galbraith had elected to skip the rest of the trial. Perhaps he had indeed gone to Montana.

He did not show up on Monday. Perhaps he would return on Tuesday, or perhaps they would stall and have him testify last. Tuesday came and went as did Wednesday and the rest of the week. The trial continued. The following Monday came and went, and that week also came and went. Since he had asked for a two-week delay, perhaps deputy Galbraith would return the following Monday. He didn't. The trial proceeded as the judge had stated without him.

Stunned is perhaps an understatement. The effect of deputy Galbraith not showing up for the remainder of the trial had a chilling effect. Was he contemptuous of the jury? Had he gone berserk? Had he left for Montana on his own volition? Or was he instructed to leave?

With the intensity of the trial in full swing, we did not have much time to wonder what had happened, though we surmised one of two things. A possibility existed that he had left the state in defiance of his own attorney, but with the fate of the three other officers at stake, that seemed highly unlikely. The other possibility is that he was instructed to leave.

Only their side knows what happened, or perhaps only deputy Galbraith knows what happened. For us, his premature departure only added another bizarre dimension and heightened the tension at the trial.

17 / Elephants and a Web of Lies: The Officers Take the Stand

On the night I was released from the jail ward of the Los Angeles County Hospital, I was forced to go home wearing the blue, county hospital-issue pants. At the civil trial, we produced them in court, along with my bloodstained jacket. I would have rather brought in my own blood-soaked pants because they would have created an impressive jolt, similar to the effect of the jacket. That I couldn't bring in the beige pants did not work against me because the hospital-issue pants worked even better.

Their mistake that night had been to compound the commission of their crimes by lying about them afterward. Worse was to continue the lie during trial.

During the civil trial, their side did not expect me to come in with those blue hospital pants. The blue pants, though clean, did not physically show anything. What it did was add credence to my version of what had happened. The pants indicated not only a cover-up but collusion between the deputies and the jailers.

Though the blue pants by themselves caused a stir, it was the cumulative effect that caused the opposition additional damage. It was similar to the effect the photographs had. The deputies testified that they had not struck me, that the injury was caused by me hitting the cement. The location of the head injury, which the photographs corroborated, showed the impossibility of receiving that injury by falling. During pretrial motions, their attorney had attempted to have the photographs ruled inadmissible, not only because of their graphic nature but also because they would have revealed that the nature of the injury could only have been caused by a blunt instrument. To have sustained a head injury similar to the one I received as a result of a fall, my nose would have been injured if not broken. My nose was not even scratched.

The tragicomic aspect of their explanation was given to them by me. It was I, who in fear for my life, had told the officers that I had fallen. I said that to them so that they wouldn't kill me while they were driving me around slowly through dark streets. Just because they had forced me under threat and under duress to say that I fell didn't make it true. If I had said an elephant had crushed my skull, they probably would have written that in their arrest report because they employed no logic in the arrest report or in the courtroom.

What could have worked for them is if they had claimed that while in the process of trying to subdue me, it was necessary to use their batons against me and that, accidentally, they hit me on the head.

If they had said that, at worst they might have been reprimanded, and even that is doubtful because they could have claimed that they were aiming for my shoulders but missed as I moved. They would have had to have claimed it was an accident because no law enforcement agency in the country condones or allows officers to strike the head with their batons.

The Prosecutor

The baton or the riot stick, as it is also known, is officially called the PR-24 Monadnock Baton. The training manuals of the Los Angeles County Sheriff's Department are careful to warn never to use the PR-24 on the head or the windpipe. Regulation XVII B states: "Do not strike to the head or windpipe!!!!!!!!!!" The regulations have always existed; however, only recently were they obtained by process of discovery in another case involving the use of the riot stick. The reason of course that officers are warned not to use it against the head is that the tremendous force of the PR-24 on the head is lethal. According to the training manuals, it has three times the striking force of a conventional baton. The manual also warns officers not to call the riot stick "The Prosecutor," which is an apparent nickname given to the baton by law enforcement officers. Regulation XVII G states: "For court purposes, the baton will be referred to only as the PR-24 BATON, NOT THE PROSECUTOR!!!!"

Referring to the riot stick as The Prosecutor lends credence to the idea that in the Black and Brown communities of Los Angeles, the police had become the prosecution, the judge, the jury—and the executioners.

In court, we did not have access to these manuals, though we did know of the prohibition against its use against the head. And though we did not have these manuals, Dr. Arnoldo Solís, the doctor who testified on my behalf described the effects and potential effects of a head strike.

The delicacy of the brain, he revealed, is such that many times damage cannot be detected even by the most ultrasophisticated equipment. When he was questioned about my mental and physical health, he stated that I exhibited signs of not only posttraumatic stress syndrome but also frontal lobe damage. When asked why the tests taken at UCLA the year before did not reveal frontal lobe damage, he chillingly replied that the only way to accurately ascertain if I had frontal lobe damage was postmortem.

More chilling than his assessment was one made by attorney Hugh Manes at a seminar in which head strikes were discussed. "The lucky ones," he stated, "are the ones who die."

The Arrest Report

More damning than the blue county pants, the photographs, or even the medical testimony was the arrest report. The entire document was not only filled with lies on top of lies, but also it was a document that once written and entered into the public record could not be disavowed.

If we had gone to trial immediately after the incident, the officers would have had trouble defending themselves because their arrest report was illogical. But if it was illogical then, trying to defend lies seven years later was practically impossible.

The scenario I had related on the stand was that of a defenseless man in a sarape being beaten by officers. Appalled, the witnesses pleaded with the deputies to leave the man alone. Without much choice, I continued photographing the events that unfolded before me.

On the stand, the three officers told an altogether different story. All three told the same story. They painted a picture of two officers trying to subdue an unruly drug-crazed lunatic wearing a sarape in the middle of the street. They further painted the picture of two additional officers coming to the aid of the two officers in distress, who they claimed were under attack from a group of 10 to 15 Mexicans. According to them, echoing their attorney, I was the leader of the gang.

In their attempts to claim that they were in fear for their lives, they alleged that there were only four officers on the scene. Nice logic until they began to try to explain how police cars were magically being moved around. At one point, while attempting to put the first arrestee in their patrol car, one officer allegedly ran through the crowd and moved his squad car, which was in the middle of the crowded intersection, in front of where the incident had taken place. According to their own testimony, it would have been impossible because the Boulevard had come to a standstill. Allegedly, he had done all of this in 30 seconds. More incredibly, he admitted that the car he moved was not his squad car because he had already testified that his squad car was parked elsewhere. Clumsily, the officer made the assertion that all sheriff's department vehicles operate under a standard issue key, that is, one key fits all. Of course, the fact of the matter is that he did not have to move the vehicle because there were plenty of other police vehicles around. But admitting this would have unraveled their concocted story that four defenseless officers were under siege. If anything, the opposite was the case. It was the witnesses who were set upon and under siege.

The officers' problem was they did not realize that each lie had to be perfect and each added lie could not contradict the transcripts from the arbitration hearing nor the arrest report. Neither could each officer contradict the testimony of any of the other officers. But their lies were far from perfect, and there were many.

One of their biggest mistakes was that the officers testified they never saw my camera. While attempting to subdue the guy wearing the sarape, in fear for their lives, they allegedly decided to isolate me and arrest me. Supposedly, after being isolated, they still had not seen my camera. Once isolated and up against one of the police vehicles, I, according to them, swung my camera at them, attacking and injuring two of them in the process. This magical camera they alleged not to have seen almost killed them. Additionally, according to them, nothing happened while I was being transported.

The key here is that officer Galbraith, being absent from the trial, could not be cross-examined about what took place on the drive from the intersection of Whittier and McDonnell. The other officer who transported me could not recollect anything significant that took place on the drive to the hospital except to say that he thought I was cooperative.

The reality was that, in addition to the lies about what took place and the failure to recollect what happened on the drive, apparently, after I was placed in the custody of the jail ward of the Los Angeles County Hospital, which is operated by the sheriff's department, jail personnel were telling those who called that I had been picked up under the influence of PCP. Who claimed that I was under the influence? If it was deputy Rapisarda, then he perjured himself on the stand. If it was deputy Galbraith, then he was guilty of willfully providing false information to the jailers. And if both or either of the deputies had passed on that false information and the jail personnel in turn passed it along, then they were guilty of collusion. But what if deputies Rapisarda and Galbraith did not instruct the jailers to claim I was under the influence? Collusion was proven in regard to the pants, that is, it was proved that the deputies, by their false assertions, conspired to deprive me of my liberty, and the jailers, in direct or indirect collusion, destroyed evidence and unnecessarily prolonged my stay. It is not entirely out of the question that the jailers, being part of the same Los Angeles County Sheriff's Department, conspired on their own not only to destroy evidence but to hold me unnecessarily.

Collusion in the Jail

During the civil trial, the arrest report was the rope the officers used to hang themselves. Fortunately for us, in questioning my character, attorney Paquette raised the issue of the two warrants that were used to prevent my early release from the jail ward. Apparently, perhaps because seven years had lapsed, Paquette had not been told that the two warrants had belonged to someone else with the same name. The guy was 5'9" tall and weighed 185 pounds. I was 5'6" tall and 150 pounds. The only thing we had in common was that we both had two ears.

When my mom testified, in attempting to trip her up, Paquette asked her why I had two outstanding warrants if I was so good and moral.

Knowing that the warrants were false, we moved in for the kill and contradicted the attorney.

But on top of committing a major error, he followed up with another major and more costly error. After having been embarrassed by attempting to destroy my credibility, he then backtracked and claimed that I had not been held against my will, that I had not after all been forced to raise the bail money for the two false warrants. We were not prepared for this. We didn't think that the issue was in dispute, especially since it was Paquette himself who had introduced the fact that I had been held for the two warrants. His backtracking began when my father took the stand to explain my family's efforts to try to get me released. When Paquette claimed my father had made up the story of having to raise the money for the two warrants, we were left with the paradoxical task of proving that I indeed had been held an extra day while my family tried to raise the bail money for the two warrants. Seven years after the fact, how were we supposed to prove that I had indeed been held on two extra false warrants? Nobody maintains those kinds of records, we thought.

When Paquette questioned my father's integrity, my father unfurled a receipt from his coat pocket for the bail money for the two warrants. It was an incredible scene. I didn't know my father had saved the receipt. I don't even think Antonio was aware of its existence. In an effort to shoot down my credibility, Paquette had shot himself in the foot, not once but twice. Embarrassed, he had no further questions.

We had not even planned to raise this issue until Paquette himself committed the error of attempting to pin me on the same false warrants that had been dealt with seven years earlier. This major blunder went in our favor, compliments of the opposition.

After having heard the deputies perjure themselves, the realization set in that, apparently, though officers lie in arrest reports, they perhaps don't very often expect to have to explain their fabrications. Because law enforcement officers are entrusted to serve and protect, they are also expected to be truthful and honest. Because of that, their arrest reports are taken at face value by society in general and the judicial system in particular.

Los Angeles Assistant District Attorney Stephen Kaye testified at the trial that his office routinely files criminal charges after it conducts an independent investigation. An independent investigation means that they read the arrest report, and if they are satisfied, charges are filed. As shown in my case, it doesn't mean that they go out and interview witnesses or the charged parties. In my case, I was never interviewed by anyone; thus the allegation that an independent investigation or an independent determination was made was completely false. And if that's the way the judicial system works, so too do juries operate. Most juries believe the police version at face value. For these reasons, once an arrest report is written, it is as good as the truth unless someone calls their hand.

And that is precisely what we did. In court, the incredible story they had concocted had to be explained by a mountain of lies. Each lie brought on another lie, burying them deeper and deeper in an inescapable avalanche of lies as their assertions were not corroborated by their trumped up arrest report.

As they tried to explain their version, their original assertion that only four officers had been on the scene is what did them in, particularly because at the arbitration hearing deputy Galbraith claimed he had been away from the action altogether. That left three officers to claim that they had fended off 10 to 15 Mexicans, while in the process of effectuating three arrests.

Perhaps unintentionally, Paquette handed us another major point by allowing deputy Taylor to reveal he was a national karate champion. Their entire fictional scenario was destroyed by Taylor's assertion that he had made all three arrests. He claimed the first arrest was of the guy in the sarape. The second arrest was me, and the third arrest was the guy with the other camera.

Perhaps in their minds, a national karate champion was able to effectuate the three arrests, thereby explaining why they didn't need other officers present. But to their chagrin, they had destroyed their own assertion that a 5'6", 150-pound individual could have injured two well-trained and well-armed officers of the elite Special Enforcement Bureau. After the karate revelation, that idea seemed absurd, bordering on the preposterous.

With the amount of lies that had been aired in the courtroom, there was no way a decision could go in their favor. Their attorney would have to pull a few rabbits out of his ears to win over the jury. As far as I was concerned, we had proved that they had invented the whole story. Besides, à la Perry Mason, we had come up with a secret witness, and on their side, deputy Galbraith had gone skiing in Montana. If Paquette could win this one with an impassioned speech, then he would have to give the speech of his career because we had exposed enough lies to impugn the testimony of all the officers combined.

With their side finished presenting their case and after cross-examination, only the final arguments remained.

The Closing Arguments

Essentially, the closing arguments went true to form. Rather than appeal to the intelligence of the jury, Paquette went for the jugular. Still, after three weeks, he continued trying to discredit me, and in public he insisted on calling me an out-and-out liar. It was a bizarre approach. We knew that it was they who were lying, but we never claimed that in court. We proved it. Paquette, on the other hand, proved nothing, yet contemptuously called me a liar in front of the jury. Morally, he didn't have a wooden leg to stand on. Legally, he had less. If it had begun as a David versus Goliath encounter, by the time of the final arguments, Goliath was on the floor, reeling from a knockout blow, trying to get up, claiming we had used an illegal slingshot.

The slingshot that felled their side was the thesis that Antonio proposed in his final argument: if anything, this case boiled down to the old axiom of the pen being mightier than the sword.

The case was as simple as that. The officers, in performance of their duties, were photographed by a journalist performing his duties. It came to the choice of what society valued more—the unrestricted use of force by a law enforcement agency sworn to protect the rights of individuals or the freedom of the press.

But it was not a debate of absolutes. It was not strictly law enforcement versus the First Amendment. The jury had to make the determination, or rather was charged with making a distinction. If they elected to find the officers guilty, they would not be indicting all of law enforcement. Similarly, if they decided to rule against me, they would not be ruling against the freedom of the press. Instead, they would have to believe the deputies' version that I had used my camera not for journalistic purposes but as a deadly weapon.

In the end, the evidence was in, the final arguments had been presented, and now the decision lay in the hands of the jury.

18 / The Verdict: No Sense of Justice

After the closing arguments, the case went to the jury. It was a Friday. Antonio had hopes that they would return with a quick verdict. So did I. There was absolutely no way their side could win. At the end of the day, the jury was dismissed for the weekend. A quick verdict was not to be. During the second week, the amount of time the jury was deliberating began to worry Antonio. He said that the longer they took, the less chance the decision would be in our favor. I didn't think so. I thought the longer the deliberation, the chances were better that the jury would be handing us a victory. My logic was that if the jury was to vote in favor of the deputies, they only had one consideration, either believing them or not. If they were to decide in our favor, they had to decide the guilt of four separate individuals, and they had to decide their guilt or innocence on five separate charges. Additionally, if they ruled in our favor, they would then have to deliberate on the amount of the award.

As the days dragged on, I became impatient, but my confidence rose. In the middle of the week, the judge summoned everyone back into the courtroom. The jury had not yet rendered a verdict. The judge had summoned us to explain to the jury the way a monetary award was determined, in case of guilt.

Though it was a false alarm, by asking a technical question regarding the awarding of monies the jury signaled that they were discussing award as opposed to guilt or innocence.

Though the judge cautioned all parties concerned not to read into the clarification, I was convinced. It felt it was a premonition.

Incidentally, we ran into one of the officers and their lawyer on the street across from the courthouse. They asked Antonio whether there had been a decision. I thought they should go find out themselves.

Friday came and went. Monday was a holiday. I felt Tuesday would be the big day. Friends and family were there. Additionally, reporters were there. The court clerk signalled that the jury was ready.

Ten days after the closing arguments, 36 days after I had received word of my trial, and seven years after the incident, it was now the moment of truth.

In my mind, I had concocted the scenario that if the deputies were to lose, one of them would go berserk and shoot me inside the courtroom. As we waited outside of the courtroom, when the court clerk announced that the jury was ready to read the verdict, I ran in the opposite direction.

Antonio asked, "What are you doing?"

"I'm mailing a letter."

"Mail it after the verdict."

"This can't wait," I told him.

Because I thought I might be shot in the event of victory, I had prearranged that, as soon as I knew the verdict was in, I would mail a letter I had written to my friend Consuelo. In it were special words for her regardless of whether I won or lost or whether or not I was killed. The irrationality of thinking I was going to be shot only existed because of the heightened tension. But also during the first week of my trial, a defendant in another courthouse had gone berserk and shot his accuser.

I ran to the mail shoot, dropped in the letter, and ran back.

My heart was pounding.

This was it.

Could the impossible happen?

Inside the courtroom, both Antonio and I stood. The jury entered the courtroom. We remained standing. The tension was building. In addition to their lawyer, only two of the deputies were there for the verdict. One of them waited inside the courtroom while the other one waited outside.

Throughout the entire trial, I had taken notes. Here, as the verdict was to be read, I stood with my head bowed. No pens or note pads. After 36 days, we were moments away. The tension was incredible. My skin was cringing. The anticipation was near the unbearable stage. The seconds went by like hours.

My demeanor was calm, but I had arrived at the moment I waited for all those years. In a moment, certain words were going to come out of the judge: "Have you reached a verdict?"

The foreman of the jury would respond, "Yes your honor."

The next words that would be uttered by the foreman would bring a finality to this nightmare. Win or lose, in a split second, it would all be over.

The decision.

"Your honor, we have reached a verdict."

"And what is that verdict?" the judge asked the foreman of the jury.

"We have found the defendants guilty."

Shock.

Incredulity.

There were screams in the audience. It was pandemonium in the courtroom. I could hear euphoric shouts and screams of victory. It was incredible. The impossible had occurred.

Victory.

I did not react.

I could not react.

My head remained bowed.

The jury award came to $204,500.

I still did not react.

I was overcome by a feeling of irreality.

Antonio spoke with the jury, then with the media. Outside the court-room, everyone was in a state of euphoria. The end of the nightmare had finally come. Against impossible odds, we had triumphed. Amid high drama and incredible tension, we had persevered.

Despite the monumental nature of the victory, I couldn't smile. Per-haps I wanted to cry, but I couldn't cry either.

In celebrating the victory, Antonio jumped in the air, clicked his heels, and shouted. My family was overcome with joy. My friends whooped it up.

It was truly an incredulous scene. I could not believe it. Year after year after year had finally come to this. The wait was over, and the trial was over. The verdict: good triumphed over evil. I was happy that we had won, but because of the draining and traumatizing nature of the trial, I wished at that moment that the whole thing had never taken place. Be-sides, what was money? Instead of getting money, I rather they were heading to San Quentin.

Perhaps at that moment, I also felt bitter. I felt the money was like a bribe. Take the money, and forget about the matter. Justice has been tendered, but it hadn't been served.

My self-respect had no price. Yet in exchange for $204,500, I was supposed to get happy because I had won. Yet they still walked free. Perhaps in time I would appreciate the victory, but at this particular time outside of the courtroom, I wondered if justice had really been served.

19 / Freedom of the Press: The Pen Is Mightier Than the Sword

For us to have won, about 15 major things had to have happened. Nothing short of watching an old *Perry Mason* episode could have prepared us for the incredible tension and the unexpected drama that unfolded.

When the first lawyer abandoned the case, Antonio came through. If he had been tied up in another trial, because of the expiration of the statute of limitations, perhaps I would have petitioned the court to put the case on by myself. Of course, if an individual can represent himself in a criminal court, most likely it can also be done in a civil court. Who can tell whether I would have won had the other attorney taken the case to the end?

The difference between the two lawyers is that one of them listened to me and the other one did not.

During the arbitration hearing, every time I spotted a discrepancy or an inconsistency, I passed a note to the attorney. Nine out of ten times, he ignored the note. He treated the notes as though I was interfering with his case. Well, of course, it wasn't his case.

On the other hand, during the actual civil trial, I must have passed Antonio well over 100 notes. Not one was ignored. For obvious reasons, he knew that, if anyone knew what was right or wrong or inconsistent, I did, because not only was I the plaintiff but I also represented continuity. From the beginning, attorneys had changed, judges had changed, witnesses had come and gone, and in the end, I was still there. For me, to be on top of the case was self-preservation. For Antonio to take my suggestions meant trusting someone who was not trained in the legal profession but who, as a journalist, was competent enough to assist in the trial. For all the stories I had ever done, for all the interviews I had ever conducted, I don't think I ever took as many notes as at the trial. I filled quite a number of legal pads with notes. From the moment we stepped into the courtroom until the final arguments were presented, I jotted down everything. The only missing notes were of my own testimony. I took the notes for two reasons. One was because had I been nervous or anxious, and the writing allowed me to concentrate strictly on the testimony. For me, there were no distractions. The other reason I took notes is that we based our entire strategy, our cross-examination, on Antonio's and my notes. Essentially, as Antonio questioned or cross-examined the witnesses, every word was being taken down. Immediately, we were processing the notes for the purposes of inconsistencies and contradictions.

As I took down the notes, I was not self-conscious about my actions. Yet at times, I would look at the deputies and notice that they were very casual about the whole proceedings. At times, they looked bored and inattentive. I thought about the jury and the images. Before them, they saw a marked contrast between plaintiff and defendants. I was attentive not for the purposes of image but rather because my life depended on it.

In contrasting the two attorneys who represented me, there was a night-and-day difference. I still wonder why the first attorney abandoned the case. Of course I know the reasons he told me and the reasons he told Antonio, but regardless of the explanation given, it is doubtful that another attorney in his shoes would have done the same. Whatever the reasons, his dropping the case created and added the tremendous tension in and out of the courtroom for those 36 days.

Then, as now, I think that perhaps it worked out for the best. Even if we had planned the perfect trial, even if we had devised the perfect strategy, it is doubtful that we could have improved on our chances because the incredible drama occurred unexpectedly. Who could have anticipated our star witness or the sudden disappearance of the main deputy from the trial? Who could have predicted that their attorney would not have been aware that the false warrants had not been mine and that he would attempt to use them against me seven years later? How could we have known that one of the deputies had been a national karate champion? One by one, from denying the motion to dismiss the photographs as inadmissible evidence to the selection of the jury to the medical testimony from our side, everything went our way.

Besides most everything going our way, perhaps the single biggest factor in the trial tilting it in our favor is that perhaps the opposition expected to convince the jury that law enforcement pitted against an uneducated Mexican gang member would prevail.

The attitude of the opposition was not only casual but pompous, bordering on contemptuous. It was almost as though they felt it was undignified for law enforcement officers to have to explain their actions. Whether they wanted to or not, they indeed were compelled to explain their actions except for the one who chose to leave in the middle of the trial.

For myself, it was a very expensive lesson in democracy. But more than myself, for all the witnesses, for family and friends who attended the trial, who saw the judicial system at work, it was an experience that won't soon be forgotten.

Freedom of the Press

Though the trial did not focus on the issue of the First Amendment, in the end, the issue was omnipresent as the case came to its conclusion. That the First Amendment issue was not pursued, I suppose, was an error by the original attorney because he apparently failed to comprehend the significance of fighting for the right of a journalist to perform his duties. Had the issue been pursued, a corollary issue on top of violation of the First Amendment would have been the destruction of evidence and the willful conspiracy to obstruct justice.

My personal thought on the matter is that my original lawyer, as well as the deputies, did not comprehend what the deputies did in a legal sense. That the deputies assaulted me and destroyed my film can be understood within the context of self-preservation. If the film had been developed, it might have put them behind bars. At minimum, it would have cost them their jobs. To this day, still etched in my mind is the brutal attack on that defenseless man in the sarape.

The mistake they made was in claiming that the camera had been used as a weapon. The symbolism did not escape the jury. It was classic. The camera as a weapon—as a recorder of history—is truly a dangerous weapon.

20 / God on My Side: The Cross and the Arrowhead

Regardless of whether or not people are religious, when they are at their lowest, in times of deepest crises, they find themselves on their knees, praying for guidance, for strength, and, in essence, placing themselves at the mercy of whomever they believe resides up above.

In life-and-death situations, most people would probably do that.

Not me.

At least I wouldn't have expected myself to have reacted in that manner. But I did. Twice.

The first time was when I thought the sheriff's deputies were "going to finish the job." The second time was throughout the trial.

After I received the news of my pending trial and after calling my friend Consuelo for strength and reassurance, for the next 36 days I went to church every day, even if only for a few seconds of silent prayer. I hadn't hung up the phone thinking, OK, now I'm going to have faith, and tomorrow morning I'm going to go to church. I didn't think that. It just happened. When I went to my parents' house in the morning, my mom gave me a cross. I took it halfheartedly, but I couldn't reject it because it was the cross my family had prayed with when my dad almost died of a heart attack. On the first day of my trial, it was in the coat pocket of my suit. It was also in my coat pocket on the second, third, and every day for the duration of the trial.

The whole trial was surreal, intense, and a blur. Perhaps I experienced every emotion possible except one, fear. Even though I was facing the officers who had attempted to kill me seven years earlier, the same officers who had threatened to finish the job, fear did not enter my mind until one Sunday morning.

Entering the third week of the trial, I woke up that Sunday ill at ease. This morning was different from the previous mornings since the trial had begun. The intensity of the trial had unexpectedly caught up with me. I had been going round the clock on little sleep, little food, and for the most part, on raw nervous energy.

The night before, one of my brothers told me that my brother-in-law called to tell me to be careful because he had had a dream in which I had been killed by sheriff's deputies. When my brother began to explain the dream, I told him, "Keep the dream to yourself. That's the last thing I need to hear right now."

"But," my brother started.

I didn't let my brother continue, "I don't want to hear it."

Perhaps being told of that dream caused me to be overcome with a certain emotion with which I was extremely familiar: fear. For the first two weeks of the trial, I was oblivious to everything except what was being said in court. I took notes on everything. While the trial was in progress, I was being told by friends and witnesses that the four deputies and their lawyer were trying to intimidate them inside and outside of the courtroom. I didn't pay much attention except to say to my friends and witnesses that their intimidation would work in our favor because the jury had nothing to do but listen, look, and observe.

Perhaps the fear that Sunday morning was a natural reaction, albeit delayed. Whatever the cause, all of a sudden, I became frantic.

I believed that every one of my moves was being watched. My calls were being monitored. A contract had been placed on my life, and today was when it was going to be executed. I went to church. That still didn't calm my nerves. In fact, it had the opposite effect. Usually when I went to church, there was nobody there, but today, being Sunday, it was teeming with churchgoers. I couldn't pray. I couldn't find solace or sanctuary there. I left. Again, I was being watched. There were squad cars everywhere. All of a sudden, the imaginary became real. A squad car pulled up behind me. Without hesitation, I pulled over. The police car kept going. I had become unnerved. I didn't know what to do. What a time for the fear I used to know, to return.

After having lived in fear, and after having conquered it, I would still get scared once in a while, but there was a world of difference between getting scared and living in fear. At the moment, as I was driving down Whittier Boulevard in the town of Whittier going toward East L.A., I had become overwhelmed with that fear. I was trembling. I was going to be shot. Where? I wasn't sure. Neither was I sure when. But I decided that by nightfall I'd be home so that if I made it to my house on Mount Washington, at least I'd be killed at home as opposed to on some unfamiliar hill or isolated road where no one would be able to witness.

Regardless of what had triggered this fear, driving down Whittier Boulevard, my body and mind began to return to the nightmarish reality I had already conquered. As I drove, I could not think straight as the intensity of the fear heightened. I was driving down Whittier Boulevard because I wanted to get my car washed at a lot near the corner of Whittier and Atlantic in East Los Angeles. I was accustomed to getting it washed there because a lot of clubs on the East Side would hold car washes there every Sunday.

When I got to the lot, I didn't recognize this group of car washers. Immediately, I suspected they were fake. They appeared to me to be a strange group of teenaged kids. Normally, it was Garfield High School cheerleaders or the Garfield band or even a car club or another school, but on this Sunday, this group of kids did not look normal. In fact, I thought they were weird. They didn't seem to be a club. I nervously parked my car. I walked away feeling like I was being watched and like these kids were plants. As I waited for the cars to be washed, some of the weird looking kids kept going to the side street. As nervous as I was, I walked on the sidewalk to see why they kept going back and forth. Parked on the side was a sheriff's car. I froze. The little kids were junior narcs! It was a setup. All of a sudden, I realized that this is where I was going to be shot. I walked back. Had the deputy noticed me? Of course. That's why he was there. In fact, he was on his radio. Flashbacks. Soon, he would have backup. But what were they going to do, or what excuse were they going to use? All of a sudden, the kids started fighting among themselves. A ruse. I had to get out of there. The deputy had apparently been there for a while, and he didn't seem to be going anywhere.

Since the kids were monkeying around, not the way normal kids monkey around, I went up to them and told them I would take my car the way it was. I didn't want to let them finish doing whatever it was they thought they were doing to my car. They got mad. I paid them and took off in a direction that would have made it difficult for the deputy to follow me considering the traffic situation.

I decided to go to Consuelo's house.

I don't know whether she had ever seen me in a frantic state of fear. Probably not. I somehow knew that all my fears were in my mind, yet there was nothing I could do to get rid of the feeling. I was trembling.

I was no longer used to living in fear. It had left me a year before and had not revisited me during the trial up to this point. The fear that had enveloped me was immobilizing. The fear not only paralyzed me, but it did not allow me to think. The only thoughts I had were those of my imminent assassination.

Ten minutes after speaking to Consuelo, I had calmed down relatively. Three hours later, we were both laughing at the thought that I had been overwhelmed with fear. During those three hours, she said a prayer for me, and I think I said a prayer for myself. Just as fast as the fear arrived, it was now gone. I left her house not only laughing but feeling strong, stronger than I had felt throughout the trial because now I knew that nothing could stop me.

With my friend spiritually at my side, there was no way I could lose. She had enough faith for both of us. At home, and for the rest of the trial, the fear never returned.

When the verdict was read, I wanted Consuelo to be by my side. She wasn't there, but as soon as it was possible, we went to the Placita Church on Olvera Street in the historic part of Los Angeles and prayed. We prayed and gave thanks for the victory.

This matter of faith and relying on Consuelo for spiritual strength surprised me. After the trial, I could either tell people the truth or conceal the fact that I was in church every morning of my trial and in the court-room with a cross in my coat pocket. It was a major contradiction be-cause prior to my trial, I had not willingly been to church in at least 14 years.

No matter my thoughts, my theories, or my ideologies, in the end, I relied on the spiritual strength of a 17 year old. How could I deny that? Or why would I want to deny that? Having faced life and death, having been in a number of crises, why would it matter to me?

It mattered to me because the basic tenets of my beliefs did not allow me to comfortably accept the Christian faith, and that was for racial and cultural reasons.

In my mind, I equated Christianity in the Americas with colonization. I could not separate the conqueror from the missionary. I blamed the church for the slaughter, for the genocide of 25 million Indians. A race nearly had been obliterated in the name of God. And ever since I could remember, I could not accept that genocide. But if I took that thought to its logical conclusion, I could find comfort in knowing that the missionizing and colonizing was not done by God but rather in the name of God. And I knew that—I had always known that, but it was a mental block. It was too easy of a way out. Besides, it let the church and the Spaniards off the hook too easily.

Still, because of my beliefs, it was hard to see Christianity as the true religion of the Americas. Because of that colonization and because of the missionary work, I knew that the original beliefs had been almost wiped out, but they hadn't been wiped out completely. And I was aware of those beliefs. Perhaps that would explain why in the same pocket with the cross I also had that arrowhead I had found in the pyramids of Teotihuacán ten years earlier. It wasn't intentional that I had them both in the same pocket. In fact, I brought neither of them to the courtroom they were brought to me. Perhaps Octavio Paz, famed Mexican author of *The Labyrinth of Solitude,* could explain the significance of having the cross and the arrowhead in the same coat pocket of a mestizo. For me, to have tossed out one in favor of the other would have been a rejection of one and the acceptance of the other.

I, the bronze-skinned Indian, could not fathom the idea of turning against or rejecting myself. And I, the Godless warrior who turned to God in time of need, could no longer reject something that I had re-jected for half of my life. So it was that after my trial, I did not feel as though I had betrayed my beliefs by praying. And furthermore, I wouldn't have cared if I had. The only thing that was important was that, through the trial, like it or not, I came to recognize the dual nature of my soul.

21 / The Bitter Aftermath: A Hard Pill to Swallow

Seeking Political Asylum

Had I lost the decision, I was prepared to take an immediate flight out of the country and seek political asylum elsewhere.

Of course it sounds funny now, but at the time, there was nothing funny about it.

After getting continually harassed for years, and after having lived in fear, I was not about to return to the past. After I had returned to Los Angeles sometime around 1982, I was so disgusted at the hypocrisy of law enforcement and the judicial system that I wanted to reject my U.S. citizenship.

Perhaps the politics at that time helped shape my ideas of rejecting my citizenship and seeking political asylum. In the early days of the Reagan administration, it became popular for the United States to grant political asylum to Soviet ballerinas or circus jugglers claiming political persecution. I don't know that anyone actually believed the Soviets were going around politically persecuting ballerinas or circus clowns but nonetheless, those artists seeking asylum provided political points for the United States in their great cold war against the Soviet Union.

In reading about the cause of Soviet Jewry and the Refuseniks, it dawned on me that according to the media, their concerns were somewhat akin to that of Mexicans living in the United States: discrimination, cultural oppression, political powerlessness, and second class status. If anything, based on what I could ascertain, the condition and plight of Blacks, Native Americans, Mexicans, and Central Americans was infinitely worse than the plight of Soviet Jews.

At about that time is when I began to contemplate rejecting my citizenship and asking for political asylum, but I would not have sought political asylum from the Soviet Union. I would not have wanted to place myself in the continuing East-West struggle. I would have asked Mexico to give asylum to one of its sons. Seeking political asylum was probably going overboard, but within the context of the repressive police behavior against Mexicans and Blacks, what more cause did I need?

Because of my pending trial, I decided to hold off on the idea of seeking political asylum, but I had already resolved to reject my citizenship. My objective was to cause an international furor, to draw attention not solely to my case but also to the plight of Blacks, Latinos, and Native Americans. I figured, if people had the ear of Soviet dissidents, then the world should also know that all was not well within the borders of the United States.

Of course, rejecting my citizenship and seeking political asylum were fanciful if not naive acts of desperation. Indeed, in those days, I had become desperate. I did not opt for seeking political asylum early on because, in the event I was to leave the country for reasons of racial/political persecution, I felt I would not be able to return to press my claims against the sheriff's department in a court of law. Though I wanted to make that political statement, I resolved to wait until the trial was over.

By the time of my trial, I was no longer in the same state of mind, but my views regarding this matter had not changed. Win or lose, I determined that after the trial I would leave the country. If I won, I would leave for the purposes of recuperation. If I lost, I would leave bitterly and seek political asylum.

When the verdict was read, and when the decision went in my favor, I no longer felt the need to seek political asylum. Nonetheless, I was relieved, knowing that I would finally leave this country, which had treated me worse than a criminal, worse than a rabid animal.

I was ready to leave immediately after my victory but could not because I knew there would be a request for another trial and there would be an appeal. And that is precisely what happened.

I won my case in February 1986, yet I was not able to spend my first penny until the last day of July. By the beginning of August, I was exhausted. Amidst the celebrations, I began to plan my departure.

Detour to Sacramento

A few days after my case had finally been settled, I found myself in Sacramento covering a protest by the Mothers of East L.A., who had come 400-strong to protest the building of a prison in East Los Angeles. After the protest that evening, I stopped off at the University of California at Davis campus, the host site of the annual Chicano/Latino Youth Leadership Conference. Although I had come to cover the conference, I was invited to address the 120 young leaders the following morning regarding my victory.

That evening, student candidates who would represent the leadership program for the upcoming year were delivering their campaign speeches in one of the small auditoriums on campus. What I heard was awe-inspiring to say the least.

Sixteen and seventeen year olds poured out their hearts, giving impassioned speeches on how they had grown up ashamed of their race and embarrassed of their culture and how, through the conference, they had found new pride in themselves. The commonality among the candidates is that they all spoke of a newfound commitment, stating that whether elected or not, they would go back home and give back to their communities. There was a touch of innocence and naivete in their words but, more important, of sincerity.

They were dreamers. All of them.

There was one student, José Pascual, confined to a wheelchair, who touched everyone's heart and inspired everyone with his courage and fierce determination to succeed. There was one student who had been born in Ecuador and spoke in Spanish regarding the beauty of her native culture, language, and the unity of all peoples. Another one spoke with the oratory of a Jesse Jackson of her determination to fight for her community, of her quest for justice and equality. Her persona was awesome. The effect she had on her fellow students was incomparable, a born leader. The standing ovation she received brought the house down.

I had almost gone back on the bus with the Mothers of East L.A., for they too were inspiring but, instead, had opted to come to the conference, and after listening to the future leaders of our society, I had no regrets.

The last speaker to come forward was a thin, humble-looking, bespectacled student. She was competing for the same office as the student before her. As she began to speak, sparks of emotion were still flying in the air from the previous speaker. Everyone looked at this candidate as though she shouldn't waste her time, that she should just hurry up so that they could vote for the candidate before her.

She began speaking in a soft voice, her head bowed.

"I was born in Mexico," she stated, "and like many of you, I grew up denying my parents, grew up ashamed of being Mexican. But not anymore."

She raised her head with dignity.

The soft light shone on her deep, bronze skin.

"Like many of you," she paused, hands trembling, her words coming forth slowly, "I also crossed the border when I was a child."

By now, everyone had fallen silent.

"When I crossed the border," she continued, "we crossed in a car, but I wasn't in the front seat."

She paused once again.

Her words were coming even slower and more haltingly. Tears began to form in her eyes.

"I didn't come in the back seat of the car either." Her voice quivered with emotion. Fighting back the tears that began to flow, she blurted out, "I came across the border in the trunk of a car."

Her tears were now flowing freely. She couldn't continue. Looking around the circular shaped auditorium, there was not a dry eye in the room. The silence was deafening, broken only by her faint sobs. Tears from all quarters began to flow uncontrollably. Suddenly, a student rose and began clapping. Then another. All of a sudden, all were on their feet, clapping, swept up by the emotion and electricity in the room. They began to hug each other. Here, hundreds of miles from home, students who barely knew each other were hugging each other like the closest of families.

Who would win the election? It no longer mattered for these students would not forget this conference and especially this moment for the rest of their lives. They had indeed become, through camaraderie, the closest of families.

I was moved, more than they could have imagined. It was an incredible experience, one I had not prepared for.

The following morning, as I stood before them preparing to address them, the images from the evening before were still clearly etched in my mind. The electricity was still in the air. I was proud of them.

These students before me, the brightest students from throughout the state of California, were destined to be the future leaders of America, our future doctors, future engineers, future lawyers, scientists, urban planners, teachers, journalists, judges, and elected officials. What message could I give them? What could I tell students who thankfully would never have to know what it is to be humiliated by law enforcement and degraded by our judicial system, of what it means to be deprived of one's civil rights, of one's human rights? None, I hoped, would ever come or would ever have to return to the same violence-plagued streets that had been my home. How could they comprehend my seven-and-a-half-year perilous journey?

As I looked around the auditorium, I felt as though I should have been at a car show instead, at a park or on the Boulevard, celebrating, somewhere where people knew what it was to be viewed as being on the wrong side of the law, who knew what it was to be on the receiving end of a riot stick.

The students in front of me and I inhabited two different worlds, yet I saw myself in their faces. What had happened to me, I wondered? That used to be me in the audience, bright, cheerful, and full of enthusiasm.

Perhaps taking a cue from the night before, I poured out everything that had been locked inside of me for all those years. I told them, in wrenching detail, of the agonizing seven and a half years. I told them of the tremendous psychological toll it had taken on me, of what it meant to have one's dignity ripped away, and of how I wandered aimlessly in search of justice, in fear, in pain, and without hope while no "leader" would step forward and help. Finally, I told them of my trial and my miraculous victory.

And finally, I closed with a plea that, as the future leaders of our society, they should ensure that what happened to me will never happen to anyone again.

There was stone silence.

I stared at them.

Drained and visibly moved by their expressions, I walked away. The silence was finally broken by a clap and then another, then followed by a thunderous standing ovation.

Yes. I was them and they were me.

That's what my trial had been all about.

I left the conference, reinvigorated and proud, proud to know that following in my footsteps was a new generation of leaders that would not only fight against injustice but, in the future, would be in the position to do something about it.

In Defense of the First Amendment

A few days after returning to Los Angeles, I was asked by a friend what my colleagues thought about my victory. I paused. I didn't know how to respond. I had never viewed other journalists as my colleagues, or rather, I had never viewed myself as a journalist, per se. Journalists, I presumed, were objective professionals who did not give their own opinions about anything. Instead, they gathered the news and reported the facts. Up to that time, I don't think I ever viewed myself in that manner. I viewed myself as an individual who wrote because I didn't like what I saw in the world. I wanted to write for the purpose of exposing lies, to change things, to make things better. So it is that when I was asked that question, in a sense I felt honored that I would be considered among the same rank of professionals who gathered the news.

Surprisingly, that same day, I was informed that I was to be one of two journalists to be honored at the upcoming annual banquet of the California Chicano News Media Association. The other honoree was to be Luis Nogales, president of United Press International, and the keynote speaker was to be Miguel Vásquez Raña, a multimillionaire media magnet who had just finished buying United Press International. It was awe-inspiring company.

I was in awe. Journalists I had grown up watching on television, listening to on the radio, or reading in the newspapers were bestowing upon me the honor for the defense of the First Amendment. Ironically, even though on the legal front the case was not fought on the issue of the First Amendment, my colleagues did in fact correctly recognize my case as one involving the freedom of the press.

Had the case been handled properly, had the lawsuit been filed based on the First Amendment early on, perhaps it could have attracted the attention and support of national and international media. I was bitter in a sense, bitter that my victory had essentially not given me a forum to discuss the prevalence of police brutality around the country.

At the banquet, it was as though the honor and tribute was the fitting end to the lengthy pursuit and quest for justice. Because I was being honored for defending the First Amendment, for taking on and beating the system rather than for my writing skills, I felt awkward. I would have rather been honored for my skills, but after thinking about it, perhaps it was better. I, the individual, was being honored by my colleagues for my character. It was an honor that almost made the whole ordeal worth it.

Despite the momentous and memorable nature of the occasion, deep inside I still did not feel the fight had been worth it. That total war had culminated in a victory but at the expense of traumatic scars, caused by the assault and the seven-year wait for trial.

For a variety of reasons, I was never did leave the country. On the night of the California Chicano News Media banquet, besides inviting family and those closest of friends who had pushed me along when I needed it, I went with Susana, the closest of friends, someone whom I used to go out with in college and whom, after 10 years, I had recently met up with again. Not long after the banquet, she called me in tears. She relayed that her brother had been killed inside a jail and that they suspected that it had been the jail personnel who had done the killing. The night of the banquet, I had spoken to her brother at length about my case, about my trial and the victory. I had not known the brother that well, but the conversation was well ingrained in my mind.

Upon hearing the news of his killing, I went into temporary shock but then recouped. Assuming that the family would not be able to think straight immediately, I did everything I could in assisting the family to get to the bottom of the matter.

Through months of assisting this bereaved family, I finally came to the sad recognition that my case had indeed been worth fighting. Based on my unnecessarily long ordeal, my knowledge was finally put to use to help another family avoid suffering for years and years of additional agony.

At that point, I stopped regretting all that had happened to me and was comforted by the knowledge that at least someone else had benefited from my trauma. I didn't feel good about it nor did I feel happy, but at least I felt that if another family was spared those extra years of agony, then, indeed, the ordeal had actually been worth it.

The Public's Right to Know

The only bitterness that remained is the knowledge that none of the four sheriff's deputies ever had to face criminal charges, much less spend a day or night in jail. To my knowledge, they were not fined, suspended, nor demoted. Instead they were promoted. Worse, I may never officially know because the department remains unaccountable. That points to a problem bigger than my case. If I or someone else wanted to know whether the sheriff's deputies were ever disciplined, by law that information is confidential. And this is not a unique situation. Around the country, the public does not have the right to know.

Somehow, that doesn't sound like a victory.

If the public cannot find out whether officers who have been found guilty of police brutality and of violating a person's civil rights have been disciplined, then what I questioned in 1979 still holds true today: who are they serving and who are they protecting?

22 / Justice:
A Question of Race

After winning my trial, I was repeatedly asked one question: had I been a white reporter, would I have won more money or would it have taken seven and a half years to achieve justice?

My sincere belief regarding this matter is that, had I been a white reporter, none of this would have ever taken place.

23 / Law Enforcement and the Law: A System Gone Awry

In fighting my case, I learned many things. Chief among them was how an entire system essentially conspires to ensure that police brutality exists and continues to flourish. I learned about lawless police departments, a discriminating judicial system, spineless attorneys, timid politicians, an unquestioning media, and a disbelieving public.

To this day, police brutality is pervasive because many people still have the mistaken idea that, under a certain set of circumstances, police abuse is permissible. That misunderstanding exists perhaps in part because most people have been taught to believe that there is a fine line between justified use of force and excessive force.

For the record, all police departments have codes that allow police officers to use force when necessary. Force can range from grips, compliance holds, batons, kicks chemical spray, saps, taser, use of dogs to the use of firearms. Essentially, the range is from nonlethal to lethal.

Deadly Force

"Deadly force" is force that is lethal. "Justified use of force" is the force necessary to effectuate an arrest and or to halt a crime in progress, which can include the use of deadly force. "Excessive force" is force that is unnecessary in the performance of the officer's duties.

The use of deadly force can be justified, and at the same time, it can be unnecessary. Although all police departments have their own guidelines regarding what constitutes "justified use of deadly force," for the most part, the guidelines are basically the same. The use of deadly force is justified when it is used in self-defense or when it becomes necessary to save the lives of others. In some states, it is still permissible to shoot to effectuate an arrest, even when there are no lives in danger.

In the old days, prior to the advent of modern law enforcement techniques, deadly force was used at the discretion of the officers. In essence, it was arbitrary. Deadly force was permissible even if the crime was a misdemeanor and even if no one was in danger. Deadly force was once allowable as a means to apprehend any suspect, but as can be imagined, the use of deadly force by police departments was never applied equally. It manifested itself in racial terms. Throughout history, African Americans, Native Americans, Puerto Ricans, and Mexicans have suf-

254

fered tremendously at the hands of officers of the law. Previous to this century, when no records were kept, these groups regularly suffered at the hands of the law—including lynch mobs—legal and extralegal. In the archives of the earliest newspapers, reports of Mexicans, Native Americans, and African Americans being killed fill their pages. And they are numerous because of the constant protest by their fellow compatriots. In those days, the use of deadly force required no justification. The law was supreme authority, and the law was the lawman and his six-shooter.

Into this century, as records began to be kept, most police departments throughout the nation still operated under the principle of shoot first, ask questions later. Not surprisingly, nonwhite victims were invariably killed disproportionate to their numbers in the population.

The unfortunate aspect of the history of the use of deadly force is that, with or without codes or regulations, an infinitesimally low amount of officers who have used deadly force have ever been found to have applied it unjustifiably. Of those who are found to use unjustified use of force, few are indicted; fewer yet are convicted. Only in the rarest of cases has an officer ever been reprimanded much less convicted of murder.

The Excessive Use of Force

The abuse of force, the excessive and unnecessary use of force, when it is nonlethal, is for the most part treated with less seriousness than the use of deadly force. The reason for this is that police normally do not have to account for bodies. Part of the reason police brutality is widespread is because in many communities, from a legal standpoint, it is not clearly understood. Many people believe that suspects, by the mere virtue that they are suspects, not only surrender their civil rights, but also that if they get beaten in the process, they deserve to be beaten. Whether or not the subject of police brutality is understood, what is abundantly clear is that police abuse is illegal anywhere in the country.

Police abuse is the unnecessary use of force—intentional or not. Unnecessary force that is unintentional is illegal and results from bad training, loss of control, or plain sloppiness. Unnecessary force that is intentional is always illegal.

Many people have the mistaken notion that to talk back to a police officer or refusing to answer questions somehow gives the officer the right to use force. There is no legal doctrine that accepts provocation as an excuse for police abuse. In fact, no crime merits the use of excessive force. Excessive force in simple everyday terms is a police beating. Police officers in the previous century were permitted to beat suspects, but nowhere today do police officers have the right to use excessive force, regardless of the reason. The officer on the street has the thankless job of detaining and arresting suspects, but they do not have the right to mete out justice on the street. That has been the traditional role of the courts. Normally, the police are not in the position nor do they have the authority to determine guilt or innocence. That is the function of the judicial system.

Normally, in the courtroom, in cases regarding police brutality, what is debated is not whether police abuse is right or wrong, legal or illegal. Police abuse is unquestionably wrong and clearly illegal under any circumstance. What is normally contested is whether the force used in the arrest constituted "justified use of force." In most, if not all, cases in which police resort to the use of force, the police will argue that their use of force was proper and justifiable. They rarely deny that they used force. In most cases, they don't need to deny it. They simply have to justify it.

But this discussion about whether force is excessive or justified is akin to discussing how many angels can dance on the head of a pin. The subject of police brutality is not complex. It doesn't exist in a gray legal cloud. Few people will argue or take issue with the police officers' rights to use force to bring down a combative suspects or to save their or other people's lives.

Police brutality in America refers to something else. It's not simply a matter of going overboard. Police brutality refers to yanking someone out of a car and striking him or her with a riot stick. It refers to mercilessly beating on an individual who is already handcuffed. It refers to officers ganging up on a defenseless individual, then fabricating a crime and a provocation to cover their tracks.

This type of brutality does not exist in any gray area. It is vicious and common and many times results in hospitalization. It usually occurs when officers grant themselves the right to punish the known or alleged perpetrator of a crime. Not coincidentally, the vast majority of the victims are Black or Brown youth.

Much of this brutality is motivated by disrespect, contempt, and hatred. Many times, brutality occurs because a suspect did not respond fast enough or did not show deference or respect to the officer. Many times it occurs when officers intentionally humiliate a person and attempt to emasculate him. When the person demands that he be treated with respect, that, in the officer's mind, constitutes grounds for punishment.

In many communities, police officers who work in special antigang details employ brutality for purposes of harassment—to send out a message. This is done for the purposes of establishing control and a reputation. The message, delivered via riot sticks, is usually received by anyone with black or brown skin.

One thing indisputable in history is that, on the whole, when police officers use their riot sticks against Mexicans and Blacks, it has been justified.

The Legal System: No Place for Justice

Although people have the idea that our judicial system is fair, the reality is that it is a two-track system. It is designed for two types of people: for those who know their rights and for those who don't—for those who know how to fight for their rights and for those who don't. It is set up for those who can afford justice and for those who can't—for those who can pay for good representation and for those who get herded through by public defenders.

The problem with the judicial system is that it does not treat all criminals in an equal manner. Some criminals commit certain crimes and get off with probation while other criminals will commit the same crime and spend time behind bars. Although the inequity exists, it is magnified tremendously when it involves an innocent person who has been charged falsely with crimes.

In fighting my own case, I learned that in cases involving assault on officers, frame-ups are the rule rather than the exception. Prior to my case, I had never seen the use of deadly force by police officers, but I had seen plenty of excessive force used against many individuals.

The Judicial System:
A Virtual Gauntlet

Police abuse has always existed, not simply because the courts traditionally have looked the other way but because police brutality has been refined into a science. One of the components of this refinement—the practice of plea bargaining (discussed in more detail in *Assault with a Deadly Weapon*—is in effect a legal insurance policy for police officers who engage in police brutality.

Most attorneys in the field of police abuse believe that in cases of police brutality, there is no crime committed prior to the altercation. The crime is the altercation itself. As a result of trumped up charges, plea bargaining becomes "the primary means of police officers covering their behinds," says Carol Watson, a prominent Los Angeles attorney, in the field of police brutality. With their behinds covered, the success rate for police officers getting away with police brutality has always been and continues to be in the vicinity of 99.999 percent.

There are a number of other factors why defendants rarely win in court against police officers. Sam Paz, one of the leading attorneys in the field of police brutality in Southern California, states that the reason law enforcement prevails in cases of police brutality is the victim's lack of money. "Most of the victims of police brutality are poor and from high-crime areas," he says.

Trials are expensive, especially if a defendant retains the services of a worthwhile attorney. Thus, most victims aren't able to secure good legal representation. Most defendants end up with public defenders who are more than happy to effectuate a plea bargain.

Another factor, assuming the defendant has time, money, and a good lawyer, is credibility. The credibility of the defendant and the credibility of his or her witnesses, even if they have clean records, are no match for the credibility of the guardians of justice. Juries pass judgment based on character and credibility.

Paz states, "Citizens have a high respect for the law. People feel that cops don't lie. People feel that if you've been arrested, you must have done something wrong, that where there's smoke, there's fire."

Finally, even if everything were right regarding time, money, lawyers, and witnesses, the intimidation factor is tremendous.

"Most police brutality goes unreported," states attorney Watson, "We only see the tip of the iceberg. Most victims don't know how to proceed. Many more fear retaliation from the police."

Witnesses also fear retaliation. In general, most witnesses don't want to get involved. In cases surrounding police brutality, witnesses become nonwitnesses faster than smog accumulates in the city of Los Angeles. Police officers are supposed to represent law and order. When a citizen witnesses an officer violating the law, the witness does not have to be convinced of what police officers are capable of doing. Testifying in court against police officers could mean putting their lives on the line. The prospects of testifying on behalf of a stranger against police officers is not determined to be worth the risk.

Prior to my case, I didn't or wasn't aware of the relationship between police brutality, poverty, intimidation, and the system of plea bargaining. As exciting as television depicts trials to be and contrary to popular perceptions, the judicial system is geared to avoid trials. Back-room deals are the norm. In this bastardized form of justice, the biggest loser is the innocent individual.

On those rarest of occasions, when a lawsuit is pursued, there is no assurance that the party will end up victorious. Defeating law enforcement in the courtroom is akin to not believing in our legal, judicial, and law enforcement system. People who comprise our juries do not want to believe that we live in a corrupt society. They continue to believe in the idea that police officers are that last line of defense in the fight against evil. Thus, victories against law enforcement are one in a million.

24 / Respect for the Law: A Moral Responsibility

Today, it is difficult to see or hear about police abuse without wanting to do something about it. Luckily, it seems that a great many people no longer accept police abuse as part of life. In some parts of the country, especially in the nation's inner cities, police abuse is rampant. In other parts of the country, it is virtually nonexistent. And though people are now beginning to win lawsuits in cases of police abuse, nevertheless it is still difficult for a victim to win in court.

The primary reason it is difficult to win police abuse cases is that society still holds onto the notion that fighting against police abuse is to fight against the police. It's true that there are some people who hate all police, but those who dedicate their lives to fighting against police abuse, for the most part, do not harbor antipolice feelings. The reason for this is that the efforts of those who oppose police brutality is to end police abuse, not hamper or interfere with the operations of law enforcement. However, because of that mistaken perception, a victim of police abuse, rather than getting support from law-abiding individuals, from people in a position to provide support, invariably ends up fighting alone.

A victim of police abuse knows what it is to fight alone, and the victim fights alone because no one else will step forward. Not lawyers. Not politicians. Not community leaders. Not the media.

When a person is assaulted by law enforcement, the victim ends up in a precarious position. In a state of panic and fear, that person attempts to reach out for help but normally doesn't know who to turn to. Law enforcement is where one should be able to turn in a time of distress, but in a case of police abuse, that is the last place to whom the victim will want to turn. Then to whom does the victim turn? Some attorneys do not even talk to a victim unless the case is a sure moneymaker. The practice of lawyering is a business. Thus, police abuse cases are treated in a businesslike manner. What's in it for the attorney? If a victory does not seem likely, then it is unlikely that a victim of police abuse will obtain competent representation. In the courtroom, for all intents and purposes, a victory is unlikely unless the abuse was captured on video, and even that does not ensure a victory.

Perhaps it is easy to lay the whole blame on attorneys, but the truth of the matter is that the reason lawyers find it difficult to win police abuse cases is that it is difficult to convince juries that the police have violated the law. That's not to say that there are not good attorneys. There are. In every city, there are a number of attorneys who know how to fight, who, despite the enormous odds, know not only how to present evidence but also how to present a credible case to a jury. However, with the amount of police abuse cases, there are not enough good attorneys to stem the tide. The solution to police abuse, however, is not simply to increase the amount of good attorneys but rather to bring the public to understand that putting away officers who violate their sacred trust is not only appropriate but a moral responsibility of the highest order. Ending police brutality will only come about when people recognize that police abuse is a crime just as theft is a crime. And just as theft is not permissible, neither is police abuse. In this regard, everyone shares a responsibility.

Contrary to popular perceptions, to fight against police abuse is to stand up for law and order. Generally, those who fight against police abuse are individuals who have the highest regard for the law and the highest regard for life. Society should never allow law enforcement to operate without checks and balances. Law enforcement officers should be accountable to the community they serve, but more than that, they should be expected to uphold the law, and as public servants they should set the example and be subject to even higher standards.

There is no contradiction in supporting the law and law enforcement while at the same time fighting against police abuse. In fighting my case, I found out the hard way that people believe that if you fight against police abuse, somehow it puts you on the wrong side of the law. Nothing could be further from the truth. Fighting against police abuse is to uphold the Constitution. The framers of the Constitution would cringe at the thought, would turn over in their graves, if they knew that people had come to grant, by acquiescence, unlimited powers and authority to law enforcement. That's what the Bill of Rights was all about—the protection of the individual against an all-powerful state.

In this respect, law enforcement itself shares the greatest responsibility. Beyond teaching their own police officers to respect the law, they should be at the forefront of educating the public regarding police abuse. Law enforcement is the most sacred of professions because, just as officers serve and protect, they also have vested in them the power to terminate life. For that reason, those officers who abuse their badges are not only a danger to society but are detrimental to any police department and the community they serve.

If police abuse is ever to end, it will come about when law enforcement itself joins with the community to educate the public to recognize that police abuse is intolerable. The end of police abuse cannot come about through an "us versus them" confrontation, and there need not be a confrontation. An educated populace and a responsive police department would not permit police abuse.

The reality of today is that those attitudes don't exist yet. Police brutality is still pervasive, and it appears that in many cities it is not simply a case of a few bad apples but rather a rotten department and corrupt city officials. If taking police to court and winning lawsuits has a deterrent effect, then perhaps, in the near future, police abuse will begin to decline. In cities where a department and city officials condone or tolerate police abuse, it will take more than lawsuits to bring about change.

Personally, since I've won, victims of police abuse call me, bewildered, wanting to know what to do. Sometimes it tears me apart. Sometimes, I'm affected profoundly because I wish I could do more than just offer advice and refer them to a good attorney. Sometimes I wish I were an attorney. The reason it affects me is that they call in a frantic state—victims or relatives of victims—and many call in desperation after they've already spoken to an attorney. I've had mothers call and tell me that their sons are in jail, victims of a brutal attack, and that their sons are the ones facing the criminal charges. A woman, who herself was abused, told me once that she had talked to every politician but that she couldn't get any to take her seriously. And the attorneys, they told her she had no case.

During those moments, I remember walking around like a leper when I was looking for help. Disillusionment is not even the appropriate word. Incredulity is perhaps a better description. The rage one feels toward the police is overshadowed by the failure of anyone to step forward. The abuse and assault by a law enforcement officer on an individual is the ultimate expression of disrespect. It goes beyond racial insults, beyond discrimination, beyond negative images. The individual is traumatized—the ultimate violation of human rights—yet no one steps forward. Cowardice? Hypocrisy? The great feelings of rage are now directed at those who should be in your corner, at those who should be able to do something about it but don't. Pure unadulterated hatred is directed at those who claim to fight against discrimination, at those who fail to speak up. The silence hurts.

Sometimes, when people call me, I'm busy, but I stop. I have to stop. There's no feeling worse than to feel that there's no one to turn to. Perhaps one day soon, a victim of police abuse will not have to fight alone. Perhaps in the future, fighting against police abuse will not only be seen as a civic duty but as a moral responsibility. And it is. Mine. Yours. And anyone who has a respect for the law.

25 / Conclusion: A Triumph of the Human Spirit

It seems difficult to relate a conclusion where there seems to be none. My trial ended in a victory, but the story does not end there. Justice triumphed but not the justice I sought and expected. The agonizing years have ended, but the mental and physical scars remain. Given the luxury, of course, I wish it had never happened, but it did.

Lingering thoughts remain regarding the many negative results of this incident—things I wish had never happened and things I would never wish on anyone else. Along the treacherous road in pursuit of justice, despite experiencing every destructive emotion possible, many positive results also occurred—things I'm thankful for and things I wish I had experienced under a different set of circumstances but things, nonetheless, for which I am grateful.

During this ordeal, I learned not only about myself but also about other people. I learned about the way the mind works and how people react under fire, how people react in times of crises, and what occurs to an individual who undergoes trauma. This is the most important thing I learned while fighting.

For many years, I was consumed with anger. For the first six months, I had so much anger I spoke with no one. I was virtually silent, afraid to let people hear my thoughts.

For many years, I also walked under a gray cloud, thinking I was undergoing the worst form of trauma possible—that no one knew or could understand what I was going through and that I was alone in pain, suffering, and persecution—until I began to listen to other people. At that point, when I began to understand that the world did not revolve around me, I came to understand that, regardless of the source of trauma, essentially all trauma is the same. All trauma affects individuals in a most profound way. A trauma is an experience that devastates the individual and leaves an indelible print on the mind, body, and soul. The commonality regarding trauma is not the cause but rather the struggle to return to normalcy, the struggle to heal, to recover, and to get back on one's feet. It is a difficult struggle, a long and slow process, but a struggle that once accomplished leaves the individual with an armor that enables him or her to confront life thereafter. Trauma devastates. It also fortifies.

During my quest for justice, I came to understand that my struggle was appreciated by people I didn't even know, not solely because I fought for my rights, not strictly because I fought for justice, but rather because the mind and the human spirit recovered and persevered against impossible odds. Through all this, I came to learn that nothing is impossible, that the mind is capable of accomplishing anything. More than that, I learned that the mind has the capacity to climb back up from bottomless pits and to rise to the top again.

I wish I could say I did this all by myself—that my mind recovered of my own will—but the truth is that at every step of the way there was someone there. Throughout those years, there were a number of people in my life who not only became close to me but also were there when I wanted to give up, when I needed to be pushed along. Throughout those years, I took something or I was given something special from each of my friends. From one I learned to be strong; from another to never give up; from another I learned to conquer fear; and from still another, I learned to believe in myself. And finally, from another, I learned to have faith.

No, I would never want to say I did it by myself. The triumph of the mind, the triumph of the spirit was accomplished by being pushed along by friends and by coming to know about grand struggles around the world – of Nigerian prisoners enduring false imprisonment, of Chileans and Nicaraguans fighting against their dictatorships, of Argentinians surviving their dirty war, of Guatemalans enduring and surviving torture, of South Africans fighting against apartheid. All of this was inspiring, but the critical strength was derived from the lives of people I met, as opposed to those I read about, who were dealing with traumas that don't make headlines, of dealing with death, of dealing with the painful decisions of abortion, of coping with divorce, of dealing with the effects of child abuse and rape, of dealing with the devastating effects of gang wars, of alcohol and drug abuse. Those friends or strangers who shared their grief and their struggles emboldened me and allowed me to go forward and defy the odds.

The sum total of all this is that I would hope that I came out a better man in this entire ordeal. I conquered fear, hatred, and every other negative emotion possible. If there is a legacy, it is that I did not end up bitter, that I believed in something, that I accomplished it and came out still able to laugh and smile. Sometimes it hurts to laugh or to smile, but another thought gives me comfort and satisfaction, that is, the knowledge that as a result of this ordeal, I met some special people whom I otherwise perhaps would have never met. For this reason alone, I cannot and will never regret that the incident took place, but this aside, I cannot regret because, if anything, that victory represents not only a lot of blood but also vindication.

In this battle, humanity triumphed against inhumanity. Justice triumphed against injustice, and most of all, it was a triumph of that human spirit—the spirit that endured—that drew strength from all quarters, from people who pushed me and from people who inspired me who never heard of me. In the end, fighting the good fight was itself the victory. The victory was never giving up, never buckling under pressure, persevering, and eventually emerging from the courtroom with a legal victory—a victory so satisfying that, no matter the future, it can never be taken away.

Epilogue

It seems a lifetime ago that I lay in a pool of blood on the corner of Whittier Boulevard and McDonnell in East L.A. A lifetime ago, and sometimes I feel fortunate that I've had a life at all.

It's difficult to compress thoughts, much less feelings, especially when they are of moments long ago frozen in time. One thing the reader might note is the difference in tone between part one and part two of this book. *Assault with a Deadly Weapon* was written in 1984 and *On the Wrong Side of the Law* was generally written at the end of 1986. Perhaps there's a difference in tone, even in this, the epilogue, written in 1996.

Of note, the first three chapters of *On the Wrong Side of the Law* are very different than anything I've ever written, then and now. Sometime after the 1986 civil trial, I went away to an isolated part of Mexico, where I spent a week reconstructing in writing what actually happened to me seven and a half years before. I did it because, as a writer, I knew that I had never written in detail about that weekend in 1979. Of course, my testimony at the trial brought it out in a most traumatic manner, and it was painful.

When I sat down to write what became the first three chapters, it too was traumatic and painful, minus the intensity and pressure of the trial. While writing, I did go back in time and relived everything anew. To be honest, after that I didn't want to relive it again. Unfortunately, to get this book published, I've had to. The only reason the first three chapters were included and the reason the book was written was because I thought people should know the amount of pain involved and the amount of trauma so that society can know what goes on inside the mind of a victim of police brutality, to know the human toll. What I lived through was very painful, and I don't plan on ever reading this again. I want to bring closure. Perhaps it was unnecessary to write this, and perhaps I subjected myself to needless torture, but everything around me tells me that society has still not learned the lessons I learned between 1979 and 1986 and is still unaware of what the world witnessed in Los Angeles in 1991 and 1992.

Today, I live far away, in distance and time, from that intersection, from that cold pavement, and even from that courtroom in downtown Los Angeles. But, of course, I still reside there, no matter where I live. And the truth is, my life did not freeze in time. In the past few years, I've taken many journeys and walked many paths. Suffice to say that my pursuit of justice is eternal.

This book took a long time to publish because for ten years no one in the publishing industry wanted to listen to what I had to say. For some, it was not the right time, and for others it was old news. Yet, as recent history has shown us, police brutality is never old news.

When I first wrote about what happened, I said I would give back to my community, and I believe I have. The only difference is that today my community has expanded. My idea of the barrio extends beyond the side of a town to include the barrio called humanity. What remains constant in my life is my pursuit of justice. My own justice was somewhat achieved, but it generally remains elusive on U.S. streets.

When I used to be out on the streets in L.A.'s cement jungle, no one had ever heard of Rodney King, and while police abuse and brutality was a daily occurrence in the inner cities, it was invisible from the nation's consciousness. In those years when I struggled for justice, I fought what I thought was a lonely struggle. No politician listened, nor did they want to. Police brutality flourished because timid politicians were always afraid to speak out and because the public tolerated it even when presented with irrefutable evidence. This was in part because police brutality was not viewed as a problem but, rather, as an excusable, if not necessary, tool in the fight against crime and the forces of darkness.

I still have hard feelings toward politicians because almost all the same players are still in place. Sometimes the faces change, but the attitudes generally prevail: law and order at all cost.

If the pols and the media had listened, L.A.'s tragedy a few years later would not have occurred. Los Angeles did not have to live the worst urban nightmare of the twentieth century, but it did because its leaders buried their heads in the sand, not once but every time the issue of legal and extralegal violence on the part of law enforcement was raised.

In 1979, I was a writer and photographer for *Lowrider Magazine.* Today, along with my wife, Patrisia Gonzales, I write a nationally syndicated column. Many people consider that to be a phenomenal accomplishment, rising from the streets to debating the issues of the day, alongside the nation's most notable writers and thinkers. For me, it's just an extension of what I've always done, giving voice to the voiceless, attempting to communicate messages that many people don't want to hear, especially when they come straight from the streets.

One thing the reader can rest assured of is that there were no short cuts involved. Getting syndicated was a lifelong pursuit, and it involved writing about justice and injustice. That kind of writing is, in effect, discouraged in mainstream media, yet my thoughts and my writing were not moderated in pursuit of syndication and acceptance.

After my victories, I did not get rich, nor did I take the money and run. Given the severity of the case, I should have gotten rich. But that wouldn't have begun to compensate for the hell I have lived.

The money I received, I returned in the form of a magazine, *Americas 2001.* Sadly, it did not blossom into a huge financial success. A large part of the reason for its lack of success is that I have a writing not a business background. Nevertheless, that's where the money went. I never enriched myself, and I never used the publication to espouse my personal views but rather to promote the debate of ideas. Much good came out of that publication.

My own views were expressed elsewhere, principally in *La Opinión* newspaper in Los Angeles. There, as I had done previously in Eastern Group Publications, where I first started writing columns, I wrote about our nation's injustices. In those, days, I still had a lot of anger. It was a time that coincided with the writing of both *Assault with a Deadly Weapon* and, to a lesser extent, *On the Wrong Side of the Law.*

Since I first started writing columns, I have purposely searched out other cases of law enforcement abuse, and in a sense, I haven't had to search very far. In some instances, I've been personally contacted by victims or the families of victims, and it's hard sometimes to see the pain. There's always pain, more so than even anger. That's something the U.S. public doesn't seem to understand. During the L.A. rebellion in 1992, people around the world saw the rage and the anger in its city streets, but few seemed to recognize the pain. That's part of the historical dehumanization of the Black and Brown masses.

People in Los Angeles, I maintain, didn't simply revolt because they had sympathy or felt compassion for Rodney King. I believe it was much more personal and much more profound. For some people, it was ancestral; they understood the historical nature of abuses against people of color. For others, it wasn't about collective memory but about a shared reality. To this day, mainstream Americans appear to be ignorant of the realities of the inner cities: that thousands upon thousands of nonwhite youth have lived the reality of Rodney King. All the blows to Rodney King can be magnified thousands of times in every major city in the United States.

When I write about this subject, I don't do so in metaphors and symbolic terms. I have lived it, have seen it with my very eyes, and have continued to document it as a journalist and columnist. Even before 1979, I was conscious of police abuse and brutality, primarily because it was prevalent in Los Angeles when I was growing up. However, since 1979, I have taken a special interest in documenting it, for personal reasons of course, but also because I have been exposed to much of it since.

Since then, I've written about many cases of law enforcement abuse and most have received scant attention. Most cases have involved Black, Brown, and Native American youth, although it has never been limited to youth. In 1991, something phenomenal happened. Instead of a decrease in police abuse, as a result of the wide exposure the Rodney King beating, it generally increased. Immediately after the showing of the video, there were more reported beating and shooting cases by law enforcement officers in Southern California.

I wrote about this increase when the public was content to believe that the video was somehow going to bring about a magical end to law enforcement abuse. It didn't. It's true that some people may have been more willing to report cases, but many human rights organizations believe that the violence on the part of law enforcement virtually skyrocketed. While gathering less national publicity than the King beating, 1991 was also the year when a series of shootings by the L.A. County Sheriff's deputies resulted in several deaths of mostly Brown and Black youth.

I returned and testified at a hearing about these continuing abuses, assuring the L.A. County Board of Supervisors that this brutality and abuse was nothing new. In fact, I was enraged that it had taken so long to investigate a situation they were all too familiar with. There was a lot of anger in L.A., but the silence on the part of the supervisors was deafening. All this tension preceded the Los Angeles uprising. After the civil unrest, law enforcement abuse still did not substantially decrease.

As a journalist, I continued to track cases around the country and have published a series of lengthy articles on the subject. What is undeniable is that violence against African American youth is well documented and at times highly visible, whereas violence against Brown youth or other youth of color remains largely invisible. This appears to be more of a media bias than anything else. The media continue to view the nation and the world as black and white.

Of the many dozens of cases I've written about since 1991, it's still a truism that if it involves a Chicano, a Puerto Rican, Dominican, Central American, or any other Latino, chances are that it will not receive national coverage unless there's an accompanying riot. And even that gets little coverage and normally is misreported.

Notably, the brutality and abuse against Black and Brown youth has obviously never been restricted to L.A This brutality has been ever-present in all of the nation's large cities or wherever people of color reside. One of the chapters in history that has never been written is that farm workers—especially those who have dared to organize in the fields—historically have been targets of legal and extralegal violence. The same is true of other workers, particularly janitors in the 1990s who have organized nationwide and been similarly subjected to law enforcement violence.

Another missing chapter involves the U.S. Border Patrol and other immigration law enforcement agencies, who historically have abused the human rights of immigrants. The incidence of violence from this branch of law enforcement is well documented by human rights groups, particularly this past decade. The incidents are well documented, but there is little to show for it.

None of this is simply history. Almost on a weekly basis, I hear of horror stories. In the last couple of years, besides L.A., I have particularly followed cases in Dallas, Detroit, Nebraska, Arizona, San Diego, El Paso, Chicago, and New York. Many of these have involved the shooting of Mexicans in the back or of brutality and the use of deadly force against

Latinos and African Americans. I write about these cases because no one seems to want to give these cases national exposure.

In all the years I have written on this subject, I have compiled volumes of cases, and one day, I would like to put them in another book. This work takes a heavy psychological toll, but it can never compare with the toll it takes upon the victims, or the families of victims who grieve and who often don't know where to turn.

For this reason, of all the cases I've written about, I am especially moved and inspired by the recently formed Mothers against Police Brutality from New York—a group of parents who have lost children due to law enforcement violence. They courageously fight for justice similar to mothers in Mexico and Central and South America.

In 20 years of writing about this subject, I have been affected tremendously. Many of my original thoughts have changed, thinking that people don't fight back or that they didn't fight back in the distant past. Now I know that it was simply the cowardice of society's institutions that has conspired to silence this protest. Pols, lawyers, law enforcement, and the media have all been responsible for silencing people or projecting silence. There has never actually been silence on the part of those communities but rather, for all intents and purposes, complete deafness on the part of society. If not for the video of the Rodney King beating, society would probably still be playing deaf. Because of Rodney King, everything has changed, and nothing has changed. Police brutality is still pervasive in all of the nation's inner cities.

It's true that more police officers are facing criminal and civil trials, and the proliferation of video cameras has had a chilling effect on some police officers who have a propensity for violence. But on the whole, police brutality continues and will continue to exist until the United States reexamines its very soul.

In all this time, I have never met more courageous people than those who fight against the scourge of law enforcement abuse. They are the ones who respect the law, above and beyond anyone else, particularly those who proclaim themselves to be pro law and order but who turn a blind eye to law enforcement abuses. Those who struggle against these abuses are to be admired because they are willing to expose themselves to both ostracism and danger. They do so simply to ensure that no one is above the law, particularly those who have sworn to uphold society's laws.

I never expected to be writing about police brutality as we near the end of a millennium. It seems incongruous. I never expected it to be a fact of life going into the twenty-first century. Of course, I will fight my hardest to prevent it from being a part of the next millennium because it is incomprehensible that we can go into a new age, an age of enlightenment, with human beings still subjected to violence under the color of law.

I have always felt that this violence and abuse have always formed part of a means of control against people of color sanctioned by all levels of government. I have no doubts in my mind that if thousands of white youths were being brutally beaten on a weekly basis, society would quickly bring this violence to an end. Mechanisms would be put in place to ensure that the police wouldn't simply be enforcers of laws but rather integral parts of the community, at the service of the community, and not in a figurative sense but in actuality.

This violence has always been tolerated because people of color have historically been dehumanized. I would submit that police brutality stems from a fundamental disrespect, from the fact that U.S. society places a higher value on certain human beings and actively or through acquiescence permits the wholesale abuse by one group over another. I would further submit that members of law enforcement aren't the sole, or even the primary, culprits in this debasement of human life. They take their cues from societal attitudes. They do no different than what the government does, nor the politicians, nor the judicial system, nor the media. They do no different than the banking, real estate, and insurance industries do and no different than what the educational institutions aren't doing.

The only difference is in the tools of the trade and that the abuses by society's other institutions have rarely been photographed or caught on video. I have no doubts that if welfare workers, government bureaucrats, teachers, judges, lawyers, and even journalists were given batons, more people of color would be getting clubbed on the head on a daily basis. Many government bureaucrats harbor the same resentment and disrespect as do abusive law enforcement officers.

This debasement reminds me of, and helps explain, why gang violence is also permitted to rage out of control. If thousands of white youth were being killed annually in gang violence, it would come to an end. It doesn't because society doesn't value nonwhite youth.

When the L.A. uprising occurred, I thought to myself that Los Angeles was now living the turbulence I had lived through for most of my adult life. I can look back at *Assault with a Deadly Weapon* and see that, in a sense, it was prophetic. Its main message was that if things didn't change, the youth of L.A. would rise up, and they did.

In L.A., it is well known that the uprising was virtually a Black and Brown affair, but nationally it is still viewed in many quarters as a Black uprising, even though most of the people arrested were Latinos. In a way, it was a Black affair because the huge East Side did not rise up, not then at least. But I have no doubts that L.A. is still a potential powder keg, as is almost every major city in the United States. I firmly believe that if there is not a fundamental change in race relations and police-community relations, the nation's barrios will be the epicenter of future rebellions.

In the past few years, New York City, Washington, DC, and Los Angeles have witnessed Latinos rise up in civil unrest, but all that will be child's play if the tension remains, if abuses continue. The barrios will become ground zero because in the past decade, Latinos have become society's favorite scapegoat. It has become socially acceptable to be a bigot and disguise it in the form of immigration reform. Society knows too well in its experience with Black/white relations that you cannot abuse people continuously without a response. It's a simple law of nature and human relations.

Now I say that if the disrespect and dehumanization continues, all the physical abuse and all the physical control will not be able to contain the rage that will stream forth. The future holds either flames or hope for humanity, respect for humanity. I believe in humanity. I have total confidence that in the near future, we as a society will undergo a cataclysmic change in which relations between peoples will be radically altered. I have total confidence that we will achieve a society in which color will cease being the primary factor by which people are judged. I believe that moral content will indeed count more than pigmentation. I also believe that if we are to judge or be judged in the future, then it will be our souls and our hearts that will be measured. To achieve this new society will require many bridge-builders and much healing. On this earth, surrounded by a sea of hate and anger, let the healers step forward.

To all my relations,
Roberto Rodríguez

Glossary

This glossary contains slang expressions in English that may be unfamiliar to the reader and also nonstandard Spanish usages not found in most dictionaries. Standard Spanish terms are not included here.

Aztlán: name of the ancient homeland of the Aztec/Mexica people, used to refer to the southwestern part of the United States

bombs: old cars, generally 1954 and older

cagapalos: screwups or troublemakers

carnal(es), carnalillo(s): brother, bro'; carnalillo is the diminutive of carnal

carnalismo: comradeship

cherry: immaculate, pristine

firme: cool

gabachos: Anglos, gringos

hopping: (car) lifting off the ground due to hydraulic action

huda: cops; also spelled jura

jammed: strong-armed, literally or figuratively

jefito: father, dad

migra: U.S. border patrol

Pachucos: Chicano zoot-suiters or gang members of the 1940s and 1950s

partner: street term roughly equivalent to homeboy

placita: diminutive of plaza

plebe: regular people

poppers/popping: dancers/dancing in a style of the 1970s-80s

Q-vo: abbreviated spelling of quiúbo = ¿Qué hubo?, What's happening?

que había bajado la bandera: literally, that I had lowered the flag; i.e., that I had betrayed the cause

Raza: collective term for people of the Americas, stressing their indigenous heritage

santito, santita: diminutives of santo, santa = saint

scraping: dragging the rear end of the car on the street, causing sparks, due to hydraulic action

se me prendió el foco: literally, the light was turned on; i.e., I had a revelation

tapados: ignorant people

varrio(s): street spelling of barrio(s), usually used with reference to gangs; barrio refers to community or neighborhood

vato loco: crazy dude

vendido: traitorous

veteranos: older (retired or semiretired from street life) vatos locos

zafado(s): ignorant and crazy people